Haunted Footfalls

by Aidan Lambourne

Haunted Footfalls was written and published in the UK, through Lulu.

This is a fictional work, despite the author's attempt to make it as realistic as possible. Any parallels with real-life are merely a fictional adaptation of their real-life counterpart and are coincidental.

All rights reserved. The author and owner of this work, Aidan Lambourne, does not permit anyone to redistribute or duplicate any part of this work without his explicit consent.

All credit goes to the author, you can contact him through his Twitter: @AidanLambourne.

ISBN 978 1 4717 2233 2

Contents

White Noise, pg 4

Fleeting Steps, pg 79

Scrapes n' Scratches, pg 185

WHITE NOISE

Painfully, the chug of engines faded. There was no longer any sign of his troops. Struggling to push aside the temptation to run out of his abandoned building HQ and try to fetch a fleeting final glimpse of his unfettered, unphased soldiers, Captain Northwood sat firmly. This was the first time that he had been ordered to operate separately from his party. He were to find an adequate location to set up his base of operations, command from there via radio contact to his troops, and that was that. Lips thin, he didn't retort, despite the squirming inside of his stomach. Could they really trust him? Especially after last time?

Even after all of his years of experience, new situations and struggles were pounced upon him. Usually one to be open for new challenges, a bad atmosphere lingered over him as he remained alone. He could feel on his face a frown of false resolution, his brow wrinkled in deceitful determination. He thought it better to start putting action to his expressions.

Looking down, his papers were neatly laid on the battered table he was shocked to find still standing and able to take such weight. Delicately sliding his papers across revealed a map with blue and red lines, dots, crosses; he just hoped everything went according to the battle map's depiction. Lines protruded from points, and crosses marked the spot for their targets. Real lives depended on the accuracy of the simple display of squiggles and circles. Under the unfurled map sat files, filled to the brim of the facts and figures of the bodies he was in charge of. To kill time, he went through them again, already lamenting the soldiers that were sent out mere minutes ago.

He had sworn never to leave his soldiers again, but he figured this time he could keep his composure.

The first file contained the names, descriptions, and accompanying equipment of the SLO under his coordination. The SLO (Special Land Operatives) were trained directly under the United Kingdom Liberation Army; UKLA for ease. They were well-trained and well-rounded for most land-based missions and were the backbone of the independent freedom army. Reading their names made him imagine forty faces of fortitude staring back at him, twenty soldiers for each truck that carried them across broken, cracked urban terrain. Given the severity of the mission, the SLO Parties were generously given one med-kit between ten UKLA soldiers, for a total of five med-kits between the force. Northwood was very grateful for such a gift from the area sergeant, especially seeming as they were packed with some of the latest medical kit that the boffins were able to stir up, from independent research but largely from salvaged and looted equipment.

He noticed a familiarity among each of the forty soldiers: they each were deployed with a Jackson Rifle 12. The JK12, A.K.A 'Joker' or 'The Fun Gun', was cheap and easy to mass produce and was appreciated for its light-weight versatility while simultaneously being able to shred multiple opponents at mid-range. It soon became synonymous with UKLA forces and when a whole team of SLOs were pointing the barrels of the Joker at their adversaries, they were ones left laughing.

Under his command, those forty SLO soldiers were to be labelled: NWD 1st and 2nd SLO Parties. 'NWD' was Cpt. Northwood's insignia and he had split the SLO into two parties to control them more effectively.

Softly slipping that file back on the table, he skimmed over the files of the other two parties: The Patriots' Siege Party and the Special Explosives Unit. It was quite the force he had under his command. If everything went to plan, victory should come swiftly. He hoped so at least.

Any moment now, they should be arriving at point A, where everything would begin. He had never faced so many anxieties before a mission; he had to remind himself that they were all capable troops, and that they could take care of themselves. He was sure of it, but he couldn't help but hear the frets and doubts that gathered a gale inside of his mind.

Before they consumed him, he picked up another file at random. It turned out to be the Siege Party (SP for short), courtesy of the Patriots. Being properly established as an independent freedom army in 2018, The Patriots were forged from the mixture of lurking death at the hands of armies of unknown motive, frightened communities ready to throw aside all differences to defend themselves, and the lack of a national body of defence. Under these conditions, the Patriots' start was one of struggle, explaining their proficiency of detonating devices and bombs of devastating capability. When recounting it in his head, Northwood felt a deep warmth of respect and pride for them. Despite their initial adversity, they had grown to be a strong and reliable ally to the UKLA. In this instance, the Siege Party would present the mastery of the Patriots when it came to demolition and bombardment.

In his deep thoughts, Cpt. Northwood almost missed the first three piercing beeps screaming from his pocket. Fumbling to retrieve his Morse radio, clicks sharply alternating in pitch shot out from the speaker. The UKLA had brilliantly constructed two devises: The Mother Morse radio, the one in Northwood's gloved hand, and the Messenger Morse radio, four of which in his troop's possession, one for each corporal leading the parties. By the press or hold of a single button, high pitch or low pitch frequencies were sent flying to the Mother radio, and after turning a dial to select which messenger radio to answer back to, the same process could be repeated in a coded exchange. Northwood was very fond of these devious devices and had created his own Morse code that was exclusive to him and his soldiers. He was insistent on everyone memorizing his code. There was nothing better to occupy themselves on the slow, tedious, and tricky journey to get where they were, anyway.

Excited to use his code for the first time, he greedily listened to the seeming random of pitches that came out. *'Point A'*. Perfectly transmitted, as he had hoped. Answering them, Northwood sent *'proceed'*, taking care to switch the dial to the 'all' setting. The brief contact between his and his troops was exhilarating, not only had they masterfully coded a response, but they had all arrived to point A unscathed nor interrupted. But it also reminded him how far away from him they now were, and how much closer they were to their potential demise. He imagined their footsteps, marching to their graves one step at a time. One footfall after another until their body fell through with their step. Never to rise again. And all the while there Northwood was, sitting, as far from the action as he could be. Protected by the blanket of his rank. Realizing he could still be of some use to his soldiers, no matter how far away they were, Northwood sat down on a pile of grey, dusty, weathered bricks, put his radio down and studied the map.

Point A was the location where the troops would dismount their transport vehicles and carry on their journey on foot to prevent the enemy from hearing their engines as they crept ever closer to deliver a surprise attack that would turn the tide of war in their favour. Unfortunately, the same couldn't be done for the AAI guns, the hulking, slow-moving Anti Air/Infantry vehicle in the SP, but Northwood didn't expect that to be a problem as they would station further away from the enemy, as will the mortar operators, at point C. Anxiously, the captain eyed the route from point A to point B, where the battle plans would finally start to come in to play. On foot, his brave pawns will march across road that qualified as rubble to get right behind the enemy's defensive line. His mind half-hoped that figurines would pop out from the map and show him their exact whereabouts so he could better guide them and protect them, but it remained a distant fantasy. Doing nothing squeezed his core. But what was there to do? So, he remained still. Waiting for a signal. Anything at all from his troops. Where were they?

Hailing from Zimbabwe but growing up in southern England, Corporal Henry Kumbi was a proud member of the SLO. Prior to joining the UKLA, Kumbi was quoted as being a shy, closed kid. But now, he was the bold and brave leader of the NWD SLO 2nd Party. The very party that would assist the SEU in the action, where he craved to be. The experienced corporal had been promoted to such a position a week before, and this was his first mission to consummate it: Operation Backseat. Kumbi had been ambitiously waiting for his position for a long time and was beyond eager to prove his worth. As long as his heart pumped, nothing would stop him from making that mission a success.

Although he had participated in many operations, he had never properly fought side by side with the Special Explosives Unit, the SEU, who were a renowned advancement of the SLO, by no secret specializing in blasting anything to smithereens, be it from their MVRPGs or their grenade launchers or, for ripping tendons apart, their rattlesnakes, a ferocious submachine gun. What was entertaining to Kumbi was the rumours that the enemy themselves had coined the term, 'the ballsy bombers' to describe them, which goes to show just how dreaded they were. Although only nine of them, they sure would prove devastating. It was no wonder Northwood added them to his roster of warriors to fill up the fourth and final space. The only disappointing aspect being that they were only given three MVRPGs for the operation. He was certain they would make them count, however.

Being thrown around in the cramped transport truck made walking seem a luxury, which he was grateful to be doing, even if it was on uncomfortable and clumped soil. All the soldiers alongside him tactically proceeded at a brisk pace, weaving in and out of debris and under and over obstacles. If his memory was correct, they were currently in 'forgotten Slough'. After the 'Dark Bang', Slough had become, alongside countless other cities, towns and villages, unrecognizable. The only thing that had lasted of Slough throughout the years was that people were certain that Slough used to be there. Wherever 'there' was – the boundaries seemed to change and develop as the unreliable word of mouth passed down the uncertainty of Slough's location.

Kumbi's JK12 was perpendicular to his shoulder, his narrowed eyes stared down the barrel at a crosshair of death. He was itching to finally end foreign invasion to the UK, and he would give his life to make sure it happened. At times like those he was always reminded of his new-born baby, Noah. Tragically, he had only been able to see his beautiful baby boy once before he was drafted for the current mission. Prepared to fight till the end for his son, Kumbi's grip on his gun tightened. Pride welled up inside him, but he quickly swallowed all his emotional thoughts. He needed to be sharp and concise if he and his siblings-in-arms were to pull the fantastic feat off.

Excited tension grew between all the soldiers as they gave each other the side-eye; they were nearing the fight. As soon as they were to cross a fork in the road, at point B, the SLO 1st party would fan out and get into defensive positions to blockade the road from any potential near-by reinforcements that could end the whole operation prematurely. The rest would push onwards, towards the battle to break the deadlock.

A smile spread across his otherwise stoic face. This is what they had been travelling for days for. Crossing minute cracks in the enemy's surveillance, dodging patrols, and waiting for hours and hours to quickly slip through to another point undetected. The sheer nerve and persistence were immeasurable, yet the soldiers couldn't claim all credit for the show of utter silence and control. Fear of detection and cognisance of the consequences pushed them more than they could have themselves to remain absolutely still and only move when necessary. Kumbi was glad to be freely moving and making small talk with his friends again as they crawled across a seemingly empty expanse. If only that were true, then the heroes wouldn't be pushing their necks so far through the guillotine that was Operation Backseat.

When he heard the news that not only was the famed Captain Northwood leading them on their mission, but that the Special Explosives Unit would be joining them too, he felt like a child again. He had heard tales of their exploits, from utterly destroying supply chains to levelling enemy buildings. Confidence in the success of the mission filled his mind, although he knew to not let it get him killed.

Finally, the troops halted. A clear fork had split the path of crumbs and chunks into two messy lines, as if created from the end of a stick by a bored toddler. Fond of Northwood's unique Morse code, he aptly pressed the button to spell out *'point B'*. It was time to get serious. The SLO 1st Party were to remain behind and protect the main force from any back up that were sure to try and counter-attack the invaders. They said farewell and boded good luck to their fellow soldiers. They could well truly never see each other again. Even with the reality haunting over their goodbyes, they embraced each other and laughed together. If it were to be their final time seeing each other, they wouldn't want pessimism to taint their memory of their beloved comrades.

Kumbi had a close friend in the SLO 1st party, one Private Adam. Their looks complimented each other, Adam's relaxed, warming eyes met Kumbi's piercing, focused orbs. The only similar feature shared between them were the great grins that blockaded their faces, from ear to ear. Kumbi had every faith that they would both live to talk about this battle, as they had always done. In childish jest they exaggerated the skirmishes they took part in. Some saw this as insensitive and juvenile, but they saw it as a fun twist to the depressant that is war. Clasping hands for hopefully not the last time, they both departed to do their duty. Their fun and games would have to be dropped and picked up again some other time. Returning the stock of his weapon firmly on his shoulder, the main assault force cautiously made their way ever closer to their fate. Wherever and whenever it lay.

Not too soon after receiving the second update on the mother radio, another report came in. During the process of decoding it,

Northwood was in disbelief. What little colour remained on his cold, creased face had crumbled. Practically biting his nails off, he tried to find excuses for what he heard. *'Maybe it was a miscommunication? Maybe he had decoded the message incorrectly? What if they had encrypted the message incorrectly?'* Similar reasons flew in and out of his head one after the other until he held his head with his hands in defeat. There was no mistake. His soldiers had already engaged in combat.

Viciously, the element of surprise had turned on them. All previous preparations had to be altered. He couldn't afford to lose a single soldier yet. Not so soon after dispatching them. How did they get compromised? Did the huge, blundering AAI guns give away their position? Surprise was the ultimate tool they had against the enemy, without it, they were lost. Their numbers were too small to defeat the huge swarms of enemy bodies and armour that had prevented the UKLA's push to the coast. Northwood stood hunched over the table, panic rising to seize his heart. But it didn't fuel fear, it fed fire. None of his soldiers were going to die. Not on his watch, no matter how far away he was.

Remaining in control, he swatted away his emotions as if they were pestering flies and got to work. Dialling the mother radio to the SLO 2nd party, he quickly messaged, *'protect mortars'*. For anticipation of such events, Northwood had assigned a short sequence to buzz words he knew would come up frequently. So only two swift sequences were all it took to order the mortar teams into protection. Next, he dialled the radio to the SEU, and sent them, *'preserve explosives'*. He wanted to prevent the enemy from knowing the capabilities of their assault force, in an attempt to save at least some surprise and to make sure the wild side of the notorious SEU was saved on causing maximum destruction to their real targets. He just hoped that the initial resistance didn't warrant the use of explosives anyway, as he hadn't the time to explain the method of his madness. *'They are good troops'*, he half-reassured himself, *'besides, their rattlesnakes are more than enough...'*

Orders sent, all that was left to do was sit. Once again attempting to distract himself, his eyes averted back to the table, where the NWD SEU 1st Party seemed to strike out at him. He wasn't bothered to read through it, but a large 'MIA' in large, red lettering brought itself to his attention. He recalled talking to Dion 'Dodo' Sammut about that missing person, Sherton, to which he had replied, "Not a clue, sir. One day he was with us, the next… gone." Desertion wasn't the first thing that came to mind, but it was the most likely. The SEU was such a closely-knit unit, they tended to take those kinds of losses personally.

Not having any idea to how his troops were faring was torturous, and all the while there he sat. The sound of sweet silence outside was deceiving; inside the captain's head a vicious war raged. But it was one of frustrating mystery. How many were there firing back? Where were his soldiers? In his mind a bloody battle ensued, but all he could see was darkness and all he could hear was pain. But from who? Releasing his built-up frustration, he threw himself up off the brick pile and started pacing. He picked up the map and estimated where they could be considering the time between their arrival at point B and their engagement with the enemy. Did they have enough cover? Would they be able to fend off the attack? No matter how much he looked at the map and considered, he was closer to answering the question, 'how long is a piece of string?'.

He caught himself listening to the silence.

How peaceful it all seemed.

Northwood stood still.

Tranquillity was still alive and well despite such times of disturbed peace. The sturdy silence remained true in such despicable times of death. The absence of noise a champion of order. A deep breath filtered through his lungs. It was his duty to stay there and command his troops. Surely his orders had been received and was being carried out accordingly.

Eventually, he couldn't bare wait a second more, he sent *situation?* to the SLO 2nd party's messenger radio. Unknown was their position and status, they could all have been slaughtered.

Surprisingly, it was only a matter of minutes when he received back, *'good no casualties'*. Relief zapped through him like a current. This much appreciated news encouraged his mind to remain firm and undisturbed by his fears. Fear was no excuse, even if he had always joined his troops on the ground. He had to follow his orders, as they had followed theirs.

Silence eventually remained longer than twenty seconds, aside the heavy panting and chinks of weaponry on equipment. The corporal looked around. All the soldiers were spread out, either crouched or prone. In the distance he saw the hulking mass that were the AAI guns just poking out from the building they were advised to hide behind and positioned near them were the skinny dashes of the mortar teams that accompanied the lumbering vehicles in the Siege Party. Three soldiers for each mortar: the spotter, the shooter, and the support. All are trained the same, so they made for very flexible teams, and more efficient fire support. Their position to set up the SP to bombard the enemy lines, point C, was still a little further up and they would be there by now if it weren't for the spat that had just ensued. They must have bumped into a patrol or something, no way had they been spotted on their approach.

Kumbi put his radio away. Nods from all surrounding troops within his vision confirmed to him that everyone had gotten wind of his plan. Risking a peak out of the dense, sharp, and brittle shrub that was his cover, he didn't see any US soldier. Yet, he wasn't to be fooled so easily. The ruse he was playing on them could easily be reciprocated.

He had planned to seize all return fire to give the impression that they had either fled or had been wiped out. The risk of the enemy coming over to check or drive them out for good was minimal, as was now far from uncommon, tricks and traps plagued both sides of the war - Kumbi had a hunch they weren't willing to take that chance - and Kumbi was well aware and paranoid that they could be falling into one, as moments after Kumbi's plan had taken action, the US had seized their fire too.

Either keen to save ammo or crafting a master plan themselves, Kumbi wasn't so sure. What he did know, however, was that this spat had been abandoned and he was considering pushing on. After another five tense minutes of waiting, not a peep was sounded from where the US forces had previously lay. Adrenaline now being replaced by impatience and a constant stabbing of fear, Kumbi decided that it was best to start moving. However, he couldn't perform such a daring move without consulting the other corporals, so using the pockets of soldiers that scattered along their stretch of defence he made a signal to be passed on as if a vital game of Chinese whispers. The first response was from Barry 'Bullseye' Brax, one of the famed SEU members who allegedly performed a perfect headshot using an MVRPG. On this mission Corporal Brax was leading the SEU Party. From one of Kumbi's soldiers he apparently thought it a good idea to proceed with caution. Annoyingly, Corporal Lee Clarke thought it would result in detrimental losses if they were to march onward. He suspected a trap was waiting for them, the same thought at the back of Kumbi's mind.

He was itching to get a move on, and eventually they agreed that Kumbi and Brax were to be the first ones to move ahead and slowly, inch by inch, gain ground until they hit point C, where the SP were to set up fully, at which point their soldiers would follow on through. Kumbi and Brax agreed. All troops barely whispering a count to three sounded like a choir of ghosts. At the sound of a distant "Three", Kumbi held his gun tight and gingerly crawled out from behind his shrub, being careful not to catch himself on it, as even the tiniest twang from it could compromise his position. Holding his breath, he looked to his right to spy small bits of movement: Brax. Careful not to step on any bits of weak debris or spindly branches, Kumbi advanced. Now ten feet from his bush, exposure pressed on him. Meticulously looking upon every potential place of cover where the enemy could be hiding, the two men drew ever closer to the row of housing that the US troops had surprised them from.

Kumbi pressed his back against a brick wall, heart beating heavily. He watched Brax disappear from view and his heart skipped a beat. Needing to be within eye shot of each other, Kumbi took a deep breath and leaped through the broken window frame; his gun entering before he did. Wildly looking within with wide eyes, no one was in sight, aside from the handful of lying bodies. He exhaled. Looking up he saw a broken picture frame. Right then, he was standing in the husk of a family home. Now shattered metaphorically and physically. The blood of strangers desecrated it, their blood splattered on ornaments and lovingly picked-out pictures. Again, he was reminded of his little boy. So innocent, his son was brought into a world of pain and corruption. It was time to end it.

Almost tiptoeing, he silently strafed down a corridor that used to be a perfect portrayal of a family home. A handful of wooden frames hung shattered, broken and pictureless. Below them, shards of fractured glass lay strewn. Carefully picking his way between the glass and the broken vase, the corporal successfully made his way to the end of the corridor, through the kitchen, and finally he walked over a door and past its frame. Sunlight greeted him, although it didn't feel like there was a change of light or heat. Now outside, he crouched, what was clearly once a garden was now an over-gown mess. Although depressing, it provided great cover. He protruded out from the long blades of grass and looked to his right again, along the back end of the row of housing. There was no sight of Brax. Especially as broken barriers and overgrown greenery blocked his view. He would need to spy out further if he wanted to find him.

Cursing, Kumbi walked out a little more, desperately trying to spot Brax while also trying not to get shot by the potential mass of weapons waiting for him to stumble into their line of sight. Suddenly, movement. Frozen, he whipped his eyes round to where he thought he briefly saw it. Friend? Foe? Brax? Not daring to move a muscle, he strained his eyes to stay trained on the spot he could have sworn he saw movement. Fortunately, Kumbi was still amid the tall grass that hugged his shoulders. His washed-out blue uniform would be nicely concealed, so he figured he could afford some movement after all. Turning his head slightly, Kumbi still couldn't see anything. Frustration slowly welled inside his chest. He was fit to burst as if a water balloon until it all subsided at the sound of a single noise. His blood ran cold. The sound was a brief, heavy thud. Kumbi's breathing quickened. He was torn between investigating and staying where he was and waiting whatever it was out.

Looking in the direction of which he heard it, he still saw the same greyscale, decaying buildings, with sides enveloped by Mother Nature clawing back her domain. It was as if the noise signalled silence to fall. Breathing and heart beats were funnelled out behind the loud silence that filled the startled corporal's head. All around, the same old nothing stood. Head swirling with curiosity and suspense, he took a step out of his grassy cover. Going prone, the corporal cautiously crawled along the ground that scratched and scraped at his chest and legs. Directionless, he just kept crawling forward. No more movement or noise alerted him for quite some time as he made it across the field that seamlessly connected to the garden and found himself back to a more developed setting as he almost stumbled out of the fringe between nature and tarmac; grass blades sliced through to the rough rock, a sudden change that tingled of déjà vu.

Still not letting his guard down for a single second, Kumbi ran his eyes across what was once windows and holes that used to secure doors. He was practically on the verge of where the SP were to station: a flattened and battened brownfield site. He could see the expanse of crumbled concrete a little way away, but what he couldn't see was any sign of Brax. He decided to tread on a little further and wait for him. Preciously stepping across the street, eyes still scanning the walls and corners, he had made it to point C, without any enemy engagement. He felt a sudden flush of foreboding. There he was, coverless. Alone. Reaching for his radio and searching for the enemy, he crouched, putting his weight on his right ankle.

Turning around, and Brax was nowhere to be found. Pulling his radio out of his breast pocket, he was going to ask Northwood to send through *'advance'* to the SEU and SP radios, but first he had to make sure Brax was safe. Sticking his head out a little, he explored a little further along point C, having a good look down alleys for any sign of anyone. He was contemplating asking Northwood to raise Brax when blinding flashes materialized and off he went sprinting. Bullets pounded at his feet and cracked through the pavement before him. All his pent-up tension was pumping into his legs as he dashed among the loose ground. Fear of stumbling didn't halt his speed, it merely made him more determined to escape the barren death field. Ears ringing, the corporal ran as bullets penetrated the air all around him. It was a miracle that he was still running. Not taking advantage of his luck he began to strafe left and right, avoiding the thicker clumps of grass on the field, hoping to frustrate his attackers. He was nearing friendly lines with each borrowed step and the fire was thickening as the ambush thrust to full swing, and all for one man. A salvo of silver slithers sliced, beheading flowers and neatly halving the long blades of grass that had not been cut for years. Not feeling an ounce of fatigue Kumbi flew through the building and was spat out the other side as if he himself was a speeding pinpoint of death. Enemy fire stopped for a moment, but that didn't stop his legs from taking him as far away as they could take him. Finally, when running the last stretch between him and the friendly line, he tripped over a flattened fence post and tumbled.

A cry of pain slipped past his barred teeth, and he got a face full of dirt. Kicking up a cloud of dust Kumbi tumbled for quite a distance before he managed to stop himself with bleeding, dirty palms before spinning to his back. Facing the sky, the clouds danced and pranced, showing a dizzying display of confusion. Instincts kicking in again, Kumbi gathered his last remaining strength and hauled himself up. His previous superhuman power had faded and pain was beginning to emerge. Trying to find out where he was hurting, his hazy focus drifted down to his legs.

A sharp intake of breath was all the emergency response he could muster.

Northwood was in a state of disbelief. How had his perfectly laid plans gone so utterly awry? Between sharp breaths he sent *'fall back'* to each of the radios, except the SLO 1st party who he had heard no news from. That was both relieving and worrying. Given that falling back was an underlined failure condition in the operation briefing, Northwood didn't overload everyone's minds with making even more morse codes for actions such as 'retreat' or 'withdraw', so typing in every letter to every radio was excruciating and felt like an eternity. An age after finally sending all his messages, he received an answer of bleeps and bloops that had decided to take their time coming through. Hurriedly he ciphered, fleshing out a chain of messages: *'surrounded', 'roger', 'h'*.

Such a diverse response spun his disbelief into confusion. Mentally, he tried to remember which radios had sent which message, eventually coming to the conclusion that the SEU were under some serious fire and that either the SP somehow didn't realize that they were so, or thought that they were, too, retreating. Either way he was worried sick. SLO 2nd party had the honour of most confusing reply. Just a mere letter was radioed through.

Scratching his head, the perplexed captain perceived that their radio, for whatever reason, was faulty or they had made a mistake somehow. But were they with the SEU? If they were surrounded, were the two parties cut off from one another? If that were so, he couldn't afford the SP to retreat, they needed to stay there and support the surrounded forces. After what could have been minutes or close to an hour of pure speculating and consideration, his mind begun to hurt. This was exactly the situation he dreaded when learning the news that he would be working separately from the team. Worry splashed onto his face

– what to do? They needed to retreat as they'd gotten themselves into another – bigger – fight, and still they hadn't reached point C. However, it had transpired that that was no longer an option. Subconsciously sending *'stay put and barrage'* to the SP, he soon sent *'situation?'* to every messenger radio. With only his imagination to guide him, only horrors transpired of every choice he made.

Then was the wait.

Letting a guttural groan seep from his gaping mouth, Northwood stared into the sky. Its grey features highlighted with blue spots. Darker dots shivered and slowly crawled across the grey, broken, and cracked expanse, reflecting the ground it looked over. Suddenly the anxious captain swelled with emotion yet again. Pride and sorrow, respect and regret. The innocent clouds were going forth on a mission nature set for them. Nature was just doing what She had to do for life to prevail. She didn't necessarily want the clouds to be shattered to nothing but drops, for the clouds so bravely pushing forth to be reduced to nothing but shadows of their former selves. It's for a greater cause. A greater cause.

Feeling the pricks of salty tears at his eyelids he snapped his head down. What was wrong with him? Now was not a time of daydreaming and losing focus. His soldiers were counting on him to be ahead of the game. All he had to do was to follow orders and orchestrate the attack into a success. A symphony of Morse shrieked Northwood back into the room.

Slightly startled, he missed the start of the first message, the sequence to know which radio was contacting him. Catching the rest however, he received: *'h'*, this time followed by some other high-pitched beeps that didn't resemble any existing code or even letter. While racking his brains, another message came through from the SLO 1st party, *'nothing to report'*. Northwood was considering sending them up to figure out what on Earth was going on. *'Assisting SEU SLO enemy engagement point C'* was what came through next, no doubt from the SP. Cursing, Northwood sat down again. US forces had somehow formed some sort of defence or offensive on point C, right where the SP needed to be a while back already. The SLO party's situation was unknown, but apparently, they were fighting alongside the SEU. Some form of relief fell through him, but he was far from feeling fully free of fright yet. Without their radio functioning properly, The SLO 2nd party were in a more perilous position. Mind set, Northwood ordered the 1st party to make their way to the 2nd party and to merge with them. Thinking of one group without contact to him worried him greatly. Although the absence of soldiers alongside point B could allow reinforcements to waltz in and put extra pressure on the invaders, he would not allow any of his soldiers to be without means of contacting him. He was sure it was the right call.

Or was it? Condensing all the parties into one location was one of the unspoken strategical blunders, and may not exactly be necessary if the SLO 2nd party were with the SEU, anyway. Adding the 1st Party not only exposes their rear, but also adds unneeded congestion and weaponry. His mind was reciting all the counter arguments, but they couldn't get through to his heart, which was adamant that sending the 1st Party was the right thing to do. That small chance of the 2nd party not exactly being connected to the SEU, so without means of a radio, worried him sick. He just had to make sure everyone was alright.

Another sigh sent his inner anguish to the wind. Closing his eyes, he listened as the radio beeped out, *'roger'*. Now was the wait. Silence had crept back again, this time interrupted with heavy breathing and a restless heartbeat. It was only now that he had realized how strained he felt. Frustration had been roughly tugging at his core and nerves. The inability to see what was going on and the reliance on mere sound alone was agonizing. Knowledge of what was going on without physically being able to do anything played on his mind again and again, eating away at his soul. Letting another sigh into the air, this one with a little more gusto, Northwood retired to the pile of bricks once more; the cold air a bandage to soothe his burning head and heart. Northwood had never felt pain like that before.

Kumbi felt an alien pain shooting up his left leg and a foreign sting ravaging his left bicep. Never before had he been shot. Blood had taken free reign of his arm as the bullet tore a small chunk off his flesh, but his leg still had the bullet wedged deep inside. The wounded corporal desperately and torturously crawled to where he had departed from, back to friendly lines at last. As he made his final stretch, he was suspicious at the empty silence, of the stillness that froze the air. No one greeted him upon his arrival as he made it past a familiar shrub. Panic began to swathe across his mind. Through blurred vision he erratically looked left and right. His gut dropped. They had gone.

Kumbi's radio had broken during his tumble and was now only able to send higher frequency beeps. Every letter and sequence included a set of both high pitch and low pitch beeps. Apart from one of them, which was comprised solely of four of the former, which he had learned the hard way when requesting help in response to Northwood's message.

Devoid of contact and now bleeding out in an abandoned position being chased by the enemy, Kumbi felt the uncomfortable prick of fear. Alone he lay amid rubble, a sitting duck on the bank. More and more air was pushed in and out of his lungs. He looked back. Nothing could be seen nor heard. Kumbi doubted that would stay the same for long. Where was everyone?

The silence shattered as penetrating gunshots snatched his attention rightwards. Conflict. How had the party moved so quickly? Lungs on overdrive to compensate for lack of movement, Kumbi knew he had to investigate, or he was a dead man. A dead, useless man.

Rejecting the ground's embrace, he forced his legs to support him, letting noises of concentrated agony rip from his chest. Profusely sweating and in incarcerating pain, the wounded corporal limped his way to where the skirmish was commencing. Each step reverberated around his walking carcass; his body jolted painfully with every footstep. His JK12 knocked his legs as it swayed to and fro. Adding to the harmony of gunshots and the pedal of cries and shouts, occasional explosions littered like a bass that vibrated and shook Kumbi's core. It was clear the SEU were getting desperate. Or bored, Kumbi reasoned equally possible.

A scarier thought reared its head at the claps of power sweeping limbs and lives. Kumbi wondered if the US had the explosive means of returning the compliment. Decimation of his troops would naturally follow, this unit was built to infiltrate and disable, not take on the entire US front line head on. Imagining the aftermath, Kumbi let his worry, anger and fear mix together and fuel his limbs and numb his pain. From slowly limping to awkwardly jogging, Kumbi's face was contorted in agony and determination.

Ping!

From awkwardly running to on his backside, Kumbi's efforts were undermined by a stray bullet that whipped past his face and bounced off a pole. Stunned and disgruntled, Kumbi fought to get back on his feet. Rule number one when amidst a fight, never stay on the ground for more than you can help it. Shuffles and rustles sounded from inside of a house a stone toss to his left. They were on to him. Groaning with every lungful, Kumbi hurried on with tears in his eyes and rolling down his cheeks. The uneven ground made quick steps too excruciating to bare, but the thought of the enemy springing up from nowhere and gunning him down spurred him through bone-shattering work.

Heat plastered on to his back; his joints and wounds boiled. Kumbi managed to vault over a brick wall and crumble on the other side. More footsteps could be heard stealing towards his final place of rest. Among his bated breaths, he heard whispers and the distinctive clinks of weapons readying.

Momentarily, all of his pain had evaporated.

Briefly, he was empty of all sensation.

Transfixed, all Kumbi could think about was his son.

His breathing slowed as the enemy made their final strides towards him.

A singular smile grew on his face as his heart swelled and his blood drained.

All of his remaining strength was put to work on producing an image of his beloved wife holding their only son.

Pure love was all Kumbi was left with as he was crumpled on the floor awaiting his death.

If it were to be over, then so be it.

He felt a tug which drew a sharp cry out of him. After being hauled over the brick wall he was plonked down again, pushing pain right back into him.

"Kumbi! We thought we lost you!" exclaimed an SLO soldier that the corporal was too weak to recall the name of. Four other figures shadowed into view, Kumbi noticing the distinguishable features of Private Stephanie 'Steph' Reed with an MVRPG slung around one shoulder. She was the most hard-headed of the SEU, who were all stubborn as a default. Another SEU troop, grenade launcher in hand, stood by her.

Relief and extreme joy washed over him like a cold wave on a blistering day. So intense were his emotions of joy at seeing friendly faces that he managed a small, hysterical laugh. New, fresh tears of joy began to run down his face and into his gaping, gasping smile. Heart fit to burst, Kumbi wanted to squeeze all of his saviours in a tight, inescapable hug. But soon his ecstasy began to fade, and his pain returned fully. He was truly a sorry sight, and his rescuers didn't wait for long before rushing to his aid.

Three SLO soldiers hauled Kumbi upright and noticed his injuries with a recoil of horror. Fortunately, Private Chris was one of those lucky enough to be given a med-kit and immediately got to work. As he neared, hands precise yet frantic in his readying of the med-kit, Kumbi remembered that he had no second name, and it was somewhat of a mystery. Some say he hadn't any parents, which were a common happenstance, and others say that he enjoyed the quirk, but Kumbi wasn't sure. Right then he couldn't care, for he was about to save his life. Chris whipped open the bag and pulled out an antibacterial wet wipe.

Disregarding Kumbi's grunts and noises of pain, he expertly cleared up all around the two wounds. "Sorry mate but I'm going to have to leave the bullet in. It appears that surgery is the only way we're gonna get that thing out," informed Chris as he moved onto the next stage of his healing. Kumbi just nodded gravely as he saw his medic take out a capsule that was protected in a cyro-packet. Kumbi recognized it as the new and improved pathophage capsule, which had been released for use not long ago. Being met with a small flush of freeze as the packet cracked open Chris, without hesitation despite the cold, clasped the capsule, twisted it open, and very delicately poured the liquid contents onto a medicated bandage.

"This may sting a little," his warning was met by a deep knife of cold that plunged deep inside of Kumbi's arm. Swiftly, Chris tied the bandage and applied pressure onto the wound, emphasizing the unbearable freezing slash that rendered Kumbi speechless.

Chris then got to work on his leg, this time pouring the rest of the contents onto a square-shaped bandage to place firmly onto his wound. The same sweep of arctic wind embraced his body and blood. His speech frozen in his throat, Kumbi accepted Chris' hand as he got hoisted to his feet. Putting pressure on his two legs again caused yet another strangled wince as the sub-zero temperatures started to work their numbing magic.

"Oh, almost forgot," remarked Chris as he started to pack up the bag, "take this." He plunged a cream tablet into his face, not even looking. Too tired to ask questions, he accepted it and gulped it down. Chris grinned, satisfied with his work, "It's a pain killer," was all he added.

"Movement up ahead," Reed vigilantly called out. Chris wasn't going to let Kumbi get injured again, so he wrapped his right arm over his shoulders, Kumbi's left arm around his, and supported him as they made an exit, the rest of the group covering them. While they were hobbling to safety, Kumbi asked, between gasps, "What are you guys doing here? Where is Brax and what's going on?"

Wallowing in fear, Northwood sat mutely, staring into the black-stricken tree trunks. Blasted bastions of nature now neutralized. Northwood couldn't help but wonder if his poor soldiers would meet the same fate. Charred, hollow husks. What to do? He felt like a pestering father, or an over-protective mother. After all, he pined for their safety and wanted them all home in one piece. From leading them into battle head on to letting them into the big scary world without him was terrifying. The last news he heard of them at all was that the SLO 1st party had merged successfully with SLO 2nd party, and that the situation was dire. A horrific firefight between his troops and the US had ensued. How had he let this happen?

Frustration twisted back up his spine. Why hadn't things gone to plan? Why had the element of surprise been so violently ripped from under their feet? Were they all going to die? He needed to draft a new plan. A plan that would break the lethal deadlock. A plan that would somehow ensure the destruction of the super turrets, Operation Backseat's primary targets, while preventing the destruction of his infiltrators. A plan that would minimize casualties and secure victory.

Desperately trying to haul himself from the sinking swamp of hopelessness, Northwood scrambled for the original operation brief. Scanning through it, he highlighted the main details for the operation to be a success.

Two were already checked off the list. Northwood had every faith that his troops on the ground could accomplish the mission, he just needed to regain control. He considered many options, including retreating to a previous position or hunkering down. The current conflict needed to be quashed or ended, and not knowing who was winning pulled at his mind. *'Which would be the safest play?'* he wondered, pacing up and down. A sneaking suspicion slipped into his mind. If a higher-up were with him, he knew they'd want his lot to retreat, as they were compromised before reaching point C. But retreat was a failure condition. Worry and fear poked at his head and body. Following orders was paramount to the UKLA's success. In such a time of chaos and madness, the UKLA remained a bright beacon of discipline.

But, weirdly, Northwood disregarded his indoctrinated directedness. Weeks, it had taken them to be where they were, and he knew those soldiers fighting for their lives to secure this mission wouldn't accept the order to retreat. And neither would he. Taking up the radio, he ordered them to make a tactical withdrawal, if possible, to point B. Northwood knew the reprimand he would have to face if his area sergeant knew of his actions, but he didn't care. The mission was beyond orders, beyond his position. Too much had been spent to get them there and too much was at stake. Stubbornly, he wouldn't let that temporary lapse of his control be the end of the operation. Not while he was their captain.

A flurry of beeps flew to the air, two radios had replied *'roger'*, with the SEU adding *'still pinned'*. Despair deteriorated the captain's determination. He knew the situation was dire, but he hoped that they could manage a withdrawal at least. The fact that even with the support by the SP they were still pinned caused a heavy blow to his new approach. With an aching heart, he knew this backtrack would be tight. People would die. But, like the clouds, he knew it was for the greater good. Either way, people were going to die. At least this way, some would survive. At least he hoped. The very thought of his troops getting violently cut down as they ran flashed before his eyes and singed into his head. Yet again, he had to privately radio to the SP to make sure they stayed bombarding until the rest had managed to evacuate. Barely managing to grasp onto his hope, he awaited an answer in the form of beeps to inform him of any progress. This operation was now out of his hands. All that could be done, was to wait for his troops to secure a withdrawal. So, he waited.

It seemed an age had passed of impassively watching the frozen life outside the make-shift base of operations; he let the bitter air prick and pull at his skin. The sun was still hiding behind its shroud of cloud. Blended into one another, the clouds formed a patch-work quilt protecting the skies, preventing light from basking on the ruined world. Full of worry and angst, the poor captain's eyes absorbed the woeful sea above him. He reflected, his posture a swan in a polluted lake. Looking around some more, he realized that none of this was his fault. It can't have been. He was just unlucky enough to be caught in the madness of a new ordering method. A new ordering method on the most pivotal mission of his career. Whatever fate befell his cygnets were out of his hands. He was doing his part. It was all out of his gloved, warm, bloodless hands. Northwood closed his eyes.

Dust and debris exploded in his face. Kumbi's eyes clamped shut, causing him to miss the movement of his eager aggressor to another position. Rapidly clearing his face of wall bits that got flung into him from a missed shot, Kumbi scanned the rest of the church that was miraculously still standing, he couldn't believe he was under its roof and not over it. Not wanting to test fate, he forced his head back behind the wall that he felt could collapse if he breathed on it too hard. More shots were fired. Without hesitation, Kumbi was quick to return it in the general direction it came from, behind a pillar in the far left of the church. Seeing nothing but the muzzle flash from his Joker, he only heard the cry and thud above the cackle of his barrel.

Panting, he recoiled. One down. He saw Chris make a brave dash for a pillar further up. Kumbi looked over Chris' advancement to make sure no one would pop a cheap shot. When they entered the church to safely join their fellow soldiers, it appeared the enemy had the same idea, just a different intention. A brief skirmish broke out, and fortunately Kumbi's team outnumbered and, for once in this operation, had the element of surprise as they jumped on the unsuspecting sneaks. Two had died, there was just one more to root out.

Breaking his cover, he pointed his barrel at every potential position the person could be.

"'Nade!" rang out from somewhere and Kumbi found himself belly-down behind the same wall he came from.

Bang!

A large explosion shuddered the church and flung Kumbi forward a few meters. Spread-eagled, Kumbi's head was filled with multiple loud, shrill rings and his body filled with a jarring, stiffening sensation.

Crack.

Havoc filled the church as quick as the explosion had shaken it. As if he had aged a hundred years, Kumbi struggled to his feet and was instantly grabbed by Chris and Reed, who had managed to get sufficient cover before the blast.

Creak.

The insufferable ringing haunted his head in the mad rush to escape the collapsing church. Kumbi had regained control of his legs as he managed to limp along the pews, debris falling and smashing beside him.

Crash!

Being propelled forward by the momentous crash that was the roof collapsing, Kumbi was punched off his badly damaged legs. With haste, he was swept up by his allies, once again being saved.

Kumbi was practically thrown away from the church as his team tumbled out of the collapsing building via a previously broken-down wall. Dust bellowed out and washed over them, suffocating their lungs and forcing the water out of their eyes. Coughing and spluttering, they all shakily stood up once again, apart from Kumbi whose legs were now rendered inadequate for use. He managed a look up and saw the lifeless body of the soldier that threw the fateful frag grenade, his body already being searched for items of use.

Being supported to his feet, Kumbi spied the distinguishable figure of Brax among the front of conveniently collapsed shells of cars. Anger spirited him onwards, his legs now pistons running on empty. Ignorant of the bullets that could end his pursuit, Kumbi made it within shouting distance of Brax, which is where he tumbled onto the upturned tarmac.

Brax was filled with jubilation upon sight of Kumbi; his dark eyes and dashing complexion lit up with excitement. Overjoyed,

Brax ran over to the fallen corporal to ensure he remained alive, as he previously assumed his death.

Craning his neck up, the fallen corporal saw Brax approaching his position with careless caution and managed to lean on his side to greet him. Initially, Kumbi was filled with rage after hearing that Brax, notoriously spontaneous, had called forth the troops prematurely after he 'was certain' that his route was safe, and that he 'was sure that' he would see Kumbi on the other side at point C. Apparently, Chris added earlier, hearing a whole host of gun fire encouraged them on in case they were all aimed at Kumbi, which was when everyone engaged in the current struggle.

Despite that, seeing Brax's reaction to his presence put on clear display that he hadn't meant for this operation to so spectacularly spiral. But it wasn't enough to put aside the suffering that had followed his poor decision-making. Brax had begun to rush to his side, breaking from his cover and already pulling out a Dense 12 Hour Breakfast Bar from one of his many pockets.

"Kumbi, lad! Thank the heavens you're here. So much has happened-" Now a plush kid's toy, Brax dropped like a ragdoll, blood spewing and spurting out of a hole in his head. Not even hearing the blast, Kumbi witnessed in horror as Brax lay lifeless, so quickly ended by a bullet that carved mercilessly through his skull. Gasps and shouts of horror and protest to a corporal dying so suddenly in front of them surrounded the bleeding corpse. Crawling backwards, Kumbi could escape the blood trailing towards him through the connected cracks, but he couldn't escape the daunting thought that Brax was dead. Around Brax, all the UKLA soldiers looked at him. unless a replacement was appointed, it seemed the young corporal was in charge of the SLO and the SEU.

As his death was, his impulsiveness was responsible for putting Kumbi and his fellow soldiers in this mess, and now it was up to Kumbi to fix it.

Taking advantage of his legs being numb, he awkwardly wobbled to the wasted life and searched the body for a radio.

Wrestling it from his breast pocket, Kumbi noticed the breakfast bar still in his grasp. With a jab of guilt, he wrangled it out of the dead, cold grip and put it safely in his own pocket.

It was time to resolve the bloody situation. Kumbi fumbled to get a message over to Northwood, now not just the pain but all sensation in his legs had evaporated. He wondered how much input the captain had in Brax's decisions.

Hunched over the table, the tired captain's brain was on overdrive. But no matter how hard he thought, his mind remained a blank plain. An abyss, void of ideas. No matter how much he groaned or shook his head or paced, nothing new came to mind. He was stuck. To make matters worse, Brax had died and apparently Kumbi went MIA for a while, which explained the broken radio situation. His two remaining corporals were as barred of control as he was, or at least the chaos of war was taking them for a spin, too. Making a quick decision to put Reed in charge of the SEU, Northwood was in despair. It was when he was about to curse to the clouds when he heard a weird, low drone.

Diving under the battered table, the captain was now truly seized by the icy hand of utter terror. The US had sent in air support. Like a predator, the aircrafts rumbled over the hiding captain, oblivious to his presence. But his safety provided no relief, for he knew who they were after. Once they had flew further ahead, Northwood desperately scrambled to get the radio, knocking his head on the battered table while doing so, causing his papers to flitter in random. Practically pouncing on it, he sent '3 EA' to all radios. Standing for 'Enemy Aircraft', all his soldiers were now warned, and the AAI guns would be ready to swat some flies. The Patriots' AAI was a menacing machine, boasting a twin flak cannon on the top and an array of infantry-slaying weapons protruding from the body. But for now, he was more concerned about the flak cannons, as they were the vital piece of kit to knock the impending death machines out of the sky.

Northwood peered up at the tails of the aircraft and roughly identified a group of three aircraft that the UKLA had dubbed the 'Thunderbolts'. They seemed to be the aircraft of choice for the US; Northwood had seen first-hand the devastation they could bring. Northwood knew, with a scratching of his gut, that if even one got within range, they could lace his force with enough firepower to spell disaster for the campaign. Once again, he found himself grateful for the expert design of the highly compact AAI guns. Those great, dense metal boxes could withstand the fire from the menacing guns that could bore down any ground unit.

Message sent, he lay on his back, his hands a bony pillow. The Americans were a strange enemy. Either they sent masses of despicable machinations and weapons to utterly destroy any UKLA effort, or they didn't. Their front line was disgustingly well-defended, and they weren't opposed to using outrageously powerful means to achieve their goals. Unless they decided not to. Some intel that had been gathered by the numerous attempts of reconnaissance and multiple recon parties suggested that the US had some sort of 'code of engagement', but sometimes they decided it best to ignore it. Northwood, ever speculating, had a gut feeling that there was something strange with the whole affair.

Not long after the sighting of the incoming aircraft did Northwood hear from the SP, *'AAI sights on EA'*. Although it did little in terms of relief, it was still the better of potential radio messages he could have received at that point. He radioed back, *'kill EA'*, which may have sounded obvious, but Northwood knew that they would get the message that it was of paramount importance to destroy all of them before they reached their lines. Luckily, the Thunderbolts were not particularly nimble and the experts behind the AAI guns would have a good chance of doing so. Faith maintained in his troops, he collapsed against the battered table, mentally exhausted.

Physically exhausted, Kumbi mustered the strength to hop off the table that he was receiving closer medical aid on and hobbled out of the half-collapsed building that Chris had announced as his field hospital, as two more injured soldiers lay awaiting bandages and medicines, with another medic rushing around trying to tend to them both. As soon as he heard Northwood's warning of enemy aircraft approaching their position, he rushed off the floor and shouted warning to his troops that were still in combat but now successfully ebbing away to point B. However, in order to combat the oncoming aircraft, the SP's bombardment had slackened and now the enemy were pushing harder, with the hail of bullets increasing to a storm that pinned the last few stragglers, Kumbi included. The SEU, although with the capable equipment to trade their fire for explosives, had to resist, as they had to reserve them for the super turrets that were their primary goal, although a few grenades were still tossed regardless. Kumbi was cautious of the trigger-happy Reed that was now in control, as he knew she wanted nothing more than to see the super turrets sky-high. But, following orders, Kumbi needed to secure their exeunt to point B.

Chris, who was responsible for Kumbi's painkillers and further pathophage treatment into his wounds, rushed to Kumbi's side. "Kumbi, I advise-" he started, but looking at the scene ahead of him, and how quickly it all turned south, Chris knew that Kumbi had to do something. Passing his corporal his JK12, Chris readied himself for orders.

Kumbi, between trying not to get shot at again, surveyed the scene. Fourteen soldiers were left cowering behind their cover in front of him, the rest had slipped off and a handful got injured in the process. From his position, he could see some troopers that had escaped getting ready to assist the others that were still pinned. Frustratingly, he knew that direct backwards retreat was no longer an option due to the heavy fire now pouring down on anyone brave enough to attempt a dash, and neither was flanking backwards to the left side, as the church entrance was completely trashed, and anyone seen attempting to crawl across the collapsed church would be seen and shot.

The right side of their defensive line was the only route of escape that hinted promise, albeit it very dangerous and it would definitely cost lives to perform. Enemy soldiers were constantly using the alley way to their right as a means of flanking, and he had no idea where it actually led them through. It could lead them to a death trap. A narrow hall of bullets. Kumbi's head ached. There were only two options: to stay put and hold out for an opportunity to escape backwards as it was the shortest route, or to follow the rough right path that could be the harbinger of death for the escapees. Either way, people were going to die, more in fact if he let them stay here, especially as aircraft were honing in. But why was it so difficult to tell them to follow him? He hesitated and halted, his mouth not letting him instruct some of his poor soldiers to their deaths. But the choice had to be made. He had to ensure that at least some of his soldiers would live. He knew the only logical choice would be to take the right path.

Shaking his head and putting on a mask of full resolution, Kumbi was ready to rally his troops to safety. A wince was felt at the back of his head, for he knew with morbid irony that not all of them would be safe. He swallowed his emotions and began to call to his troops.

No sooner had he started to speak, his shouts of command were drowned out by the thuds of the AAI. Not long after hearing the anti-aircraft guns blast away did the sound of explosions follow. All soldiers, on either side of the conflict, flinched and cowered further, this time hunting for aerial cover.

A new sound chimed in the mix of thuds and blasts, a higher pitched rattle that could only have been the aircraft's own weaponry countering the beasts that were the AAI's guns. The battle raged on ferociously for a few minutes as the AAI's guns managed to engage the aircraft a while before they could return fire, but now that they could, it meant that they were only a few seconds away from unleashing their wrath on the stragglers.

Pressed for time, Kumbi considered taking advantage of the weakened gunfire to spirit his troops nearer towards him in hopes of making a quick escape, but his soldiers would never hear him over the ever louder fight behind them. One rash decision later fuelled by adrenaline, Kumbi was off. Fear chasing him and the Grim Reaper haunting his every footstep, he ran across the line shouting for everyone to sprint to the 'hospital' behind him. Bullets started to whizz in his direction, but he was far too wired to stop now. Confused and shocked glances met his request but given the situation they all followed his orders. Kumbi heroically managed to run across the uneven ground with bullets and fear at his feet before a shadow was cast over him, finally making him halt. Spatters of bullets seized as Kumbi spied two aircraft looming over the battlefield. Like small yet raging fires, the guns of the Thunderbolts were lit up as they relentlessly sent messengers of death upon the SP and all troops who managed to make it to the failing safety of point B.

   Faltering not for long, Kumbi quickly picked up the pace and made a mad dash for the many troops still stuck and none the wiser to their corporal's suicide mission. A deafening explosion cracked the sky for the second time. Startled, as this one was the closest yet, Kumbi staggered yet again and was forced to look in the direction of the blast. On this occasion, Kumbi wasn't so keen to pick up the pace again. An exhausted bird, the aircraft came lumbering down, both engines burning a vicious red and black. It was going to crash right where he stood. In those few split seconds, Kumbi had to make the ultimate choice.

  Not hearing back from them generated unbearable anxiety. He could hear the familiar boom of blown-up aircraft in the distance, and he counted two. Had one made it through the AAI's curtain of fire and released death upon his soldiers? Frustratingly, there was no way to tell. Knowing that he will eventually receive word from his soldiers, he just sat, letting his imagination tell tales and paint pictures of his wildest fears and concerns. A blasted, bloody battleground jumped in front of him, mangled, meaty piles of soldiers lay strewn, filling the gaps of the broken, upheaved ground, patriotic, American songs filled his ears after their success of pushing back the spontaneous invasion. It became too much to bear.

With his organs knotted and tightened, the captain risked a stroll outside the confines of the half-walls. Making sure his radio was in his hand, he stepped over the wall and heard the crunch of a brittle twig. Northwood realized that that snap was the only noise he had heard for a while that wasn't his heartbeat or explosions of a distant conflict. Like a wash of fresh water over his weary face, the silence came back. That deceitful silence. The silence that hinted at death. The silence that clasped time and yet provided nothing; was nothing.

Looking around, Northwood saw his pathetic base of operations, creased and broken roads and pathways, all reminders of an ancient civilization and way of life. Shakily, his hand rested on the back of his head with tears in his eyes. This was an old war. A war that raged on as if it could be sustained forever. He was getting old. Or at least the constant fighting was aging him. Attempting to dig up old memories of before the 'Dark Bang' proved uneventful. All he knew was this life. An alien wondering in a failed race of being. Divided by differences that brought no difference. Perhaps this was all inevitable?

Strolling across two metal cages that used to be cars, he gingerly picked his way across the pebbles that used to be a pathway. Walking along the broken trail he thought about the pathway humanity had set for itself. Limbs operating with opposed objectives, controlled by a split mindset distracted by contrasting motives. *'What an awkward machine,'* Northwood thought to himself, imagining a sprawling spider with each leg wanting to take the body forward, but in different directions. The legs soon turned on each other, making the poor spider stumble and lay lifeless. Mind spinning like an intoxicated ballerina, only one thought was clear: *'How many stumbles can humanity take before it dies of exhaustion?'*

During his existential exploration, the captain was finally brought to his senses by an ordered row of beeps behind him. Halting in his tracks, he snapped around. The radio. During his trail of thought he had dropped it. Briefly back to his captain self, he hurried along spindly bushes and hopped over rusted vessels. In his hurry, deciphering the message was interrupted but he got the main gist. Still making his way in the direction of the radio, he pieced together, 'EA... survivors... point B'. What was thankfully a lengthy message was reduced to but three words, and he missed the identification sequence. Kicking himself, the dismayed captain unprofessionally asked all stations to repeat the message if they had sent one. What if his soldiers were in peril and he just missed vital information? Knowing that it concerned the enemy aircraft and point B shook his core, but not for long. The frustration and annoyance boiled down and washed away, as if folding in on itself.

Letting a pained sigh yet again tear into the wind that lightly caressed his face and fatigued head, the captain walked back to his base. Feeling sharp twigs and protruding, rusted wires scratching at his feet, his mind yet again alluded to the fate of his soldiers. Maybe it was humanity's destiny after all, to be plagued with pain and violence. Was it all in vain, then, to be fighting this war and protecting his soldiers? Why not just let them all die? It was their destiny. Northwood thought of the chilling conclusion that it was Humanity's constant struggle for superiority over fate and life and death that was their horrifying hamartia. Shivering for a moment, Northwood's eyes were pried open by dread and thought. Despite this, he still tripped and fell over a car tire. Hearing the contact of the radio with the ground sent alert to course through his veins.

Thrusting himself up from the ground, he picked up his radio. Repeating "No!" over and over again; he ignored the bleeding scratches along his legs and dusted off his radio once again. As if to answer his prayers, the radio came to life and delivered a message, *'EA KIA, survivors rendezvous point B'* from the SLO 1st party. Mixed emotions swirled inside him. Exhilaration from the aircraft being defeated and relief from them finally securing an exit to point B and terror at the word survivors greedily filled his mind and sloshed around recklessly. He figured he would wait until they were all at point B until he commanded them further. As a precaution, he replied, *'enemy status?'*. At the sight of his base, Northwood felt tiredness on his muscles and mind. Sitting down on his uncomfortable pile of rocks, he rested his face in his palms.

Why was he carrying on? For the sake of orders? The sake of humanity? Was he as bad as everyone else? Why hadn't his revelations changed him in any way? All of these questions led to more questions which led to a deeper feeling of sorrow.

There he was: a person of high regard among his fellows. Instructing them on a suicidal activity for the greater good. Following orders, they were to take the matter of death and inflict it upon others. The great machine would fall, the spider would snap, yet here they were regardless. Just another limb. One arm wrestling another on the ultimate road of progression. Striving to make it just that extra mile, that extra step to freedom or paradise. But this man knew that they would fall eventually, and it wouldn't matter how far they got in the game. The aspect of life in his hands, he daren't clamp them in defiance because no matter the wisdom, he was just as human as the rest of them. Resistance was futile, just a bug among a hive. So, he played on.

No matter how he articulated it in his mind, the guilt remained unchanged. But he wasn't ready to confront that.

"Where's Private Stephanie?" Kumbi called out. Point B had transformed from the back-up line to an all-inclusive zone. In the backrow, the SP tried their best to maintain bombardment on the scurrying US forces and the uninjured SLO manned the front, most in exposed positions due to the lack of adequate cover. It was chaos. Injured and dead lay in the middle ground, huddling behind the little cover awaiting medical attention from the soldiers that had more experience dressing and healing wounds from fragments of debris and bullets. Bravely, the medics ran between open patches, risking their lives to the inconsistent spray that were the enemy bullets, to perform concise and swift treatment.

The despaired corporal looked upon the injured with a guilty lens. So much pain and death, all because he failed to get everyone to safety. For a few moments he was stunned, until his instincts kicked back in. Kumbi radioed to Northwood that all had reached the underperforming haven that was point B before he had noticed Reed missing. Hunched over, he spirited from point to point, trying to root out where she was. As far as he could feel, his legs didn't exist. The painkillers and pathophage treatment had done more than enough to eliminate any pain. It made any form of movement almost comical, as if he were drunk. His suspicion was ever rising that she had impatiently skulked off to take the operation into her own hands, which would explain why the only two SEU soldiers left were injured. Kumbi ran up to them, repeating the question.

"I've no idea, I haven't seen her around," replied Private Mayeb. A complexion of worry and concern spoke those words, and the corporal's mind instantly formed a story of Reed's exploits. Knowing that these two were in a committed relationship and that their marriage is on the horizon ("After this forsaken war is finished," Steph would add every time their marriage comes up in a conversation), Kumbi knew that the stubborn, new leader of the NWD SEU would be doing something she deemed very important to leave her fiancé wounded on the ground. With a frown, Kumbi knew that Steph was after the super turrets.

A plan was required to find Reed and extract her, something Kumbi assumed the stubborn private didn't devise before heading out to her doom and taking the rest of the SEU with her. Whether in a hurry or on a suicide mission, he didn't know. Kumbi also needed a small team to accompany him into the fray. With a small grin, he knew exactly the people to count on.

Flirting among the bullets but playing hard to get, Kumbi ran over to Chris, who was taking cover behind a fallen tree and tending to someone. At site of Kumbi rolling behind the tree next to him, Chris was beside himself, "What the-"

"Chris, we need to find Steph. I have reason to believe she has gone after the super turrets herself and she needs our rescue," Kumbi quickly sprung on Chris.

"Firstly," Chris started, "you need to be resting! All of this running around won't allow your wounds to heal, you could cause permanent damage, I don't care if you're a corporal, you're no use to us dead," the medic methodically pulled out a rather large and bloody fragment of explosive shell from a leg of a squirming soldier.

"I will survive these wounds, thanks to you," Kumbi started his case with a little flattery, "but death is something you cannot fix."

"Tell me about it…"

"Stephanie, and whoever else went with her, is in imminent danger and needs immediate backup." Chris considered this for a moment as he poured pathophage solution on the open wound, which was met by a cry of pain that Kumbi could more than relate to. It was true, they could die, and the death and loss of such explosives and experts would cause failure of the operation, no doubt.

Chris buckled as he tied the final knot of the bandage, "Alright then, but I swear if you go running into bullets again, I won't save you," he said with a smile, and sending off the soldier he had just treated with a firm pat on the arm.

With Chris on board, all he needed now was to grab a few more bodies. Kumbi had considered the ramifications of his absence in point B and realized that Clarke would be in charge as he would be the only one left with a rank higher than private. He decided to quickly check in with him before disappearing off again.

"I need a mag!" called someone from somewhere, which triggered another horrible thought, ammunitions. Kumbi knew they couldn't keep fighting waves and waves of enemies, and their bullets might run out before their lives or fighting spirit. This needed to be ended quickly, *'and that's exactly what Stephanie intends to do'*, grimly thought Kumbi. Pressed for time, he sent

Chris to round up two more soldiers while he went to Corporal Clarke. This time, however, Kumbi decided not to chance getting shot and tactically rolled behind a car. Surprisingly, the fire raining down on them had reduced to a trickle, then a splutter in an instant. Bewilderment plastered on his face, Kumbi looked out of his cover to see no one on the other side.

"They must be regrouping," he informed everyone within earshot of him, "we should use this time wisely to regroup ourselves, take stock, and wait for orders from Northwood." No one argued, "But let's be careful, it's most likely a trap," and with that, Kumbi decided against going to Clarke himself. He practically grabbed and pulled the uniform of the closest soldier and told him to relay his message. He was not going to waste this opportunity of not being shot at, even if it was exactly what the enemy wanted him to do.

Quickly sending a message and report of the current situation to Northwood that Corporal Clarke oversaw point B as Kumbi and a few fellows went out hunting for a rogue, he awaited confirmation. A mere 'y' in return, which Kumbi deciphered must stand for 'yes', meant the mission was greenlighted. Using renewed energy, the corporal ran to where Chris had accumulated two volunteers and were waiting for his return. Briefly stopping, Kumbi asked, "Ready?" which was met by three firm nods.

"Righty then, let's go." They had barely left point B, when their radio beeped again, *'form fireteams infiltrate confused enemy positions target'*, which halted Kumbi in his tracks. Momentarily he debated if that was the wisest choice, but then was it really a choice if it were the only option? The corporal considered that it was the only course of action that made success seem possible. If they were to take advantage of their confused positions (Which Clarke must have informed Northwood about) and manage to destroy the super turrets, then it would be mission accomplished.

"Change of plans," started Kumbi to his little team, "we're no longer Steph's saviours. We're now her backup. Let's get a move on," and then off they started again, but this time, with a new motive.

A change of plan was needed, and Northwood was quite satisfied with it. At least the most satisfied he had been changing a plan so far. Other times hadn't boded well for him. But this was different. They were all going to die if they just sat there, at least this way they can be given a hero's death even it made no difference. Death is not a thing, just absence of life. And he wouldn't make a good captain if he was scared of nothing.

Grinning like a mischievous fox, Kumbi and his teammates crouched low and steady as they pressed on into enemy territory. Heads on a pivot, they remained sharp and vigilant. Tactfully turning around the fiery infernos that were the three aircraft that caused the confusion, the corporal shook his head clean of their victims with a slice of guilt. He couldn't afford to be distracted right now. Carefully stepping over corpses and burnt limbs and holes and clumps of mud, the four troops proceeded past their defensive line and truly further than they had been before.

Looking at the clouds gave the illusion of peace, silently moving onwards together and all wearing the same uniform of grey. A colour without importance or conflict. A monotone without risk or foreboding. In unison, the carpet rolled under the sky. *'If only'*, Northwood thought, *'if only we could have been like that,'* but he knew the price of their hubris and intelligence would have to be self-destruction, otherwise there would be no catch. Morbidly, the captain knew that that isn't how life works.

Feeling adrenaline start to crawl through his veins as if from a leaky tap, Kumbi started to feel a thrill prick at the back of his neck as they crept ever deeper into the hornet's nest. Now they were standing at point C, where they were supposed to be such a long time ago. Strangely, there was still no one to be seen. The feeling that this could be an elaborate trap grew on the suspecting victims, as it had been an ambush before, but it just added to Kumbi's marvellous grin and adrenaline.

Interestingly, the captain was the most at peace then as he ever had been. His place was secure. Just a captain, giving cannon fodder a target. The operation was doomed from the get-go, it was only a gamble that high command took. A risk. A slight chance that maybe the war could be eased if this daring operation took place. "But the thing is," Northwood mumbled to himself, "life doesn't reward war. In fact, war is our punishment."

Gunshots finally sprung from the darkness. Snapping left, the corporal realized that it must be from another fireteam. He dismissed the urge to pounce on the enemy and assist the other team as their directive was to help Reed. Keeping their eyes peeled, they proceeded ever further, vaulting over obstacles, carefully turning past sharp corners, they probed deeper, still undisturbed.

Lifeless eyes once again looked impassively at the scene before him. All previous emotions that spawned from its powerful imagery stopped. All that was left was absence. No life populated the bushes or the trees. This war had stripped it of its root, the habitats that contained life. Ironically, humanity was to do the same. Eradicate the root of the problem. Themselves.

Explosions. Huge, deafening, devastating, unbelievable explosions. Left leg buckling and almost being thrown clean on the floor, Kumbi had a feeling he had located Private Reed. "Go, go, go!" he shouted. Adrenaline pumping through his legs and mind, the sweating corporal led the charge to the epicentre of the blast. Assuming that the enemy would be gravitated to her position, they quickened the pace ever faster. Pressure spirited them across untraversable terrain. What almost halted his progression, was the sickening realization of what it was that got blown up.

Northwood wasn't blind of the fact that he himself were taking part in the machinery and cogs that continued the cycle of war and death, but he brushed aside any feeling for it. "This is how it goes," started Northwood to himself, "one faulty cog, and it'll be replaced." Hopelessness no longer morphed into sadness and fear. Alongside his newfound nihilism they amalgamated into freedom.

Along their advance, they encountered their first grouping of the enemy that were sneaking between cars. Letting loose a salvo of fire, Kumbi and his fire team got the jump on them. Within seconds, they had been riddled with bullets from the Jokers, clearing the pathway. A great plume of smoke was a giant flare in the setting sky, letting Kumbi know of Reed's exact whereabouts. With the sense of urgency rising, they began to sprint.

There he was, sitting on his pile of bricks, his pale and lightly pinched face a passive complexion peering at the passing clouds. Whatever happened, happened. Whatever would become of his troops would become of them. Whoever would win this war, would win the war. Then it would start all over again. Any part he played wouldn't change a thing. His actions, a useless sense of direction on a straight road. Such bliss beckoned from that fact. He had found happiness. But he wasn't enjoying it.

"I've found Stephanie!" shouted Kumbi, alerting his squad to the position of the wounded rogue, "Chris, they all need medical attention!" Chris was already opening his first aid kit as he slowed down and crouched beside them. The NWD SEU had been reduced to six surviving members, including those at point B. They had been located huddled in a shop that had dusty and ripped garments on display. Mannequins with limbs missing had their felt overlay crisped back by old flames. Glass and jewellery lay mixed on the floor, the precious gemstones lay untouched, what once held so much power and value, were reduced to nothing overnight. Such luxuries were dropped as soon as the fight for supremacy spun into a fight for survival.

Running grinding to a halt, Kumbi looked Reed in the eyes as he asked, "I cannot believe what you've just done." He wanted to say so much more, such as *"How on Earth are you all alive?"* and *"Why on Earth would you just run off like that?"* and *"Well, it turns out that the super turrets aren't so super after all, then."*

"Believe it. Got sick of standing around and wasting my bullets," she said breathlessly blunt, "besides, it was a good show, right?" Her wicked grin only exemplified her love for blowing things sky-high. In the case of the first super turret, that was quite a literal statement.

With a hand gesture, Kumbi ordered the SLO to protect the storefront. Like a veil of armour, the SLO surrounded the SEU as they received medical attention. Chris quickly surveyed the damage. Steph only suffered a few flesh wounds on her limbs and torso, but she was visibly exhausted. Taking note of her developing bruises, Chris asked, "Were you in a fist fight?"

"Yeah, after blowing up their super turret they were instantly on our tails and we quickly got surrounded," she answered before taking another gulp of air, "Without time to properly engage and shoot our way out, we decided to rush them head-on. A hand-to-hand quickly ensued," she gestured to her bruises and waved a hand to draw attention to the others, "It was a close one, but we managed to escape." Analysing the rest of her team while hearing her heroics, he concluded that although in a bad state, they could carry on. Courageously, the SLO defended their position from any US stragglers and pursuers as Chris swiftly fixed them up.

"Hurry up Chris," Kumbi warned, his bloodlust still raging, "we need to get a move on, now!" He wanted so desperately to murder as many of them as he could, and just standing there fending off curious or brave soldiers didn't meet his demand. He didn't know when his fighting spirit had transformed into bloodlust, but he wasn't going to let it go to waste.

Their position had gathered more and more attention, and although more than happy to blaze them down, he wasn't stupid: they all needed to vacate that instant if they wanted to make their way to the next super turret with relative ease.

Clink. Bang! A second's flash followed, startling everyone on the scene, and managing to wound those too close to the unexpected blast. An SEU soldier had thrown a frag grenade, scattering the approaching enemy. For now. Only seconds after the blast, soldiers were crawling back to the fringes of the fire fight.

"All done!" announced Chris, recovering from his crouched position, and helping up another. Taking advantage of the respite caused by the grenade Kumbi, although a little disorientated by the sudden explosion, started to make headway to the destination of the next super turret, some way east of the first. From the look in his enemy's eyes he could tell they weren't expecting such a daring charge, but they weren't staring for long as the Jokers silenced all the bodies in Kumbi's wake.

"Cheers for the rescue, Kumbi," Reed had a scratchy undertone, probably due to the intense heat and dehydration.

"No problem," replied the corporal, "you can make up for it by helping us finish this operation."

"With pleasure," and with a smile, the explosive enthusiast quickened her pace at the thought of causing more destruction. As they ran, a new sound had joined the ambience. Clinking around the SEU's belts, grenades bobbed up and down, swinging in a manner that would tantalize the Grim Reaper's bony fingers. He suspected the only thing bringing those insane troops through the chaos of battle was their sheer arrogance of death.

The constant running and fighting begun to take a toll on Kumbi's muscles, especially seeming as he had a bullet wedged into his thigh. Even with the knowledge that permanent damage may be caused to his leg; the determined corporal took advantage of the treatments and painkillers and chemicals surging through his veins and pushed on like a bullet himself. Albeit a wonky bullet, for he had to keep glancing down to coordinate his legs.

En route to the second super turret, they had crossed paths with a fellow fireteam. It consisted of seven SLO bodies, with one grenade launcher between them. Apparently, the injured SEU back at point B had distributed their arsenal to the fireteams in order to assist their objective, in other words actually give them a means of exploding the super turrets.

"You're better off with us," was all Kumbi had to say in return before hurrying off and leading the charge once again. Now with even more firepower at their side, the group felt a lot more confident that they could achieve victory.

Skirmishes lit up the streets everywhere, it sounded as though every fireteam had engaged the enemy. Frustratingly, the motives and plans of the US were unknown and confusing, which made it all the more difficult to plan ahead. It was as if they had been instructed to find and eliminate the invaders, unorthodox and unusual given the normally fleshed out plans of attack from the US, but it told Kumbi that they had really stung them where it hurt. A pride arose from seeing their adversaries so unprepared and panicked, even if it meant more drastic measures would be made.

Resistance stiffened as they reached the outskirts of the second turret. Kumbi could see it, a tall, grand behemoth of a thing. One huge barrel reached out from a heavy, thick body, its arm almost reaching out to claim the lives of his allies. Multiple other barrels and guns poked out like needles, all independently movable and independently dangerous. Awe struck Kumbi. Resembling a mantis' pincer, the sleek yet buff gun foreshadowed swift assassination to all his allies. Like a god, the silhouette blackened out the stars and imposed on the invaders. By sight alone, it gave the impression that the operation was futile, as if nothing on Earth would ever topple such an omnipotent being. If the soldiers weren't so driven by fury and revenge, they surely would have fled long ago.

While admiring the giant, he almost missed the grenade being tossed at their position. Being thrown aside by his instincts, his life had just been spared from the fragments that arced the sky, rainbows of death. One thing he hadn't dodged, however, was the intense ringing that startled his senses. As he began to process his eyesight, he realized he was a sitting duck, lying on the floor. Instincts once again carrying him, the next thing he knew he was bundled next to another SLO troop as they both took cover behind a corner of a building.

Scattered and disconnected, Kumbi needed to reunite his force to make a spearhead to give the SEU enough room and line of sight to swiftly secure the super turret's defeat. And all before they were killed by the advancing defenders. Taking rapid and deep breaths, his fury and bloodlust blinded him to the fear of death. With gritted teeth, Kumbi leaped into the open and quickly scanned the field. Four hostiles had hatched the same idea. Unleashing merry chaos and running through, he let his gun do the talking. Thankfully, he was joined by other soldiers that were inspired by his madness. The rattle snakes of the SEU shook down the opposition, providing safe passage to advance. Kumbi knew they got lucky and didn't know how much more of those small spats they could shrug off.

"Come on!" rallied Kumbi, not wanting to stop for a second, as his rather large fireteam broke their cover to push onwards. Counting the bodies that followed him, Kumbi realized that he was a few troops down. Deserters or dead, Kumbi would have to find out later. Right now, they needed to get a move on. After a few moments more and a taking of a right turn, the super turret was more visible, its grand design stood out in the distance between halved buildings. Steph called out that they should be able to send that turret to cinders. The party halted, the SLO took defensive positions around the SEU. Steph and Private Reece Spence, crouched down on one knee, mounted their weapons of mass destruction on their shoulders, and on a countdown of three, two rockets blasted their way towards their target, a blaze left in their wake. Reed and Spence had to regain their balance – the rocket launchers had quite the kick – and then they marvelled at the now specks of deadly explosives barrelling towards their targets.

Undermining the all-powerful pose and presence of the gun, only two rockets alone were responsible for its ultimate destruction. A few seconds later and another huge explosion shook the heavens. Everyone had to clamp their ears shut and close their eyes out of fear of being blinded or deafened. If someone dared open their eyes, a sense of beauty came from the eruption of yellow and red, a dance of destruction. Multiple smaller explosions followed, properly sending off the super turret. Like a broken toy, the barrel jerked up, then, now detached from the turret, plummeted down to earth. Upon its contact with the ground, no explosion followed, just a thud that people could not only hear, but feel. Little time remained to savour their handiwork, as now all the troops in the vicinity knew their location and would be coming right after them.

"Time to go," Kumbi called, but people where already running. They still had another two turrets to destroy, and the opposition had reorganized their defences, and by that they had just congregated around their most prized constructions: the super turrets. Although it made sense to defend the obvious targets of the invaders, Kumbi was off put by the lack of alternative means of defence than just infantry. Was it just one huge underestimation? Or had this front truly been ill defended?

Afterall, prior to the operation, the UKLA had expertly tricked the enemy into thinking that they had plans to infiltrate their most heavily guarded HQ, in London, by dropping false 'top secret' records and plans into the enemy hands and by gradually increasing attacks and bombardment there. In retaliation, the US forces had upped the ante by increasing numbers on the London front by drawing infantry, armour, aircraft and artillery from the surrounding areas, including Slough, to converge in London. In theory, this meant that Slough would be a much easier target and the operation, if done according to plan, an easy success. To further develop the ruse, an assault was led just on the outskirts of the London front six hours before Operation Backseat had properly begun, drawing their attention elsewhere.

Kumbi was still uneased by the total lack of diversity. The small squadron of aircraft was the least he was expecting to aid their fight. Where were the Wreaths, or the paramilitary? The bombers or the tanks? Although thankful, he was still surprised of their absence.

While shredding down the roaming soldiers that were in the party's way to the third super turret, another ground-breaking explosion swept the streets, derailing his train of thought. He was mesmerized by the night-splitting light that was a distant super turret being destroyed. Jubilation filled the party, another fireteam must had managed to destroy a target without the use of any SEU bodies present. An admirable feat. Hope and joy electrified the atmosphere. Just one more to go.

Dread and shock rolled over him like a pile of bodies. His mind a parrot, the radio message replayed in his head over and over again, each repetition becoming a shade more human. Beeps formed into cries. Happiness and relaxation had collapsed like a curtain, a bright, hard light now exposing him to reality and fear, with ghosts as the audience and witness to his act. Foolishness jabbed at him, and self-loathing swallowed him whole.
'One target left.'
It was all his fault.
'Heavy bombardment unknown position.'
They were all going to die.
'SP bombardment drowned out exposed.'
What had he done?
Sickness rose whenever he looked at the radio. He didn't dare answer back. By his hand, a whole team of people would lose their lives. So what if they were to die anyway? So what if it were human nature? So what if death was their punishment for war? Had he truly sent his loyal parties to their deaths and been content with it? Northwood took to trembling, time had slowed around him, allowing more time to relish in his darkest thoughts. *'Heavy casualties'* was the most recent message to come shooting through his ears.

Wincing at the new booms of the distant artillery, Northwood felt tears escaping his experienced eyes. One shot after another; the cries in his mind intensified. Screams now bounced around his skull, magnifying, and multiplying. Hugging his knees, the defeated captain's eyes glazed over, droplets forming on his chin. So what if they were to die anyway? It wasn't his to decide when. All he had to do was follow orders, and his orders were to make the operation a success, not to follow the path that Humanity has pathed itself. He felt like dropping everything and laying down. Done.

Eventually, the thuds of the artillery raining down death upon his soldiers seeped into the background. Familiar silence draped around him. Laying down now, exhaustion clawed through his limbs. Projections of people being blown to bits; faces he knew well contorted into displays of utmost agony. Returning to his conscious, the thuds exemplified the chaos letting loose in his head. With each shell that unleashed through the air, another ghost haunted him, joining the entourage. He could feel the last breaths of the dying raking down his back. He could feel the guilt weighing on his own soul. He could feel himself giving up. He just wanted it to stop. He was fed up.

A small light lit his shadowed mind, prompting him to leave his little base. There was no reason to stay. There was nothing for him there anymore, all of his troops were dead or soon to be so, and he didn't dare face the UKLA after his actions. They were fed up with him anyway.

No physical confines trapped him. His mind was trapped in a prison of his regret, but he was still a free man. Thanks to him, his troops were truly dead anyway. Thanks to him, they had entered a place of no return, the only life being spared was his. Thanks to him, he could leave without a scratch. Hauling himself up off the floor, the epitome of despair considered its options. Did he deserve to walk away? Did he deserve to have that freedom when he condemned so many to a death trap? It wouldn't make a difference, Northwood concluded. Either way, his soldiers were corpses walking and there was nothing he could do about it whether he lived or died.

He wasn't sure what option he chose, and soon enough his conscience slipped into the back of his mind, becoming little more than the background noise that harrowed his head.

'We're done for', thought Kumbi, as the remainder of his fireteam was pinned down, vicious enemy guns on one side and a sudden artillery barrage on the other. So much for lack of diversity. Returning their fire with fire was fruitless, as many more would replace the one soldier that he was lucky enough to shoot down. Reed to his left and a dead man to his right, fear began to grope at his internal organs. Remaining firm, Kumbi denied those feelings indulgence and popped his head over again, just to dip it back down to avoid a volley of fire. Attempting to get hold of Northwood resulted in nothing. Cursing the linear design of the Morse radio, Kumbi realized that if their own captain wasn't responding, potentially due to faulty radio, then he would have to bring the SP there himself.

"Steph, we need to bring the siege lot here to pin down the Americans," he schemed, gesturing to their attackers, "captain isn't responding so we'll have to go get them."

"Are you mental? We can hardly look over this wall, let alone leave it entirely," she sensibly countered, being interrupted by a line of fire that hit too close for comfort, "and besides, how do we know the SP aren't gonners? What are those lot compared to the artillery now breathing down our backs, anyway?"

"Ah, too many questions," dismissed the corporal, "time for answers." Arrogant of sense, he grabbed Reed's rocket launcher and haphazardly positioned it over the wall he had his back against. Pressing the trigger, the rocket launched right amidst the enemy positions. Shouts and cries of alarm broke the gun fire right before an explosion cracked the air, gifting everyone a shower of dust and debris. Despite Reed's complete disbelief and retorts, Kumbi threw the MVRPG back to her, its last rocket gone.

Seizing the seconds of safety he created, he scampered out of his cover and made a dash for it.

No sooner had he done that, bullets came attacking his footsteps, which just spurred him on. Deftly strafing a corner, the corporal had escaped. Adrenaline was back and coursing faster than ever, as a sense of invincibility began to surge in his brain. Making a quick estimate, he guessed that the SP would be around south of their position, in the direction of the surprise artillery barrage. Already running towards where he desperately hoped they were, Kumbi wondered why they weren't already covering them. Whether they were busy elsewhere supporting another fireteam of trying to navigate the awkward AAI gun through the challenging terrain or fighting for their lives against the sudden barrage harrowing the battleground, the quicker he got to them, dead or alive, the better.

Running among familiar faces, Kumbi leapt over arms and over-spilling corpses. Undeterred by the blood that splattered at his soles, Kumbi panted on. Soon enough, the hardened corporal bumped into another group. From his distance it was difficult to tell if they were friendly or not. A sudden whistle followed by an explosion disrupted the group and pushed Kumbi back. Taking the blast and still standing, Kumbi got bodied by a soldier that took the full force of the explosion. Managing to shift the dead weight off his torso, Kumbi quickly realized, by the colour of the uniform alone, that that was a team of hostiles that got swiftly ended by their own artillery. The irony was barbaric, whoever oversaw that barrage clearly didn't care or was being fed inaccurate information. Surely no one would order such death among a mixed battleground.

Deciding to think about it later and move while his path was conveniently cleared, the corporal lolloped on, his body finally suffering from his exhaustion. In the distance, he thought he heard a distinctive shout among the gunnery and roars. Briefly pausing, the same shouts came again. Changing course, they eventually took form into taunts and challenges.

"Give em no mercy, boys!" it was clearly Corporal Clarke. Now cracking a limp smile, Kumbi sped towards the stoic commander of the SP, still alive and hopefully well. Among the shrieks of aggressive gunfire, Clarke coloured the atmosphere with even more aggressive language, "Keep them coming, I dare you!" Peaking round a corner, Kumbi saw the legendary warrior standing up on the tipped-over AAI gun, a pillar among the plumes of fire smoke that rose from the damaged engine. Below him were a moat of bodies, with only a couple people alive, plastered against the metal wall that the lumbering AAI gun provided.

"Clarke!" shouted Kumbi at the top of his lungs, "Clarke!"

He snaped around with a wild look in his eyes, for a split second taking Kumbi for the enemy. Lowering his weapon but maintaining his craze, he jumped down, his eyes scowling at Kumbi. He approached, "See? I told you lot it was a bad idea to go galivanting into enemy lines! But you lot had other ideas, didn't you?" he shouted, stomping right up to Kumbi's face. Although just an SP commander, Clarke had the reverence and respect of an area sergeant.

"It wasn't my idea to call you lot forth, alright?" having hastily clarified that to avoid further conflict, Kumbi quickly changed the subject to the matter at hand, "There's only one turret left, and we're all pinned down."

"I suppose you wanted some of our assistance?" He almost laughed.

"Correct, but I see that's quite impossible now," Kumbi looked over Clarke's shoulder to the heap of burning metal, "We should rally up whoever's left of the SP." Both walking towards the AAI, it appeared that they had already assembled themselves, an injured mortar operator and a healthy one. Or relatively healthy, at least. At the sight of what remained of the poor Siege Party, a tune of sorrow played on his heartstrings. Doubt quickly surpassed his upset, for he couldn't get himself to believe that this rag-tag bunch would be the liberating force that would free the pinned forces, especially without any of their bombarding equipment.

"What's next, captain?" sarcastically quipped Clarke, erratically regarding Kumbi with one eye, "Right, it's down to us now," he began a riveting speech, "everyone's pinned and we're the ones to free 'em." He eyed them all, as if sizing them up through his squinted, contoured eyes, "We go in fast, aggressive and relentless. No mercy, for if we fail, this close to eliminating all four targets, then all our lives would be lost in vain." He concluded, his Irish accent brimming with aggressive passion. And madness.

The two privates replied, "Yes, sir." Kumbi was very close to doing the same. Waving away the thought that he almost addressed someone of the same rank as if one of his superiors, Kumbi started to move, not liking the idea that the burning AAIs were like flares, and the enemy the moth. Not to mention that it could blow any minute.

Running through the alley where Clarke had just mowed down several bodies, Kumbi once again spearheaded the assault, with Clarke hot on his heels. By the end of the alley, Kumbi had explained the plan: to provide enough cover fire to inspire the trapped soldiers to move out and push back the resistance that was now coming in fast to protect their final super turret.

More and more shells were being hammered upon them, with nothing much to do about it other than keep running. Shots rang out from the end of the road they were on. It looked like a group of reinforcements had made their way into the area. He cursed in his head, if only the operation didn't turn out to be such a bloodbath, then the SLO 1st party could've stayed at point B and fended off the newcomers. Desperation to reach their allies and push for the final target started screaming in Kumbi's soul. Not even bothering to retaliate, Kumbi sprinted on, with Clarke chancing a few pot shots in their direction.

Kumbi's brain whirred into overdrive. How would they do it? How would four soldiers – one of which was injured – fare against a wall of guns? As they neared the battle zone, anxiety cracked at his mask of stone, until he heard the familiar sound of the rattlesnakes. Clarke heard them too, "Well they're not too pinned then, eh?"

"No, they're not!" by some stroke of luck, another group of six SLOs had previously scurried onto the scene, attempting to escape American reinforcements. Having burst in, they disrupted the line of fire and gave the few remaining SEUs and SLOs a window of opportunity to shoot back without a guarantee of death. Without cover, the startled saviours ran towards the enemy, guns blazing. As Kumbi and his own party of four came sprinting on with renewed hope, they were met by an inspirational scene: his previously trapped allies now properly taking revenge all the while one soldier, with three dead bodies trailing behind her, persisted through gunshots, apparently immortal. Scared by the bullet-consuming soldier, the enemy had to adapt their line to properly finish off the super soldier, exposing their flank. Never ones to waste an opportunity Kumbi, Clarke and the two mortar operators pounced on their exposed flank without mercy, unleashing a laser beam that cut through the huddled mass. Just as Clarke had ordered.

Guttural war cries from the old commander assisted their insane dash towards the enemy. In a few crazed seconds, they were pouring fire on their adversaries on three fronts. Although they had managed to kill off the first fireteam to come their way, Kumbi's team had encroached on their line too much for them to reorganize. The remaining dozen frantically tried to wrangle their way back into a solid line, but it was futile. They had no option but to retreat.

In a matter of moments, they had pulled off the once-believed impossible: the wall of guns pinning them down had been demolished and forced to retreat, with soldiers leaping out of the way and running off, but all came at the cost of multiple brave, selfless soldiers that gave the ultimate sacrifice. Kumbi vowed in his mind to make their deaths worthwhile.

"We'll finish 'em off, won't we lads?" Clarke volunteered, already eyeing his prey in the distance, "Make sure they don't form a counter offensive, the cowards," his shoulder jittered, "Don't say us Patriots don't do nothing for you, now."

Kumbi nodded to Clarke, "Thank you, we couldn't have done it without you lot." Clarke nodded back and was already off giving chase with the mortar operators following close behind.

"You really are crazy, you know that?" which was Reed's way of saying 'thank you for saving us'.

"Yeah, whatever," Kumbi couldn't be bothered to jest back, as his mind was consumed by his want to finally complete the operation, "we need to move, double-time." With reinforcements coming in, and artillery fire increasing, it was only a matter of time before the invaders were finally wiped out. The pressure was on. Despite the treatment Kumbi received, the painkillers, pathophage serums and the medicated bandages, blood had started to fully saturate and leak out of the bandages on his arm and leg. Through constant movement, despite the bandage's design to prevent blood loss, too much blood was being pumped around his body for too long of a period for the bandages to handle. Beginning to slow and lag a little, Kumbi worried he wouldn't last much longer at that pace. Tantalizingly within reach, he didn't want to give up yet, not so close to victory. Panting steadily increasing, pain spilled onto his expression.

Shocked shouts of alert called out in the dark, the recognizable American tone showed that the small group were once again going to be under fire pretty soon. Sure enough, after a few more strides bullets littered around them, incredibly claiming two victims that fell, never to fight again. Pushing against the pain, Kumbi didn't want to be next. If they wanted to survive, they had no choice but to take cover wherever they could and sit tight, as they would amply get cut down trying to outrun bullets on a straight road. Frustration ebbed at the party, just another corner and they should hopefully have it.

Only two minutes had passed, but it felt like an eternity of yet again engaging the enemy. Like an inescapable curse, the American forces haunted over their every move, ready to fight them off however far they escaped. More and more bullets and bodies made their way to the dwindling UKLA force, grabbing their chances of victory and smashing it to pieces. The distance between them was closing, as reinforcements had finally arrived in their full. A few artillery shells exploded among both sides, murdering everyone in their wake. Only a few friendly soldiers remained in Kumbi's vision. He could see Reed along the road, she had just emptied her last magazine and slumped behind her cover. Kumbi himself only had one left. Hope was all but lost.

Out of the corner of his eye he saw a heavy object get thrown across the street. Holding his attention, Kumbi saw as Reed caught it. With a strangled, sharp intake of breath, Kumbi saw that she had requested someone's MVRPG shell.

Reed looked round to Kumbi a wicked yet desperate thought behind her eyes, "I'm gonna do it," she mouthed, as Kumbi couldn't have possibly heard her over the onslaught. Reading her lips and expression, Kumbi knew, with a certain dread, what she meant.

Madness ensued; the crazed captain's mind was wracked with grief. *'This is all your fault!'* came beeping out of his radio, again and again. A spikey bush drew blood out from a clean cut on his calf, but he did not stop walking.

Tears once again put their presence in his eyes, as death and defeat loomed ever closer. Reed, ever brave, volleyed all of her grenades at the advancing enemy, stripped off all of her equipment, leaving only the MVRPG, loaded with a lone missile.

Ghosts danced and accused in front of him relentlessly. No matter how far he walked, it would never be enough. With eyes glazed over with guilt and distress, faces flashed fluorescently, full of unfathomable rage. *'This is all your fault!'* came screaming into his ears, reducing his body to a trembling mess.

Now a bleeding heap, Kumbi lay, unable to return fire as he watched through blurred vision Reed, in the distance, stop, crouch, and pull the trigger, right before she was spun around by a savage stream of fire. The fateful missile ripped through the air, carrying everyone's hopes and dreams with it.

Soon, all feeling in his legs had ceased, just like the rest of his body. Onwards, he walked, unable to mentally think of anything else but the soldiers he had plunged into peril. Backseat joined the others, and together they shook his very being. Walking on, he couldn't bear it anymore. His soul had, at long last, died. Right next to his morality, although that grave resided in Oxford.

A final explosion signalled a ceasefire, as everyone stopped shooting to appreciate what the destruction of the final super turret meant. Relief washed over the wounded – almost delirious – corporal, the operation was a success, and soon UKLA forces on the Slough front would be converging on their location, no longer suppressed. A strangled cry of victory broke out from the invaders, revealing a few other pockets of alive allies near their location. Their celebration was short lived, as enemy forces were now powered by avenging their defeat, so were more dangerous than ever before.

Loading his final mag, he rolled out of his cover, letting rip among the pressing forces. Two soldiers were killed at point-blanc range, the others jumping aside, retaking their cover before shooting back at the sudden gun in their way. Holding against the pain, he rolled back behind his cover, before using it as a support to stand up.

As soon as his two feet were supporting him, a sudden wash of dizziness and light-headedness knocked through him, impairing his vision, and causing his arms to flail for support. It had quickly subsided, but his head was left with a throbbing pain. Zapped of all energy, his body was refusing to move. Only out of sheer will to save a dying Reed did his legs cooperate. It felt as if a thousand bayonets were pressing and stabbing at his limbs and head.

Reed's body lay still on the middle of the road, her operation winning MVRPG laying empty beside her. Only a few steps from his cover and Kumbi was already receiving shots, but not as many as he anticipated. Barrel trained where the flashes were coming from, he, despite pain throwing off his focus, let out bursts of fire, suppressing the few troops that remained. Although he couldn't see it, he heard another friendly gun chip in. Had the other enemy soldiers run off? Did they know that the UKLA were free to advance? Whatever the case, Kumbi was grateful. After a small while, no more guns were being aimed in his direction, thanks to him and one other SEU soldier. Knowing of Reed's sacrifice, they both ran (in Kumbi's case stumbled as fast as he could) to her body, sprawled out among the disturbed tarmac.

"Stephanie, can you hear me?" the SEU soldier shook her hard, before bending over to check her heartbeat. It looked as though three holes had been carved in her right shoulder, and they were bleeding out, a puddle already forming, staining her hair. The other soldier pulled out a piece of cloth that was crudely cut and started applying pressure to the wound that was already too big for the cloth scrap. But it would have to do. Kumbi attempted to get hold of Northwood again, to tell the good news, *'couch few survivors'* was messaged through, with code word 'couch' meaning that the operation was a success. A flurry of movement drew their attention behind them, as five other injured, barely surviving, soldiers ran up towards them with expressions of hysterical joy on their faces. Kumbi recognized one of them as the healthier mortar operator that accompanied Corporal Clarke. It was clear the other two didn't make it.

"We won!" spluttered an especially happy soldier, clutching his arm with blood trickling down his face. At sight of the SEU leader on the floor, one of them rushed over with a lone pathophage syringe in his hand. Without a medical badge strapped around his arm, it was clear their medic had also, ironically, died in action. Stabbing the site of the wound, the pathophage liquid was forced in. Another had brandished a bandage, ready to wrap the awkward wound.

"She's breathing and her heart hasn't given up yet," reported the SEU soldier, "She'll hopefully live," he added, not sounding too hopeful himself. Despite the situation, the atmosphere of celebration and victory reigned supreme, with unerasable smiles beaming from their battered mugs. In the midst of the celebration, a mortar shell struck very close to the cheering survivors, almost knocking a few troops off their feet. That was when a very good question was raised, "What now, corporal?"

What was next, was to tell their captain of the good news and then proceed with joining the advancing troops that were rushing to their aid to truly push back the enemy and flank their lines, not giving them a chance to recover and hopefully ending the stalemate and actually advancing the war in their favour. But Northwood wasn't responding. Whatever happened to him would have to be investigated later, as right now the lives of the remaining invaders were in his hands.

"We need to rendezvous with the approaching reinforcements, now that the super turrets are done for," his speech was surprisingly strong despite the agonizing pain his body was in, "we just need to find out where they are," he finished, sounding more breathless near the end.

"Well considering this is the east-most tower, we should probably head west," suggested someone who pulled out a compass and pointed it eastwards.

"Yeah-" started Kumbi his speech instantly deteriorating. His eyes were beginning to close as darkness quickly descended. Too much blood had escaped the tight confines of his bandages and he had pushed himself too hard. Pure adrenaline was what was mostly keeping him upright, and now it was starting to give in.

He collapsed to the floor, not feeling the impact.

"Screw that, we're staying here. We've done enough fighting and running and dying! Let's just let the others come to us," the SEU woman put her foot down. The impromptu medic saw to Kumbi, confidently reassuring him whilst checking for any other wounds. Not that he would be able to do anything, he had no bandages.

Numb pain felt like his body was evaporating and condensing all at once. He had accomplished the mission. The others would come soon. A sigh releasing a portion of his built-up tensions, Kumbi let himself wander off to sleep, next to Private Reed, who hadn't woken up.

From a distance, everything seems a smaller problem than they actually are. Below him, rolled out the theatre of war. Smashed urban streets split off and fused together to form a labyrinth of death. Skeletons of society: battered buildings and empty parks lay strewn, hosting the tug of war that just spawned more and more devastation as far as the eye could see and further. Silence befell the artillery that sent shell after shell after shell, in an effort to ruthlessly stop the invaders that sneaked right behind their lines, but only momentarily.

Like an aimless child, his legs dangled from the infrastructure from a block of flats that used to house civilians, poor innocent people. High up above the chaos and death, above the enemy and the invaders, above the actions and the orders. Up there, the air smelt of pure refreshment, the winds cleaving through him like icicles. A softer atmosphere enveloped him, but the phantoms that stalked his mind were more than present. The same feelings, the same memories, the same flashes reeled past his eyes as if a projector lay at the back of his head. Visions of twisted faces lay spread out amidst the blackened trunks and reaching infrastructure that struck up towards the sky. Wisps of the wind filled his ears alongside the blood-curdling shrieks of a tortured death. The only difference up there, was that it was ever slightly easier to tune it all out as white noise of a distant battle.

It was still night; the stars were bullet holes in a rug of concealment. Alongside the pictures of people dying by his orders, he even spotted a few figures weaving between the upturned cars, just another addition to his mind's performance of his evil.

Gunshots. Actual, real gunshots. Shouts of challenge. *'It must be the UKLA, finally attacking after all,'* the thought played out across his mind like a cloud. *'The operation was a success,'* also floated around, right behind his eyes. *'You won,'* briefly flashed in his heart. *'But at what cost?'* came beeping back from his imaginary radio, his real one laying right below him, its parts scattered from the drop.

Emptiness. No more emotion. Tears welled and fell down a toppled mountain, carrying with them any trace of feeling left in him. Pure nothing now pressured itself on his shoulders, but only for a second before they slipped down and suffocated him. Nothing remained in him, no will to continue if more suffering was the consequence. As if the ghosts were getting their revenge, his windpipe compressed, strangling him. With a final *'sorry'* in his head, the captain accepted the darkness that fell before his eyes. Slipping, he let the tight embrace of the dark take him.

Clink!

Booze sloshed from the lip of their mugs, spilling over their fingers, and splashing on the floor. The mood was electrifying, radiating off the packet of legends: the survivors of Operation Backseat. One lone mortar operator, four SEU soldiers, including the slightly recovered Private Reed, paler than ever, sitting right next to her wife to be. Alongside them were the five SLO soldiers, and their corporal, Henry Kumbi, still recovering but, given the circumstances was allowed to rejoice with his comrades. Unfortunately, their captain that had fought with the SLO soldiers for many a battle, War Captain Northwood, was reported MIA. His body was never found anywhere near the battle scene and beyond. His base of operations was clear of any sign of previous occupation, perplexing the search party. He vanished without a trace, somewhere near the completion of Operation Backseat. Such events happened regularly, so they didn't bust too much of a sweat locating him, but it was a crest-falling loss all the same. They had lost one of their best.

Despite the fearsome battle that they had suffered mere hours ago, life beckoned from their eyes and laughs, bellowing hearty cheers and songs and jokes. The only weight on Kumbi's smile was that he wasn't sharing it with Adam, who he dearly hoped would be joining him in celebratory alcoholic activities. But people die all the time, it was just unlucky that it was Adam's turn. Downing another mug in his best friend's name, he silently rejoiced the life he had. Other silent heroes would be dying. They all needed to be appreciated.

A sudden, physical, weight re-emerged itself to Kumbi. Patting his right breast pocket, the crumbled but still consumable breakfast bar that was now a memento of Corporal Barry 'Bullseye' Brax was discovered. He allowed a small chuckle, but he was still nerved by the near failure the operation had almost suffered due to one hasty decision. He decided to put it back in his pocket.

What lay ahead of the NWD party lay unknown, this war was constantly changing and turning like a stormy sea. Their war-changing and life-saving actions were a resounding success, the UKLA finally able to charge down the US defences and not only disrupt them, but open pockets of divine opportunities that if struck correctly, would spell catastrophe for their opponents. Never-ending and legendary was the legacy of Operation Backseat, and it was appreciated among all the ranks and all the people of the UKLA and beyond. All of those brave bravados would be rewarded and decorated accordingly and rightfully, including those of the dead and missing.

But for now, none of the future brought too much concern for the invaders. Priority number one was to drink to their success. "Well, I believe that a lot of drink is in order, if we are to celebrate *all* of our successes today," remarked Mayeb with a devilish grin, her right arm wrapped tight around her fiancé, not daring to ever let go again. And so, they drunk. The night dragged on, and still the invaders were high on spirits, and in some cases intoxicated on spirits too. After their fun, all had to return to their regiments they had been hand-picked from. Farewells were boded and hugs generously given. Corporal Henry Kumbi, or soon to be Corporal Henry 'bullet-eater' Kumbi, walked back to the Slough front

UKLA Base Hospital, where he was to finally receive the expert medical attention he needed.

Grinning like a school kid, the legend couldn't wait to get right back into the action and finally run the enemy off their proud island. But before he would go defying death some more, he would finally spend a day with his family. To say he was looking forward to seeing his wife and son, Noah, was an understatement. Close to a week of expertly traversing and weaving to get right behind the US Army, to slip past right under their noses, had all paid off. A deep breath entered through a parted grin as he looked up at the sky. He was still alive.

The cogs of human consequence still clogged on, and Kumbi would be there till the end to make sure Humanity saw it through. Afterall, that's how life works, and he was damn sure he wouldn't buckle before its entropy. Humanity is more than that. They should rise to the occasion, not succumb. After all, if death truly is the final destination, whatever the cause, of human hubris or cosmic catastrophe, surely it would be better to go out fighting than to go out already dead.

Fragmented Horizons
pt.1

    This is absolutely disgusting. Why didn't I think of all of this? They didn't exactly warn us, surely they would have known about it. It was their idea, after all. Every time I look into another burning body's sullen eyes, I feel sick punch the top of my throat. Horrific, irregular patterns of burns and flesh create a nauseating mosaic on the densely packed bodies. It's far too late to go back now. Not that I had known any better when it counted.
    Gotta think of the bigger picture. The bigger picture. This will all pay off eventually, we had it coming. Our joke of a government, our self-destructive nature of consuming and consuming until nothing would be left. We had to intervene; they were all leading us down a worse fate than this.
    Let's put another down here, I can tuck it under where the floorboards have sprung up. Such interesting things. Still got six more to go.
    To think I was a homeless only what feels like months ago, now I'm working for the new world order. It was about time we restructured society under a better banner.
    Yeah, I am not going over there, too many... corpses. I'll search over there? Should be good.
    It's not as hot as I thought it would be. Strange. Well, it is quite hot, but I assumed it would be roasting. That's Hollywood influence for you, I guess.
    Is that someone else? I'm sure I'm in the right boundaries. What's he doing?

God, better watch out, there's a lot of unstable shit lying around. *Fuck!* That's gonna leave a mark. What was that? Is it that guy again?

"Hey, this is my area, what are you doing here?"

Is he ignoring me? Bastard. I think he went around here somewhere?

"Oi, you!"

Right, got a runner. Should I pursue? Could be just one of my lot but could also be a survivor? Shit, what if people survived? It doesn't really concern me either way, I don't think. This is actually a great spot to plant another one, right below a till that harbours now useless tokens of past greed.

I'm getting poetic in my adolescence. What the fuck is wrong with me? I'm walking among dead people, so many corpses just littered around the place and I'm really acting like this?

oh my God oh my God oh my God oh my God what the fuck

Remember the bigger picture. The bigger picture, man. Gotta get a grip. Gotta get a fucking grip and do what I have to. This is the better path for us all. They would have ended themselves, had they continued.

Damn, I need to wipe my eyes before all the dust starts clinging and irritating them. I need to blow my nose. Ah fuck of course, no tissue. I guess I better carry on planting and then they might give me a tissue after. They must have tissues.

I remember this place as a kid. The memories with my best friend. He's probably dead now. Well, the memories will last always. The fuck? It's that guy again. Is it a kid?

"Hey, kid, over here."

Poor guy must be terrified. I might actually try and catch up, it's a lost kid at the end of the day.

"It's alright, come here."

Fast little shit. I wonder if its parents are still alive. Oh my god, there's another. His sister? Where did they go? They can't keep running, this place is too unstable.

"Hey, come here! This place could collapse!"

Where the fuck are they? They're gonna get themselves killed. That's footsteps on the upper floor. If they go any higher this place will cave in.

"This building is going to collapse!"

Why won't they listen to me?

"I'm not going to hurt you! I can help you." I might leave them to their fate. No way I'm gonna give chase, the floor will collapse below us. It won't be the most tragic thing that's happened today.

The survivors won't last long, anyway. Poor kids. They could've grown up in such a better world. Ah, that's another good spot. Might be a bit close to the one inside but it'll be well hidden, so they can fuck off if they have a problem with it.

The fuck was that? No way did the kids jump off the second floor.

"Hey, over here! Stop running for fuck's sake."

They need to just stop running and they'll be safe. I'm starting to get tired, man. But we didn't do all of this for them not to appreciate the better society they're gonna live in. Woah, what the fuck?

"No need for that, guys. Put that down and everything will be alright."

Where did they get that from?

"I know you guys are scared, but everything will be explained, okay?"

How do I even address kids, how old are they, even?

"Let's start with names, okay? What's your name, little girl?"

They're terrified. Scared kids with dangerous shit are never a good mix.

"How about you give me the knife, and I can bring you some place safe, yeah?" I don't know about edging closer to them, but it might show my friendly intensions? God this is so difficult.

"That's right, come here, it's okay, you're safe, it's okay."

The girl at least is on my side, hopefully her brother will join me. He's the one with the knife, after all.

"Good girl, I'll dust you off, okay?"

She's filthy. God damn, she has dust all over her. Oh fuck. Oh fuck oh no. I should've expected that.

"Hello."

"I don't know. Maybe weeks or days, I don't know."

"I'm very hungry."

"It's okay. I was with my mum when it happened. Well, not really but before I was. I was eating and mum had to pop out, to work or something, while I ate my cereal and watched the TV. She stared at me for a while before she left.
  "I watched TV for ages. I don't normally get to watch it that long and when I noticed I had watched it for a long time I started to get worried. I looked all over the house, but mum hadn't got back yet. I went to call on the landline to her work when the house fell down on me with a big crash."

"I don't know I think I went to sleep."

"No, she didn't."

"I was very scared. When I was awake, I was bleeding a lot and had to crawl out from under the roof, it was hard to breathe. When I was standing, everyone else's houses had crashed too, and people were everywhere on fire and dead. My neighbours and friends were all on fire and I couldn't wake them. I wanted my mum and I tried to find her after that."

"Yes, I do, she works at the secondary school that is down the road, but it was all burning and exploded. I don't know what happened. I still tried to find mum and I went to the secondary school and bits of the school were breaking off and falling down, crashing on the floor."

"I went in, yes."

"No I didn't hurt myself, but I was already hurt from the roof falling over anyway."

"The gates were all destroyed so I walked over them and into the front of the building. I couldn't see my mum, so I went to try and find her classroom. Bricks and wall were everywhere, and glass was everywhere too."

"No there was no one there, but there were dead people. It smelled really weird, and I didn't like it. I was even calling out for my mum, but no one answered. After a lot of walking I couldn't find her, and I reached the other end of the school where I climbed over a window.
"That's when I saw the other people. They were walking away from each other and not saying anything."

"No I didn't go over. My mum has always told me not to."

"As I watched them go and they still didn't say anything at all I crept over to where they were and saw nothing."

"I don't know, I was scared."

"Well, I kept looking for my mum. I went into the store that we sometimes went into for ice cream or a Moshi Monsters magazine to see if she was there.
"The store was exploded and on fire. I walked a bit on it and looked around. It was a big store so I was there for a lot of time as I walked everywhere I could, calling her name. That's when I saw more of the other people, but it was only one person. He was walking along loads of dead people, sometimes kicking them. I was scared."

"I couldn't do anything, I just stayed hidden. It was scary. At one point he bent over and placed something weird. When he was gone, I went over but I couldn't pick it up. It was a circle, a metal circle, and was put under a lot of broken wall pieces."

"I left it."

"I still didn't know where my mum was, and I tried going back home because I didn't want the other people seeing me but on the way home, I started to think that they had taken my mum away from me."

"Yes, I made it home, but I couldn't find anyone I knew, and there were more and more other people walking around and putting the circle things down. I tried not to be seen and I don't think they did, but I didn't know what I was meant to do. I wanted my mum."

"Yes, I don't really remember when, but the girl found me wondering around my street. She was different from the other people and her name was Sophie. She had brown hair and brown eyes with a crooked nose like this."

"Well what we did was we talked for a bit and her mum was missing too, but also her dad. She knew I was sad and scared, and she wanted to help me find my mum."

"But I never had a dad so it was worse for her because it would be like losing two mums."

"I don't know but I think she is old enough to do secondary school."

"She got me by the hand, and we walked away from the other people, but they walked away from us anyway. Sophie told me that she thinks she knew what happened to my mum. She looked scared, too."

"We were going quite quickly in a straight line, and sometimes she stopped to look at the circle things and told me to back away from them."

"No, she left them alone every time. She says they could be dangerous."

"Well, more and more other people were putting the things down, and I didn't know where we were going but I trusted her. She was nice."

"At one point, we were in a place that was far from my house, but I went there a lot of times with my mum and my friends and sometimes I went there with my cousins. It was a giant building with swimming pools in it, but it was really scary because there were so many people floating in it and broken building bits were all over the place."

"Well we were really careful, and I had to tiptoe around. But then it happened."

"I don't know if I should say."

"It's scary and I don't like it."

"Well, I saw a snack machine that was broken and had crisps all over the floor. I really wanted one so I went over to get it, but then more of the upper floor came breaking down and Sophie was yelling at me to run away so I did. I didn't know where I was going but I knew that I had to go otherwise it would fall on top of me."

"Yes, but that's later."

"I saw another person as I was walking around trying to find Sophie and my mum, and I went to run away from him. As I was, he started shouting out to me and I started to run even faster and fasterer."

"No, I got away, but then I got lost and I bumped into him again, so I ran off as he was calling me over, but my mum always said not to go with strangers, even if they said they knew her."
"I did find Sophie though, she came out of a corner and started running with me away from the stranger."

"We went up the stairs, because if we went outside there could be even more of him to try and catch us."

"No I don't know, but he was very scary."

"When we went up the stairs his footsteps stopped, and Sophie grabbed my hand again and went really fast, even though my feet were hurting. After that we stopped, and we caught our breath."

"No, he stopped chasing us. Sophie then checked if I was okay and then gave me a cutting knife. She told me it would keep me safe if they try to chase me again. But she didn't have one, so she must be really good at fighting. I've never been in a fight before."

"She told me to be really careful with it, but my mum has always told me about that anyway."

"She started to guide me out of the second floor from a different way whilst telling me that she thinks the other people have something to do with both of our mums going missing. I didn't know but she seemed sure of it."

"Yes, I believed her and no, we couldn't get off the second floor another way because the building had all fallen down."

"We were really scared of the other person coming back or something so we agreed to jump to escape him quicker, otherwise we would have to be close to him again."

"Well, as soon as we hit the ground, the other person was there again and was swearing at us, it was really scary, and I started to cry a bit."

"We ran away, but we hit a dead end, where the swimming pool place stored all of its bins. We went to go back but the other person was right there. He tried to get us over and Sophie went but I was so scared and I put the knife in his back because he was going to hurt Sophie and I was so scared."

"It was really scary because he started screaming and Sophie was also screaming and then we ran off again."

"Yes, that's all that happened before we got revenge at them, for taking our mums."

"Yes, I still had the knife and brought it with me."

"No, it's okay."

"If you go, can I at least have a bed please?"

Fleeting steps

Part One

"Pass me a mag, mate," asked Sam, and Ziven Smiert complied, quickly handing one over. The impending mission was said to be a quick and simple hit and run, nothing major. The scouts had concluded the mission possible, and everyone was confident that things would go well, which was surprising given that it was Finchingfield's first ever military mission.

Finchingfield hadn't an army, so all the people that were readying up and preparing were volunteers out of their own free will. Including Ziven, although the real reason he tagged along was because he didn't want to disappoint Marta, his sister. Being each other's only living relatives, him and Marta were inseparable. Their parents had either died or went missing and died later after Britain turned dark, so they were brought up in Finchingfield, a village located close to a couple others that had formed a tight bond over the past few years or so.

That mission was going to define the bond between the villages, with people from all over joining the first ever attack against the Preservative Party, who had been harassing them all for too long. At first it was merely propaganda, but had recently been using violence and fear to try and win them over. Everyone had had enough.

Marta gestured Ziven over, and he kicked himself off the wall and looked up as he walked over. Marta had a plump face yet a defined jawline, with brown, short, choppy hair, so it didn't get matted. Years of distress and trauma had slowly kneaded her forehead into a crease of seriousness and determination. She always had Ziven's back, even during the times he didn't think he deserved it. She smiled at him, "You ready, hm?" He said he was, and grinned. She always had his back, and he always had hers, "How was the garage?" Ziven worked at the only garage Finchingfield had. There they stored their vans and what little cars that could still operate.

They also took in any vehicles that the Preservatives had thrown at them, in their light attempts to 'encourage' them to join their party, to study them and in some cases scrap them. Ziven wasn't exactly a mechanic, but he shadowed people and did the lighter work around the garage. It was thanks to the mechanics that the old vans had been converted into battle vans, by removing the top of the former tail gate, to decrease weight and increase comfort for the people being transported. It was those vehicles that the volunteer team were to ride in the hit and run.

It did expose them to the outside but getting caught with their pants down wasn't part of the plan.

"Yeah, it was alright, thanks. Just a lot of cleaning up to do after yesterday's final preparations," he paused for a second, considering a joke in his head, before Abdul came out of nowhere.

"Well, it's time everyone. Time to show 'em that we're not to be fucked with," he announced with a beaming smile, clasping Ziven's shoulder.

With his head facing the ground, Ziven smirked, "Yeah, we're really *preserving* our place as an independent village," he shot a look at Marta just under his eyebrows, who looked at him emphatically as Abdul laughed, shaking his head.

"You don't let up, do you?" her hand was placed on her hip. Dario entered the huddle and nodded firmly, his SIG Pro firmly in his grip, and Sam soon got up from his seat.

Ahead of time, the battle vans had been driven to the outskirts of Finchingfield, and volunteers from the other villages had walked over, excited, and nervous. There were twelve battle vans in total, and people were travelling in groups of five, including the driver. Abdul was theirs, and Ziven couldn't think of a happier man to drive them to their deaths.

Waving the pessimistic thoughts aside, he looked up and took his hands out of his pocket, his pistol with it. Although his first time handling one, Marta had helped him practice. His aim may not have been the best, but he was sure he would be alright with Marta by his side. They had been through thick and thin, but he wondered if this would be pushing it too far.

"Let's get this show on the road then," piped up Abdul, breaking off to climb into the van's front seat.

"Well, this'll mark history, lads, I know it," confidently reassured Sam, looking at Ziven whose murky brown eyes were trained on the floor.

Marta wrapped her arm around Ziven's shoulders, nudging him on, "It'll be alright. We're going in and out, nothing to fear, alright?" she told him, patting him on the back as she jumped onto the van after Dario and Sam. Ziven paused for a second. He had never done anything like this before. There was no way he could pull it off, although thankfully there were twelve battle vans of people who could be relied on. They were waiting on him. With his face made up of straight lines, he stepped into the van and took a seat, his heart dropping with him.

A canon of engines bellowed to life, and a cheer whooped from the bystanders and volunteers. Ziven's stomach twisted and tugged; his light breathing had gone ragged. His ripped grey shirt swayed around his lower torso, his ribcage pushing against the thin material. Around the gun held his bony fingers, *'it wouldn't take me long to decompose,'* he thought, his cheek pinching slightly.

A wave of good-byes later, and all the vans pushed off from Finchingfield, ready to make a mark on their slice of the world.

The journey was pleasant enough, little was said. Abdul hummed a song every now and then and Dario joined him, but Ziven ultimately shut himself off, letting the outside blur past him as he crawled deeper and deeper into his head.

Marta made small talk with him, but he couldn't focus properly on what was being said. At some point or other, they had entered the urban mess, and the vans had split off from each other to better traverse the bumpy and disrupted roads. He clutched his SIG Pro ever tighter as stress pressed in on him.

Passing more and more ruins of civilization past, more bittersweet reminders of a life long ago flashed by his mind. Usually, he would bat away the unwelcomed throat-blocking memories of his family and life before the Great Malfunction, but now he decided to welcome them, in case he never got the chance to remember them again.

His beautiful wife, his gorgeous kids, his son's last birthday, the water park trip, all of it. As expected, a solitary tear journeyed down his gaunt face.

"Chin up," Nudged Marta, he could feel the heavy expression on his face, "this mission needs everyone to be on high alert. Only then will we be able to return home." Ziven remained silent, she was right, as always.

Another while of getting jerked around by the uneven ground whilst Ziven played more memories of his family in his head went by. It was exhausting. He needed to get out of his head.

Still toying with his pistol, he looked up over the battle van's tailgate. At long last, it looked like they were finally exiting the built-up urban ruins and now traversing the decimated fields and rocky plateaus.

Their scouts had reported that the target, Outpost E, the nerve-centre of their local Preservatives, was located just beyond the urban mess, the tell-tale sign they had warned to lookout for was post-built structures among the ruins. Post-built structures were obvious to spot, from hallmarks such as dodgy infrastructure, and primitive designs and handiwork.

Bumps lay out all across the route, throwing the van up and knocking it from side to side; Ziven just hoped they didn't pop a tire or cause any major damage.

Behind them, the rest of the battle vans escaped the maze of concrete, roaring from the darkness into the cloud-covered light.

Occasional cheers and whoops could be heard, and he was half-tempted to join in, but decided against it to just listen contentedly.

Pulling himself away from his pistol, he consciously re-joined his surroundings, that being Dario sitting next to him, with Sam and Marta opposite.

Marta's blue, crystal-sharp eyes cut through the horizon, no doubt envisioning their future success.

He wished he could be imagining the same.

"I wonder if they'll throw a welcome party for us," remarked Dario, a slight smirk apparent.

"I'm not sure you have the same definition of 'welcome party' as they do, Dario," came from Marta.

"Well, we'll find out soon enough," chirped up Abdul, "Something tells me that we are going to be the party-poopers in this situation," he added, not expecting a response but getting an involuntary snort from Sam.

Ziven went through the plan again. They were to drive up to their target and cause as much chaos as they wanted. Killing, destruction, and mayhem were all on the table. They hoped it would make a statement, by striking an important asset of theirs. Everyone back home speculated that Outpost E was responsible for organizing the military operations in the area, including their violent acts on Finchingfield. If they managed to shut it down, all the better.

At that moment, a huge explosion over-turned a battle van some place to their left, summersaulting it before it crashed in a devastating landing. Without a word being said, Abdul cranked up the speed. All around them, the other battle vans swerved and sped up, not wanting to meet the same fate as the mad mess of metal and meat.

Instinctively, they all clutched their seats and scanned around them, trying to find a source to the sudden destruction.

Another staggering explosion uplifted and spun another van at the far left end, but this time Ziven saw it happen. There was no smoky trail left in the air, no sign of anything shot at them. With a pit opening in his stomach, he knew the source of the destruction.

"Mines," he spluttered, "We're in a mine field."

The driver only tightened his grip on the steering wheel and pressed harder on the acceleration. Ziven only feared that all the explosions would attract unwelcome attention, which would spell doom to the whole mission, if the minefield didn't finish them off beforehand. Through the bumps and rocking, he tried to focus on distant spots where sniper nests could be present, or an ambush could be waiting.

Another explosion sounded; the van right next to them was hit. The shudder and shock slipped his pistol right out of his hands. *'Damn it,'* he thought as he scrambled to grab it again. Thinking about the potential ambush of sniper rifles and bazookas and automatic guns while trying to get his small, measly SIG Pro was a strange reality check. Of course they didn't know for sure what weaponry the Preservatives truly boasted, but it didn't stop Ziven from thinking the worst.

Spiralling down, the van came crashing from the air in front of them, causing Abdul to slam on the breaks. There wasn't enough space, however, and the van charged right into the metallic husk of flames and corpses. Almost flipping right onto the crash, the van reared up, throwing Dario out of the van and into the bonfire with a choked scream. Ziven could only hold on for dear life as the van threw itself onto its side, spilling the passengers out like a dropped packet of sweets.

As soon as he stopped rolling, he remained deathly still, trying not to flinch at the strangled gurgles of his incinerating friend. Lifting his head up, he saw Abdul boot open the door and clamber out, falling onto the ground. Marta was also flat on the ground but started to pick herself up.

"Marta!" he hissed, "Marta get down!" if she triggered a mine, then she would surely die. Not to mention everyone around her. Including Ziven. He could hear the other battle vans racing off in the distance, with another one triggering yet another mine. By his calculations, that left eight more vans going, which should be enough if they run into some heat.

Sam was already squatting down, "Guys, we need to go, if they've heard us then we're dead meat just staying here."

"But the bloody mines!" cried Abdul, Ziven fearing the same.

"We're dead either way," joined Marta. As much as it frustrated Ziven, they were right. Taking the plunge, he rolled around. No mines yet. Then he hauled himself up, still shaky from the crash. Checking himself for injuries and the like, he exhaled. Sam continued, "We need to travel with enough space between us to mitigate the damage any mines will do if we stumble into any." They didn't argue with that.

Before they got going, Ziven shot Marta a look, his face plastered in concern. She looked back with a firm glare of determination.

With everyone up and going, they quickly checked the van that crashed in front of them for any survivors. The sight was sickening. Dario was still twitching, the flames scolding and ripping his skin. People they knew were wrangled between chunks and plates of metal, viscous tears exposing meat and bone. Faces warped around the bent, melting metal scraps. Ziven quickly turned the other way.

Everyone dispersed from each other, with Marta a distance to his right. Walking along felt as though they were tip toeing on eggshells, only with higher stakes. Sweat and terror preceded every step, with fleeting relief every time an explosion didn't follow after pressing his foot firmly on the Schrödinger's soil.

The tension was almost as tangible as the intense heat that seemed to wrap itself around them in a demon's massage. Chest rapidly rising and falling, Ziven tried to keep control. It was those instinctive jerks and urges that he had to control with an iron fist if he wanted to traverse the minefield alive.

Glancing up, and the other battle vans had thankfully made it through alright. He could only hope they didn't run into an ambush. They didn't have too much stretch left to go either, but every step was a pain-staking process. And a blessing. The key in such situations is to ensure that you don't let the monotony of it throw your attention. Every second was vital, and he had to make sure he was fully utilizing each one.

Fully down the line to his left, a concentrated stream of power and a fray of dirt erupted, closely followed by an ear-splitting boom. Ziven was knocked off his feet as the ripped body of Sam spun in a gory glory through the air. Back on the floor, Ziven recoiled in pain, yet was frozen in fear.

He thought he could hear the muffled cries and screams of others near him, but he wasn't so sure through the brain-wracking echoes and ringing in his mind. He so desperately wanted to writhe around in pain, but he was pinned down by the greater fear of imminent death.

There was no time for remorse, although Sam's death was a sobering moment for everyone there. No one would be getting their hopes up until they met the fringe of the folded tarmac and disrupted streets.

Sweat protruded from his brow, his heart rate quickened as he hoisted himself up, and began to continue, albeit with a tremble in his feet. Being exposed and in the open like that was a strange type of fear, fear of the unknown. Anyone could be watching them, and all they could do was slowly creep over the rotted earth.

A few more agonizing paces in, and Abdul broke under the pressure. Ziven could feel the anticipation, as Abdul screwed up his face and bolted. It was the same panicked feeling as a wasp landing on the back of your neck or seeing something inhuman move out of the corner of your eye, watching Abdul follow the whim of his instincts, yet suddenly Ziven and Marta were both compelled, too.

Under such fearful, pressuring circumstances, seeing one person flake off was all the spark needed to properly light their terror, bringing action to their fears. Sprinting in unison, the three smashed down on the ground with every footstep, not breaking stride. The world flashed around them as tunnel vision blinded them. Tension and fear peaking higher and higher with every second of running was almost too much to bear but stopping wasn't an option now.

His chest tightened and seized, yet his legs carried him further and further until they all graced the safety of the crumbled, ruined concrete, throwing them off their delicate balance.

All tumbling to the floor, their adrenaline exploded in a fit of exasperation, extasy, and a final bombardment of panic and tension. Swallowing deep breaths, they couldn't believe how lucky they had just been.

Ziven wanted to shout and scold Abdul for such an irrational action, but he was too shaken and breathless to do anything. Staring at him with narrow, sharp eyes, Abdul looked back, a slight shudder to his breaths. Rage subsiding, Ziven knew he didn't need to say a word.

Next, he looked for Marta, who was leaning against a wall with wide eyes. Looking at Ziven, she hurried over to help him up, which he gratefully took. "How are you?" he breathlessly asked, making sure she had no major wounds.

"I'll be alright, you two?" she went to help Abdul, but he was already bent over holding his knees. Ziven said he was alright, and Abdul just let out a sigh, looking at them to make a point.

Pangs and cries jumped their way into ear shot; their allies ahead had entered combat. They suddenly started to make their way towards it, at the cost of a large throbbing in their heads and another wave of breathlessness.

Ziven was without his gun, he didn't notice it at the time, but it must have flung from the van when they crashed. As long as he was with Marta, he considered himself relatively safe, especially as she had managed to keep hold of hers.

"We better watch out, in case of a stray bullet or Preservative," whispered Marta, in the lead.

Edging around a corner, and what looked like a pre-built cul-de-sac, with houses standing in solidarity bearing the scars of war, was revealed. Turned on their sides were two of the battle vans, with a few corpses flung around the impact of the crash. They quickly passed, their allies were in trouble and they really didn't want to see such a sight again. Leaving the street with a brisk pace onto a main road, they made a left turn. More sounds of action filtered through the air, with shouts and shuffles and the sliding of metal on metal.

A huge multi-lane road was the setting for the battle, resembling a stormy sea with sharp cracks and what looked like waves of tarmac washing over debris. With a few seconds to react and absorb the situation, a sudden impression of loss hit his eyes. The irregular uniform of the Preservative military broke cover and dashed along the frozen sea, automatic weaponry pointing in the direction of the huddle of bleeding, terrified Finchingfield soldiers and allies.

Battle vans littered the scene, all upturned and decorated with bullet holes. They must have been ambushed after all. Finchingfield residents and their counterparts were scattered in a horrifically failed attempt to try to form a defensive line. Ziven, Marta and Abdul could do nothing as before they knew it, a dozen enemy troops vaulted over their little cover, and executed all on sight.

It was a massacre. No remorse, no mercy. Their pitiful SIG Pros were kicked aside, their bodies grabbed and dragged like garbage. In a sickening display of efficiency, Ziven's friends were butchered and put down in seconds.

They stood there for a few moments, staring wide-eyed and terrified. One of the enemy soldiers, who was already sliding Oliver over the scratchy, slicing road, looked up to the group of three standing in disbelief.

"Oi! Over there!" she rallied, already drawing out her gun. It was time to go.

Spinning around and sprinting off, bullets had already joined the rush. There was no time to organize or prepare, but there was a mutual understanding between them: don't slow down, don't get caught, and don't get shot.

Sharp breathing flowed with Marta's quick breaths, and Abdul was grunting a little. All running down a straight road, Ziven knew that eventually the enemy would be able to align a straight shot. Between breaths, he tried to say, "Over there," whilst gesturing to a right hand turn. Thankfully, they all understood what he was getting at.

Scurrying, they managed to flee the road before the bullets started whizzing down it. Briefly out of eye-sight, they wanted to throw their pursuers off whilst they had the advantage. Ziven was more eager to do so apparently, as he motioned onto another turn and scrambled to bend around without falling, but as he glanced around, Abdul and Marta were too carried by their momentum to stop.

Before she went completely out of sight, she made a circular gesture with a pointed finger. They were to press onwards and reconvene wherever the paths join.

Trying not to think of yet another irrational decision, he stabilized himself, swallowed his fears, and pressed on. The rumble of the Preservative military could be heard, with their guns clinking and their boots stomping.

He so desperately didn't want to see the corpse of his sister later down the road. Thankfully, the alley he parted through joined a road that went parallel to where Marta and Abdul were legging it, so he took his chances and continued to sprint up.

He could hear the chilling sounds of guns letting off a murderous stream of bullets towards Marta and Abdul. Pace quickening, he couldn't operate his legs fast enough. Dread poked at Ziven all over, especially when he heard a cry of pain. The roads merged just ahead, a little closer and they would be able to escape the streams of bullets, but all it took was a couple good shots to end their lives.

Marta and Abdul practically tumbled into his road further ahead, Abdul holding a bloodied arm and Marta screaming for Ziven to run away.

In those few split seconds, so much happened. Far too much to process. Struggling to turn around, Abdul tripped and fell with a cry. There was no saving him now. Ziven didn't look back. He didn't linger, or let the immense guilt cause any hesitation. It was either Abdul or everyone.

They only had a few seconds before the hail of bullets were let loose again, silencing Abdul's cries of pain.

Running side by side, Marta gave Ziven a look. He hadn't seen that look for a long time. She looked worried. It must have been sibling instinct, for he knew exactly what she intended to do.

Splitting up in situations such as that seems like a good idea from afar, but in the heat of the action it was a gamble of the highest order. He might never see her again. There was no energy to argue, and they sharply turned in opposite directions, carrying themselves out of the line of fire and into a side alley or road.

Ziven just prayed he could see his sister again.

Gravel gritted under his feet, threatening to unlevel him. Fatigue and exhaustion wriggled its way into his muscles and laced itself thick around his bones. Thankfully, the alley he had dashed into split off into streets and highstreets, and he picked at whim what branches he wanted to escape into.

Echoing footsteps reflected his beating heart, his breathing providing an unsettling base. He stumbled out of an opening onto another road. His sweaty, red, and wild face looked around. There was no sign of anyone. Proceeding with caution, he lightly jogged away, being vigilant to take as many turns as possible to really shake his pursuers off, if they were even still after him.

Although satisfied he had escaped them, there was no time to celebrate. Now he needed to find Marta, and then get the hell out of there.

There was only one problem, he had no idea where he was. In the mad chase he sprinted as far away as possible, the whole thing was a blur, spare the shocking image of his friends all being slaughtered.

Walking around for a bit, he had figured out he was well and truly lost. Lungs screaming, he let himself focus solely on breathing, squeezing his eyes shut and letting shudders and shivers shake his spine and shoulders. Hurting all over, he let his body collapse onto a flattened park bench.

Was it truly just him and Marta left? Anxiety clawing through his gut, he forced himself up and ignored the exhaustion that followed.

Activity became apparent to his right, after walking for some time trying to subdue the growing sense of panic. Sneaking around a corner, he saw a group of soldiers, which he would later know as the perimeter guard, walking together. They were talking, but he couldn't quite understand their conversation.

Making their way past him as he reduced himself behind a car, he got the impression that they had given up, with only one escapee. His heart beat out of his chest and into his ears. Trying to contain the panic just condensed it until it felt like he was trying to suppress a rhino from stampeding.

Had they caught Marta?

Managing to stay relatively quiet until they had passed, he let his shaky breathing loose, and grabbed at his legs in a small frenzy. He couldn't breathe fast enough, his lungs were contracting and expanding at a ridiculous speed, with his hands clamping and shaking on his legs or the ground.

After about five whole minutes of fighting for control and trying not to make himself a target, he closed his eyes. Regained control of his breathing. Released his hands. Now standing, albeit with his guts in knots, his eyebrows wavering, and his jaw clamped shut, he had to develop a plan if he wanted to escape and find Marta, if she were still alive.

Deciding to follow in the direction the group of perimeter guards had travelled, he brainstormed. He had no idea where he was. Besides, even if he did know, the route they took to get there would be riddled by guns and malcontent. Could they be considering a counter-attack? That would be the death of Finchingfield for sure. Something told him they were getting sick and tired of their resistances, and now their attack would be the last straw on the camel's back.

As he walked, the afternoon sun caressing his neck, many ideas flashed by his mind. Sneak all the way back home? Impossible, the distance would be too straining on foot, especially considering how exhausted he was. He would die of starvation or exposure or something of the like. Surrender? That was morbidly appealing, the odds were against him, and perhaps a swift death would be a better alternative than any other death that awaited him. Besides, he hadn't yet given up on his sister. She always had a way out, always had a plan

What about infiltrating the perimeter guard and stealing a vehicle? The perimeter guard proved a large force, there was no way everyone knew everyone. Blend in, steal a ride and then he was home free. Light excitement bubbled in his gut, but he knew any plan he set his mind to was bound to fail, especially without Marta by his side. Oh God, he needed to find her.

It was moments like those when Marta would step in, encourage, and support him. He knew she would want him to trust his gut, not his head. It was difficult, however, when his head was outlining all the ways in which he could screw up or make a mistake. But that was always his excuse.

Straightening his eyebrows, he committed himself to the half-baked plan. He would steal a vehicle and drive out of the place, hopefully with Marta by his side.

From his brief glances of the perimeter guard soldiers, it was clear there was no strict dress code or uniform, but they all stood out by their weaponry and neon green straps around their arms and legs, just above their boots. For his plan to work, he would need to acquire those straps and a gun.

Something told him it was going to be easier thought than done. Still wondering down the path the perimeter guards had traversed down, the distant rumble of conversation once again crept into earshot. Ducking low, he quickened his pace until he was shifting along a mess of upturned cars, with dust wrapped all over them.

Up ahead was a large open area that seemed especially destroyed despite obvious efforts to clear the debris out of the way; it was hard to tell what the space used to be. It was hosting a gathering of soldiers, all milling around. For reference, he dubbed it the meeting point. People were entering from multiple different roads and paths, to sit down or stand idly. At a guess, there were about a few dozen milling about, no doubt all talking about the breach that they had swiftly ended.

The rumble of conversation materialized into three soldiers exiting an alley and walking towards the meeting point. As luck would have it, he heard them talking about the two losses they had endured, and that they would do something about their bodies a little later. That was an opportunity Ziven would gratefully accept. If he could find a body in good time, he could steal all of the stuff he needed, ditch the body, and then try to bluff his way into the fold.

The thought inspired anxiety and doubt. He tried his best to ignore it.

He didn't want to waste time; he had to find at least one body before it was too late. In his brief visit, he made sure to mentally note the direction back. From how they were talking and addressing each other, he didn't feel they were particularly close, a weakness he made a mental not of.

Guessing that the lethal conflict had to be around there somewhere, he branched off, keeping a keen eye out for flies, or an attractive neon green slash among the grey rubble and ruin.

The husk of urban life not only was riddled with dust and decay, but painful memories. Memories of walking down the dense streets of strangers, all leading their own little lives. The simplicity of walking on mostly intact concrete pathways and crossing the road was all in the past. Now, it was hard to tell where the pavement stopped, and the road began. The choking pollutants of progress be it adverts, factories, or corporate scams, all lead up to the big wipe-away. No one was expecting it. He just went to sleep one day and was woken up by the bone-shaking, mind-numbing explosions…

He fell over and sliced his forehead on a particularly sharp chunk of stone. Grunting, Ziven touched his head. It stinged to the touch and dabbles of blood latched onto his fingers.

It was then when he noticed a couple of green reflections as he straightened up, and widening his focus, he realized he was across the road of where he stood before. Where he watched as his friends died. Swallowing his pain and grief, he walked over the final battleground of his friends, to the body of a fallen perimeter guard. She had a bullet wound that burrowed deep inside her ribcage. Must have been a lucky shot, or maybe even friendly fire.

Relieving her gun and reflective straps, he hauled the body over his shoulder. She had long, filthy blonde-turned-brown hair with two scars that ran down her face. He figured that people's lives and stories still carried on, even when the book they all knew had closed and another had opened.

He eventually located a suitable spot to dump the body, under a large slab of collapsed roof. Momentarily putting her down, he grabbed the underside of the slab and hauled it with all his might. It didn't budge. Trying some more, and he managed to shift it sideways a bit, but not enough to achieve anything.

Cutting his losses, he went to pick her up again when he heard walking. Scrapping his plan, he decided to pick her up and ungracefully dump her in the corner, a place where the collapsed roof hid the body out of plain sight.

Grasping his new gun and donning the reflective straps, he hastily jogged onto the road. Now was the time for action. He prayed he didn't mess up, or his shallow, rapid breathing didn't give anything away.

As soon as his presence was made aware to a group of four, they immediately regarded him as one of their own.
"Where the hell have you been, man?" asked one of them, with flat black hair and matching dark eyes. There was somewhat of an accent under his breath, but he couldn't discern it properly.

He only hesitated for a couple seconds before his lie developed in his head, "I was chasing down that last guy," he blurted, tightening his mouth shut as soon as the words left his mouth. 'Dammit'.
"Really? He gave you the slip too, huh?" asked another, his gun in a surprisingly relaxed grip.

"Yeah," Ziven tried to sound as conversational as possible, after a brief splutter and coughing fit. His mouth was dry, "Bastard rounded a corner and as soon as I passed, he wacked me in the head with a rock," he really tried to sell his story, even if he did sound like a talking corpse. That trip from before was a life-saver. Quite literally.

"Jammy sods," the first one spoke up again, "Those fucking Finchingfield lot have definitely got some guts, coming at us with sidearms." Everyone burst into laughter, and Ziven had to painfully join in. In hindsight, it was stupid being so ill-prepared, but then again the mission didn't exactly go according to plan.

He joined their group and walked back with them. It was obvious now that the perimeter guard was a large force, how may were running about?

"What's your name, by the way?" asked one of them, and only hesitating for a second he gave 'Thomas'. He probably could have got away with using his own name, but it didn't feel right. They didn't bat an eye, not knowing people must have been a common occurrence.

He settled his mind, as easy as closing the lid on box bursting with bees. He was in. Instead of celebrating that he had passed on as one of their own, he wondered how long it would last, no way would it be enough. There were so many possibilities, he could slip out of character or accidently give up his plan or crack under the pressure…

For now, though, he laughed at jokes making fun of his own dead friends and socialized with the very same murderers that wiped out the entire assault force. Except him. And hopefully, Marta.

Part Two

Ziven used to have a son. He was just a child, a little past one-years-old. Not old enough to appreciate anything in life yet old enough to be incredibly adorable. Patryk, his name was. He would've been five or six years old, had the bombs not gone off. It struck Ziven as unfair to call them 'bombs', as that would put the deplorable, nuclear, inhumane 2,400 pound death machines in the same category as stick of dynamite.

He tried not to think about him much, especially when he was trying to behave like a merciless member of the Preservative's perimeter guard, and not a terrified, shaken Finchingfield resident.

It had been a small walk back, and upon entry of the meeting point, he faded right into the mass of bodies and guns. People were sitting around at random, chatting and every now and then scanning the rooftops and alley ways, before doing some more lounging around.

Following suite, he sat down upon a broken bollard and felt immediately uncomfortable. But not wanting to attract attention, he remained still. It was surreal, being among the hive that had been pestering his village for so long, trying to score them under their political puppet strings.

"Hey, you good?" approached a random soldier, with a flask of water and what looked like a cotton pad, or at least something similar. He gestured towards his forehead, which he had forgotten was smeared with blood.

"Yeah, thanks, just a scratch," jested Ziven, maintaining his casual tone.

"Well, take these anyway," he handed him the bottle and the pad, "and clean yourself up," he seemed keen on staying and chatting, so Ziven prolonged the process of dabbing the pad in water and then applying it to the wound in the hope that he would eventually go away.

He wasn't so lucky. At least thinking to utilize the situation, he asked, "So, were you at the fight?" It was quite a risky question, but it would cement his place among them. Or at least with one of them.

"Hell yeah, although I didn't get in on the action, I just saw as a load of the others," he paused and recounted their names, "piled in on the unlucky fuckers." Suppressed rage strangled his fake laugh, which he played off as a small coughing fit.

They exchanged names and then Ziven told him the same story of where he was at in the action, the same story he told the first lot.

He didn't want to compromise himself by asking a stupid question, but luckily Matt did that for him, "When are we supposed to be switching with team B again? Is it tomorrow or the day after?"

"I've no clue," he gave himself some considering time beforehand, "Maybe someone else knows."

"Yeah, maybe," Matt soon broke off and asked someone called Aryana.

"In a few days or something," she answered matter of factly.

Ziven could only assume that they had different perimeter guard teams that rotated every so often. He would have to leave before that happened. Thankfully, there were multiple nights between then; he could use the cover of darkness to jump into a vehicle and slip away.

Matt then stood idly by, like everyone else. Ziven had a horrid feeling that they were waiting for orders or waiting for the clean-up to be completed. He would have to wait and find out.

Right on cue, someone wearing yellow reflective straps and a heavy presence walked in the centre of the meeting point, needing to say nothing to grab everyone's attention. He must have been the leader, or supervisor of the team. He was muscly, large and Ziven most definitely would not want to take him on in a fight.

It was unusual to see such a display of muscles and broadness, they must be eating well.

Voice punctuating his stature, he announced that all par one of the Finchingfield 'assailants' had been killed, and that the only escapee was long gone. He was disappointed in them for letting one slip through the net, although it wasn't a big deal because he was sure whoever it was wouldn't make it back anyway.

He also announced that a scout team had been dispatched to scour the route they believed the invaders took, which, with a stab in the gut, turned out to be the right one. It was highly uncomfortable listening to his enemy talk about his butchered friends in such a way, it took all of his willpower to keep his composure.

"Nothing has been stated by the director yet, but if you wanted my opinion, I'd say that it was a desperate attempt to show us who's boss, and nothing to worry about. I heavily doubt they will be performing any other theatrics again," he was probably right, "Alright, everyone return to normal, and if you see that one escapee, just kill him, and get it over with. Keep your eyes peeled." He walked off, with a final scowl.

Everyone ambling away, Ziven quickly wondered if there was a strict patrolling schedule or particular patrolling route they were expected to take. He would need to blend in seamlessly to maintain his fake identity. In his fretting, everyone had already walked out of the four roads to begin their patrols. In that moment in time, he sat alone. Usually, he would be sat in those tough situations with Marta, and she would be the one to come up with a brilliant plan. He would have to come up with one by himself, at least until he found Marta.

Brainstorming, he tried to reason the best probable place for vehicles. *'Probably some place important, near where the leader would be?'* With that sudden lightbulb, he quickly strode his way towards the exit the leader took, in hopes that he was going someplace at least of value, if not with transport.

Skipping along the meeting point, the same yellow strap wearing, big-built leader came striding back through.

"What's this then? Felt like you had some time to mosey about? Didn't feel the need to follow my orders upon ordering them, did you?" he boomed, puffing his chest up.

"Just lost my orientation is all," he didn't need to fake the lackey-scared-of-his-superior act.

"Who are you?" that's the question he desperately didn't want to hear.

"T-Thomas, sir," he stuttered.

"Thomas who?" there was a hint of disbelief in his voice.

"Thomas Grant, sir,"

"Right," he gave him a suspicious look, "off you go, then." He took his leave, keeping his composure, but as soon as he was ten steps away he let out a shaky breath and felt a shiver run down his spine. That was too close. Only moments in and he had already almost ruined it. He was going to have to steer clear of the leader until he found his getaway car, which he was hoping to find sooner rather than later. Marta would have definitely handled that situation better than him.

The idea was to locate the vehicle now, and sneak out in the night to steal it, granted there were no night patrollers to get in his way. Although on his own, he had faith in the plan. He couldn't find anything wrong with it yet, which he was pretty sure he would do soon enough.

Walking further down the road, and all of the pieces of the perimeter guard puzzle were perfectly in align; everyone was walking up and down their designated spot, which happened to be quite a stretch per soldier. The sense of being out of place loomed over him, he could almost feel their quizzical eyes on his back as he scurried from road to road, trying his best to adopt the perimeter guard look: plain face, straight back, barrel pointing anywhere but the ground.

Weaving throughout the separate roads and houses, he found the guard to be everywhere. He couldn't believe how far-flung they were, and how they kept organized in the urban jungle. Their presence was known with every street he passed onto, every road he walked down.

Charles and Michelle were the scouts that concluded the hit and run to be possible. They must have missed the fateful minefield, having stationed their vehicles well away and taking an alternate route in for maximum stealth. Shakespeare couldn't have written a better tragedy.

In the distance, he spied signs of post-built infrastructure, as the roads had been filled with dense, pact dirt and the buildings had no holes in them, although there were a few large cracks. An imposing, solid mass of grey bricks and metal fencing sat in the middle of the contrasting, weak ruins. He was nearing the end of the perimeter guard presence and was on the brink of their fateful target. Outpost E.

The very building they had been tasked with attacking was in front of him. Out of all of the people sent on the mission, he was the only one who made it. If only he could finish off what they started, but he knew that was unrealistic. At least he knew where the vehicles would roughly be located. Or at least it was a start.

Slowing to a casual pace, he considered the best way to go about finding where the vehicles were parked. There was no way he could walk up and gain access to the outpost, there must have been security measures put in place. Deciding to play it safe, he changed course. Instead of walking towards the outpost, he was going to walk around it, keeping a keen eye out for a setting that would harbour vehicles, be it a garage or parking lot.

Pacing briskly now, he had walked for quite some time, with no luck. After about twenty minutes of walking, he spotted an entrance. There were four perimeter guards and around half a dozen other, burlier, outpost guards in fixed positions. He didn't want to pry out any further than he was to avoid detection, but he did get a good look around it.

A long walkway was the direct access point, and the main outpost was surrounded by a line of barbed wire right before the high metal fencing. At first glance it seemed impenetrable, which, thankfully, was of no concern for Ziven. Unless, of course, all the transport was located *inside* the outpost, which was a worrying thought. Waving it off, he latched onto the hope that they were within reasonable access for him to sneak into later that night.

After a while of walking, interesting sounds reached out to him. Hushed cheering and quiet tapping. Curious, he changed course towards it. Growing louder, he could make out individual voices between the whispers of excitement. He kicked a pebble as he neared, and silence dropped. A light shift here and there pointed him in the direction to investigate. Following his hunch, he walked into a building, his footsteps filling the empty expanse. Pressing on up the stairs and he found himself staring at five perimeter guards, all staring at him in anticipation hunched over a game of cards.

"Did someone invite him?" whispered someone.

"You alright, mate?" cautiously branched out one of the two players.

"Yeah, thanks," he let the silence linger for another couple seconds, "what's going on here?" a little more silence remained, before another whispered something about them already being exposed, so what's the harm. Ziven was clueless.

"Well, now that you've discovered us, congratulations, by the way, I guess it wouldn't hurt anyone," he looked around the gathering for confirmation, "okay right, come here then." Ziven did as he was told.

"You're Thomas right? The guy that got outran by that Finchingfield rat," laughed someone, the others contributed a little chuckle. Word must travel fast. Ziven was about to retort, but remembered that right then he wasn't Ziven Smiert, he was Thomas Grant.

"Yeah that's me, dickhead," he laughed. The expletive got caught on his throat.

"You know how to play rummy, right?" asked the one sitting cross-legged. Ziven had never played the game himself, but Marta was somewhat of a professional. If only she were with him.

"Roughly," he shrugged.

"Well, it's simple, really." He then explained the basic rules of the game, but no tricks or strategy, Ziven would have to learn that by himself. They all gave him their names: Jack, Kobes, Will, Lillian and Juliette. Jack taught him how to play, and the rest were friendly to him. It felt strange, being a part of these new people without Marta to cling on to. It was very strange. Stranger still, was the thought that he was *socializing* with those monsters, who appeared a lot less blood-thirsty when they were hunched around a card game. The contradiction upset his stomach.

It was Jack and Kobes who were in the middle of a game, the two champions of the tournament facing each other off, hence the excited hushing. They decided to pit Ziven against Juliette, as she was in last place.

"We'll do our match later, I'm more looking forward to see how good you are," stated Kobes. Before long Ziven was sat cross-legged with seven cards in his hands facing off against Juliette. She had her game face on. The match wasn't particularly exciting, but everyone else seemed to be having a blast. It brought a smile to his face, which was dashed when the unsettling thought crept into his mind that he was having fun with the very same people who had riddled his friends with bullets.

But he couldn't let himself get distracted now, they could prove useful.

In his hand, Ziven was neatly building a frayed run of spades, from the ace to six, needing only one card. He was feeling pretty confident and allowed himself to feel good about it.

A couple turns later, and Juliette threw her winning deck onto the floor, the seven of spades he needed along with it. 'God damn it,' he thought, to think all that time she was clutching the card he needed for victory. Not to mention having been beaten by the worst of the bunch.

The crowd cheered in suppressed joy, "You're not so bad, Thomas," admitted Will, "maybe next time you'll go after cards that are actually in the deck." Ziven noted the use of 'next time'. They had adopted him in their little group. It was a mixed feeling. It felt good to be a part of the little community, by himself without him using his sister as a shield. But then it felt despicable, for they were the very people who had killed her. Allegedly.

"To the victor goes the spoils?" she dragged out, looking at all the others.

"Hey, this was just an initiation match, this don't count," rebutted Kobes, "Oh yeah, Thomas," he gestured Ziven over. Hesitantly getting up, he was led to a pre-built basement. At first glance, it looked like a load of old junk scattered around the place.

"We've all got a surface," he started to explain, "and whenever someone wins, they take something from the loser," he waved at the now obvious five distinct arrangements. No one's name was allocated to any of them, yet the piles stayed to themselves. All the items were worth one point each, no matter the size or previous function.

"We're nearing the end of this season, there's only a couple tournaments left so only a few opportunities for the likes of Lillian or Will to get first place, but I don't think that's gonna happen."

It struck Ziven as very interesting, that this whole thing was occurring right under the leader's nose. He must never patrol himself.

"What about when team B rolls around?" Ziven asked, now curious to the whole affair.

"Well that's the thing, the season ends when we switch, and we're pretty sure some of the guys from team B do the same as us, as when we return to start the next season all the shit seems to be in a different place." Ziven took another few seconds to marvel around. In the smallest pile were random pieces of broken car engine bits and bulbs, with occasional household items, such as picture frames and lamp shades. Strangely, all of the items were broken memories of a largely forgotten time. Some things he couldn't recollect the meaning of, or even what they should have looked like all those years ago.

He stepped down to walk around. Brushing his hands on old paint tins and springs and the occasional glass bottle or cap, he was reminded of such weirder times. On the wall, above the piles of junk, was a tally chart. Initials of who he could only resume to be the five players had a number of scratches in a line next to them, every four bunched together with a fifth line crossing through them. Kobes was in the lead, but not by a large margin, Jack was only a few points behind.

As much as he hated them all, it was interesting to see them living ordinary lives that mirrored his own back in Finchingfield. He didn't like to think about it. Assigning humanity to those evil people didn't sit right in his soul.

Finally, he stopped at the biggest pile. It was in close competition with its neighbour, which was when Ziven noticed the beautiful, rusted, pair of bolt cutters. He could have laughed. Sitting right there, on top of a load of rubbish, was a tool he would most definitely be going back for. Already he was imagining cutting the surrounding fence some place no one would see him. Now he could get in the outpost anywhere he wanted, as if he held a master key.

All he needed to do was pilfer the cutters during the night and just hope his new card playing buddies didn't notice. Not that he especially wanted to spend all of his time actually playing with them. Suddenly remembering that he was not alone, he snapped out of his thoughts and walked back over to Kobes.

"Pretty cool," ended Ziven, and they both walked back to the ground floor, where everyone else was joking around.

"Can we expect you next season?" asked Lillian, her head to the side.

"Of course," he lied.

"Feel free to pop in whenever," smiled Jack, "Oh yeah, and remember, don't tell a soul." With that he was off with a final nod. He certainly would be popping in later, but a little later than they would be expecting.

Before he departed, he asked whether the leader knew anything about their card games, to which Jack replied, "What? Jordan? You're kidding, right?" Ziven quickly sprung a smile as if he intended whatever joke they were now laughing at.

Leaving, the sun had started to set, and his legs had transitioned from a painful thudding to a sharp, bone-penetrating ache from all of his walking around. He was unsure of how the night patrolling worked, or where they went to for sleep, so he cautiously made his way back to the meeting point.

Although glad he had found the bolt-cutters, worry returned and was grabbing at the corners of his mind, his shallow face highlighting his concern. The horrible thought of the vehicles being inside the outpost daunted on him once again. He hoped he could at least find where the vehicles were, otherwise, he may never escape. He'd may as well just surrender.

He hoped it wouldn't have to come to that.

Upon arrival of the meeting point, there was a presence through it. Smaller than before, but still slightly busy. Not wanting to get caught out, he slowly idled his way towards a smaller group of people standing around.

"Put you on the nightshift too, huh?" drearily asked someone.

"Yeah," Replied Ziven, pretending to sound bummed out but secretly rejoicing. Now he was 'in' the nightshift patrols, he would have an excuse for being out.

"What route he put you on?"

"Oh you know," he started, now a hair's breadth from being caught out, "the usual."

"Right, gotcha," he neutrally responded. Surprise at that response was difficult to contain, so he looked to the floor as a grin emerged.

Pushing his luck, he then said, "I'm gonna go ahead," without providing an explanation and walked off, in the direction he hoped was 'the usual'.

Taking a turn into a side road, he heard the leader's gruff voice as he rounded up the others. 'Oh no,' was all he could think as he began to speed up. He didn't want to take any chances; no way was he going to wait around and be found out. If anyone said anything, he would immediately be compromised. He needed to find a vehicle as soon as possible.

Why did he have to push it? He could have easily lingered in the back and proceeded in their regular fashion and there would be no possibility of suspicion. But, typically, he messed up.

With his head start, he ran through streets and roads and between houses, but there was no sign of anything significant. Hope dwindling, he doubted he would ever find access to anything. Although a vehicle was his best shot of getting out of there, he would use anything he might come across that could help him. There could be other structures aside Outpost E, there could be literally anything, yet all he stumbled across was more and more ruins. His heart beat ever faster, he had to find a way out. He had to.

Whispers. Slowing down and trying not to breathe despite the cries of pain from his lungs, he strained his ears. Nothing. Not trusting that, he crept closer to where he assumed the whispering came from: his left. Not daring to even let loose pebbles or debris give away his position, he tiptoed, easing his weight onto his every foot.

Replacing the whispers was general shuffling from passive activities. Craning his head around a corner, and past the large metal fence that wrapped itself around the outpost, were two people, presumably outpost guards, patrolling a short circuit. He hoped they happened to be guarding a conveniently placed truck.

He resisted the urge to quickly flit past them, as he realized according to them he was an innocent night patroller. Gradually walking past, he appeared unbothered, barely managing to hide his nerves. He skirted along the metal fence, the border of the outpost. A few more outpost guards were milling around, but nothing to worry about.

Filtering through the darkness, a faint, dull glimmer caught his eye. A reflective strap? Were they on to him? After quickening his pace, he felt a cold band pressure on the back of his neck, and his lungs lose capacity. If they caught him, he would be shot on the spot. Just like his friends.

A few more buildings onwards, and the glimmer was there again, and undisturbed. Unmoving. He looked closer. It was beyond the fence, the light reaching out through the wires. Steadying his breathing, and a shape protruded from the darkness. A bulky thing, and more lines of light reflected off what Ziven soon saw to be a bonnet.

He had found his ticket out.

"Yes!" he harshly whispered, almost exclaiming to the world. He couldn't believe his luck, as his eyes lapped up the gorgeous, sturdy, green vehicle ahead of him, with a whole host more ahead of it in neat lines. He recognized it as what his lot back home called the cruisers, as they had seen a good few quickly tumbling down the horizon. Being a mere four-seater, *without* a gearbox, most likely to reduce weight and expenses. All the mechanics assumed the cruisers was used to transport information and papers and such like around, and in his case, would be used for a grand escape right under the Preservative's noses.

He knew the cruiser to have a great suspension to match the large, gripped wheels which maximized speed and minimized damage, and the result was quite the nice balance. At least Ziven hoped so, he would be relying on it.

He quickly found himself asking, 'What would Marta do?' Now he knew where it was, the next step was to figure out how to actually escape in it. Fishing around the border trying to find an access point for the bay, and he soon over-stepped his boundaries. A quick crinkle of clothes somewhere near him. He froze. Movement slithered from the shadows and night, nothing solid until a silhouette materialized from behind the metal wiring. *'She wouldn't have done that…'*

A flashlight suddenly sprung to life, illuminating him. Highlights of a tired face bore down on him. He had been compromised. Using diplomacy to get out of that rut, on the basis that the outpost guards had probably already been alerted about him by the perimeter guard leader, he didn't think was an option. Not wasting any time, he darted.

The harsh spotlight withdrew, and shouts of alarm broke free. He had no intention of finding out who would answer the guard's call.

Crunches of gritty pavement rhythmically sounded behind him: the chase was on. Unsurprisingly, given his fatigued legs, the chaser was gaining ground. Brain throbbing in anticipation, his neck tingled. The flashlight's incriminating beam was violently thrown back and forth as the pursuer gained more and more speed. No matter how much he tried to pump his legs, they were getting slower and slower.

At this rate, no matter how many corners he turned, he was going to get caught.

In the disrupted shadows ahead from the ever growing flashlight beam, he saw shadows of the guard's arm attempting to grab him. Ziven could almost feel the presence of his hands around the scruff of his neck. Legs beginning to buckle, he strafed left, but threw his right leg out.

As intended, the outpost guard bolted right into his improvised trip wire, forcing a considerable blow to his leg, making Ziven fall down himself. Thankfully, the guard got the brunt of it, as he went headfirst into a brick wall. Scrambling to get up first, Ziven feigned strength as he stood over the fallen guard. He tried desperately to suppress his need to breathe to keep up the façade.

But the guard weren't to go down that easily. Faster than Ziven could register, he grabbed the flashlight and beamed it into his eyes. Startled and stunned, he couldn't react as the guard then threw himself onto his feet, and before Ziven knew it he was being grabbed and thrown against a wall, knocking the air out of him.

The guard was gearing up to throw a nasty punch into his stomach, so he quickly twisted his body to his left. His hip got grazed as the clenched fist went powering into the wall. Taking the opportunity as the guard cried out from the knuckle-jarring punch, Ziven delivered a quick jab to his face before charging at him, his shoulder ramming into the disorientated guard. Barely recovering from being thrown around, Ziven forcefully grabbed the sidearm from the attacker, and extended his arm fully to aim it at the guard's face.

That's when time froze. Both were panting hard, clutching areas of their body that had been slammed or hit. Ziven had the gun, so he was in control. Like a tower of cards, his mental composure was a breeze away from crumbling. He may have the gun, but there was no way he would actually use it. *'I'm too weak,'* he thought as the gun started to waver in his grip. He had never killed anyone before, and for good reason. He would probably miss or slip up somehow.

Slowly, the guard started to stand up, and Ziven's built up tensions released themselves as he kicked the guard back down, his breathing shuddered. He may have had the gun now, but the guard had it all along. Which prompted the thought, the guard could have killed him at any time, but he chose to chase him down. He couldn't help it, he had to ask, "Why didn't you just kill me?" his arm lowered slightly.

His hostage just looked right into his eyes, a small smile curling into his right cheek, "I didn't know who the fuck you were, boy. But now I see. You're that deserter, aren't you? The one that you lot have been rumouring about for weeks now." He didn't expect that reaction. Paranoia had rooted deep in his mind. The perimeter guards weren't on to him at all. The leader hadn't alerted anyone else. He could kick himself.

Playing along, he ordered him to let him pass, twitching his pistol to make a point.

"Alright, I know when I'm beat," he subsided, letting his body collapse onto his elbows. Ziven shifted past, keeping the pistol pointed.

About to make a run for it, two hands grasped his shoulders from behind him, causing shock to run riot in his head and spine. Being spun round, Ziven was face to face with a night patroller he was talking to earlier. Burley laughter sounded from the outpost guard.

Instinctively, he jammed the barrel of the gun into the night patroller's side, not letting any time go to waste. He scarcely had time to think, all he knew to do was to fight, whether he could do it properly or not. Striking the night patroller's side several times with the gun loosened his grip of Ziven's shoulders, to which he wriggled out and spun back around to stick the gun between him and the fast approaching outpost guard.

There was no way of getting out of this by running again, he was simply too exhausted. One hasty, dangerous thought developed in his mind, and the sound of the night patroller lunging at him was the catalyst it needed.

An ear splitting *bang!* lit up the night as the guard fell to the floor, arms flopping to his side, just as the night patroller bodied Ziven to the floor. Trapped, with panic and adrenaline zooming through his veins; the cocktail drove his brain to do the only thing it could think of at the time.

As the gun recoiled and he got barged, the pistol fell out of his hand, so he summoned all of his might to tuck his forearms under his chest and launch himself up. The night patroller hadn't the time to properly adjust himself to keep Ziven down, and so, off balance, he went cascading to Ziven's right.

With his last remaining strength, he forced himself to reach up and grab the pistol and with a hiss of effort, all he recognized after that was the flash of light followed by a twitch of a finger.

Reduced to a trembling mess, he couldn't bring himself to look at the horror he had made. Night patrollers and outpost guards would be swarming to the location of the gunshots, right to where he was standing. So, he ran as hard as he could. Fear replenished his energy as he felt as though he were floating along the roads he shot past. He couldn't feel his legs. All injuries were postponed. He didn't pay attention to where he was going, as long as it carried him as far away from his crime scene as possible.

Slowing down, he briefly checked himself for bloodstains and finding that, miraculously, there was none, he stopped. If he wanted to fit in, he would have to be among them all and appear as clueless as them.

Only problem was, he was holding the smoking barrel. He threw it so it landed on a two story ruin. Out of sight, out of incrimination. Through the ramblings of his frying mind, he knew he couldn't appear at the scene how he was.

But he couldn't calm down. Trembling and panting as if he was malfunctioning, he had to sit down. He barely felt in control of his facial muscles. His hips were jerking uncontrollably. Marta wouldn't have murdered those two people; she wouldn't have been in that rut in the first place.

Dozens of thoughts ran through his mind. He could pretend he was assaulted by the mysterious Finchingfield invader? That could explain why his gun went missing. But everyone must have been suspicious of him after pushing his luck at the meeting point, they would question him on the spot. But the outpost guard didn't know of him, as he thought he would.

His bout of paranoia had caused his hasty decisions, and now he had to make another one. Was it safe? Should he take the opportunity to check out the vehicle bay again? It would be free of anyone if they had all rushed over to the gunshots which were a considerable distance away.

He half-considered turning himself in, he couldn't handle another situation such as that. Paranoia and recklessness had taken over his mind, it wouldn't have happened to someone such as his sister.

He knew the sensible thing to do would be to clear his mind before making any rash decisions, but it was quite difficult to do after committing his first ever murders.

Fast movement echoed some distance behind him, people were rushing on to the scene. He had to make his choice: rush over and blend in or make a run for the hopefully empty border. More and more bodies could be heard moving. He made his choice.

Vaulting upright, he quickly jogged away from the area before arcing his path around to where he had met the outpost guard. As suspected, nobody was around. Just up yonder from where he got caught was an entry point for vehicles, with a long metal arm controlling the access. After seeing some kind of toll booth, it was clear that the person he murdered must have been the barrier operator, to control vehicles in and out of the bay.

Ducking under the bar and there he was, in front of the cruisers. If he weren't so anxious and nervous, he would be over the moon. Nerves and tension spurring him on, he quickly leaped into a front seat. It was then when another obstacle presented itself. He didn't remember the route back. He didn't even know the path out of the urban mess, let alone the whole journey back. He started to sweat when he also noticed they needed a key to start the engine.

Cursing and smacking the steering wheel, he knew he wouldn't be leaving any time soon. He was so close; he was sitting in the damned thing. He had to get a key. More movement started shuffling in his direction, at that point they must be trying to find the one responsible for the two murders, so he quickly rocketed off the cruiser and legged it out of the outpost, but not before scanning the toll booth and spotting a lever that presumably controlled the bars, and three other buttons: a red one, a blue one and a yellow one that was lit up to show it was on.

As soon as he was out of the vehicle bay, he lost himself into the turns and corners and twists of the ruined urban streets, until he bumped into the perimeter guard leader.

"Where the fuck have you been, then?"

Part Three

When he was younger, in the time before the Great Malfunction, Ziven was quite a mischievous kid, and hence had a lot of excuses and lies in his arsenal for any such occasion. It wasn't his fault that his army action figures had kidnapped Marta's Barbie dolls and were taking them hostage. It was actually Marta's fault for not paying the ransom of a packet of skittles.

Although he renounced his past of lies and excuses, his skills sure did come in handy.

"I was near the gun blasts and caught whoever it was legging it down a road, so I gave chase," was his quick reply, looking the leader directly in his eyes.

"And you didn't catch him?" he angrily growled.

"No, sir, it's pitch black. I can only assume it's the guy who escaped us earlier," A good lie will always retain elements of truth. He also wanted to distract the leader from being mad at him specifically.

"The guy who escaped *you* earlier, you mean," he looked around, before beaming into Ziven's eyes, "You did a little escaping yourself, didn't you, when you thought it best to start your patrol a little ahead of the others?" So they had noticed after all, "As memory serves, Grant," He got closer, his teeth bared, "I don't recall putting you on the night patrol," he was so close to getting a ride out of there, and now his cover had been blown, "You better watch your step, or I'll have to report you to the Director for your insolence." He spoke slowly, ending with a tone that would suggest that the Director was the furthest up the command chain that could give out punishment to a lowly perimeter guard.

Instead of feeling fear, he felt extremely relieved that he had no suspicions of his identity, and that Jordon thought of him purely as insubordinate. He took a second to thank God, before moving off with a deliberately guilty expression and walk. Although his identity remained intact, the leader would only take so much more of his slip ups and mistakes. Trailing behind the leader to the scene, the outpost and perimeter guards he had killed were being awkwardly examined, as people assessed the damage, presumably to find out what the rogue was capable of.

A stab of guilt followed after looking at the blood puddles that pooled out from beneath the bodies.

"That guy is going to become a real fucking problem," the leader muttered under his breath. Ziven slowly joined the mass of people walking away, his nerves still on edge. But that didn't stop him from feeling a swallowing fatigue. Seeming as he wasn't supposed to be on the night patrols anyway he thought it shouldn't be a problem if he flaked off and got some rest.

Keeping an eye on everyone else, seeing the slight highlights of the straps disappear round bends and corners as if stalking cats, it turned out they moseyed off to bed wherever they saw fit. Some people crashed in abandoned buildings or inside alleys, where it was a bit darker. Ziven decided it best to choose a random ruin with a clear view of the stars.

Peering up at the patchwork of cosmic fabrics, held together by forgotten constellations, he was pulled back to a time when he would look at the night sky with his family and close friends without being reminded that they were all dead. What once was looked upon with such awe, admiration, and wonder, was just a sickening reminder of isolation.

All the stars, constant observers of the unfurling destruction, held the memories of him and his wife sitting together in a pasture or field. With no worries, the night sky refreshed their minds of the wonders of the universe, and how much lay ahead of them. Now all it did as he looked up at the bullet hole ridden void was reflect the nothing he felt every day.

It was scary to look at. From day to day the constant worries and activity distracted him from his loneliness. And now not even Marta were there to remind him that she was always there for him. Where was she now? Even if he did make it home against all of those odds, what would happen then? Would he find her before that happened? She had always told him to put himself before her, right before he called her a hypocrite. He snorted, a small smile pinching his cheek as a tear rolled down it.

Marta was the only one he had left. Sure, he had friends in Finchingfield, but he never felt particularly close to them. He wasn't entirely convinced they thought of him as a close friend, either. To top it all off, now they were mostly dead.

He couldn't finish his thoughts as sleep swept over him and soon a new day dawned and pried open his eye lids. Getting up revealed a pang in his back and a pain in his neck. Must have been from sleeping on stones and rocks all night. After stretching, he quickly made it back to the meeting point, it was the safest bet given he didn't know their morning routine. Everyone was already standing pin-straight, listening to the leader as he hurriedly walked over to join them.

Trying to sneak into the back, the leader lingered his gaze towards him for a few seconds to make a point. He was already in deep trouble, at this point he was just slapping the leader in the face.

Nothing important was said or ordered, it was just a general briefing. Or so he hoped, he wasn't there for the first bit. Mechanically, everyone branched off, either to patrol or to receive breakfast, consisting of a 'nutrient-rich porridge' which looked like it violated the human rights of anyone who ate it. Ziven had to reminded himself, in that day and age, no one had human rights. It seemed hardly any of them were even human.

He decided to mix into the group who went first to get breakfast. Twenty minutes was all they had to eat, before switching with another batch. In total there where three groups, to keep patrolling up and to feed everyone within only an hour.

Asserting himself in the line, he hoped they made spares, otherwise there would be one other person left hungry after taking their meal. *'Although,'* he reminded himself, *'after last night, there's one person less in the camp anyway.'*

After collecting his fresh hip flask of preboiled water and 'porridge', he woefully dumped a spoonful into his mouth. Bracing himself for the worst, it came as a pleasant surprise to find that it didn't taste too bad, but the texture more than made up for it. Automatically, his mouth was resisting the sludge and it took a great effort to overcome his gagging and to forcefully swallow the blob down his protesting throat.

It was awful. Although starving, he immediately lost his appetite.

Half-way into shovelling the porridge into him, people started to put their plates away. Time was up, thank God. Hurrying off to patrol, the pressure was on. He needed to scout the vehicle bay in case they had upped the security, and he needed to formulate a plan to counter their new defences. If they were good enough, then he would have to think of another way to escape.

His mind was a mess, he just hoped a plan would unearth itself in his mind when he started visually seeing his target.

People seemed a little tense after last night, from their perspective it must be terrifying. A hidden rogue capable of killing an outpost and perimeter guard, all before scurrying off. The mental portfolio of the hidden assailant brought a smile to his face. He was right under their noses, in plain sight and was able to pull off feats like that. A hint of pride shone from within, before being buried by sudden guilt and regret. Marta wouldn't have done something so stupid. He killed those two people out of sheer inadequacy.

Before long he was almost face to face with the border of the outpost, so he spun on his heel and made his way towards the vehicle bay, trying to drown out the melancholy thoughts with methodically constructing the next part of his plan.

First things first, he knew he would have to be inconspicuous, so he shouldn't stare for too long, linger or break his composure. He was simply gathering information, there was no need to do anything stupid or improvised. Upon passing the final corner, what he saw made him groan internally. At the toll booth was another guard replacing the one he killed, but there were two others standing by the barrier, unwavering, observant. Additionally, he saw a couple more bodies break off their usual patrol from inside the outpost to weave throughout some vehicles before walking back inside to resume their patrol. They had definitely upped the ante.

The vehicle bay was large, however, and he could easily roll under the vehicles or skulk past them. His original plan of stealing a vehicle and shooting off didn't have to change, there was just more room for error. Unable to help it, memories of James Bond, or Mission Impossible were recalled. Grand heist operations that had all the odds against the protagonist were his favourite films as a child. Remembering them brought a little smile to his face, the sweet memories of watching them on a weekend with his dad. As a kid, it was his dream to partake in such nail-biting adventures, but now he was faced with one, all he felt was dread. There would be no coincidences or plot holes to save him.

Amidst his childhood fantasy, he remembered he would need keys and a map of sorts. Altering his plan slightly, he would have to break into the outpost and pick those up before driving off into the sunset. He knew it was practically impossible, but then again, what else was he to do? Unofficially become a permanent member of the perimeter guard? He would just rather be shot and killed, and rest among all of his friends.

He was now making his way past the bay. What would Marta do? She would probably be up for a grand-scheme operation. But could he pull it off? Probably not. But that wouldn't deter Marta. With a strange excitement, he accepted the challenge. There were only a couple days or so before they switched with team B, he would have to perform his getaway before then. Unless it could be used to his advantage?

If only he had Marta.

He was distracted from his thoughts as a perimeter guard cut out in front of him. Startled momentarily, he apologized and went to go on with his patrolling, but the guard started to talk to him, "So, apparently you've had two run ins with that escapee, right?" She had her left eyebrow cocked up and her weight was being pushed onto her right leg. She had short, black hair and lighter eyes, and her face was marred by red flushes.

"Yeah, that bastard's just got away twice from me now," he sounded suitably fed up.

"What does he look like?" she asked, leaning in slightly.

"Well, I couldn't get much out him, but he had light hair and was skinny," he realized that most people around there were skinny. Apart from the leader, but he isn't subject to the breakfast porridge. In fact, he didn't know what he ate at all.

"I'll keep an eye out then. What's your name?"

"Thomas Grant, yours?"

"Pecky Blank, I'll see you around, I guess," and with that, she left, a boyish grin that immediately flashed Marta's face in his head. Suppressing a jolt, his head was the last thing to turn as he walked away.

Trying to forget the strange ordeal, he thought it peculiar that they didn't really know who they were serving with. Ziven would hate that, working with strangers. Sure, they were bound to form some friendships, but the point remained.

It reminded him of his friendships back home. Everyone was nice enough to him and included him in all sorts of activities or jobs. But all of his memories of life in Finchingfield always included Marta, save from the garage. Had he ever lived a day without her? Was she the only reason he tolerated anyone else?

He always knew that Marta was a comfort blanket of sorts, but now she was gone, it felt like all the colds of the world were sweeping upon him. With a solemn sigh, he realized he had taken her for granted. That looming thought was always present whenever she introduced them to someone new, or she encouraged him or helped him, but now he was telling himself that, with no distractions present. It was a sobering moment. And the flash of her face on Pecky's was still fresh on his mind.

All he could do to prove to himself that he wasn't some sort of lost cause without her, was to succeed in his mission. And he couldn't do that walking away from the bay.

Stopping, he backtracked, his eyes narrowed. Going to stake out the vehicle bay again, he started to form a mental checklist. To start with, he would need the bolt cutters from the card-playing lot's basement. The bay was large, and he could easily break in at the other end to where the toll booth was, giving him an undetected access point. He would need to go in with a plan, a purpose. Could he sneak past the guards into the outpost? Surely not, that would be suicide.

Rounding the bay again, and this time he properly noticed the barbed wire. It shouldn't be any match for the bolt cutters, granted he could pilfer them. Once in, he could do whatever he needed. Ziven knew the bay must be a wealth of opportunity, he just needed to think a little more.

Multiple ideas flashed through his head, but the more he dismissed, the smaller he felt. It was an infuriating battle. He wanted to prove to himself that he could pull off the escape, and yet was still stuck on the first hurdle. He would just have to take more risks, if he didn't want to rot in the urban mess, patrolling forever for the Preservative military. At least he would have the card-playing lot to keep him company.

At that thought, he ambled off to where he thought he remembered them to be. Not only would it be infinitely more fun than walking around and thinking till his brain hurt, but he may be able to extrapolate more information about the outpost.

Searching through familiar roads, he finally recognized the same building in still relatively good standings. They were silent. So silent, that Ziven almost passed on, until he heard the quiet flip of a card. Grinning, he entered the building.

A row of eerily mute smiles greeted him as he entered, he guessed they only remained completely quiet whenever they felt like it. It was Kobes against Will, and despite the greeting grin, concern and frustration screwed his face. Kobes looked suitably worried too, unless that was just his poker face.

Jack gestured for Ziven to sit down with them, so he slowly pattered over, having a good look at Will's cards as he did. He had a set of three, but a discombobulated spare four cards that, somehow, weren't connected to each other at all. In the next five turns, Will's frown had grown to a neutral smirk, one that was dashed when Kobes threw down a winning hand.

"Oh for fuck's sake," Will projected, and the others laughed, trying to suppress their noise. As they settled down, Ziven thought to try something.

"So, that attack last night, huh?" he left it open to the floor, and luckily Jack took the conversation.

"He must've got lucky. No way is that deficient villager able to shoot down two guards," Jack snorted.

"Well, how do we know that it was the Finchingfield punter?" proposed Will.

Kobes made a few false starts as he realized one thing after another, "Thomas, it was you wasn't it?" Ziven's heart thumped, until he added, "You saw the rogue, didn't you?"

"Yes, I did," he struggled. Clearing his throat, he continued, "You know, I was making my way there and the bastard runs into me. He barged me to the floor but I got a few quick swings of his head before he fled again, taking my fucking gun."

"Ain't that the second time he's got your gun now, mate?" jested Will.

"Just my luck, eh?" he laughed, sweat slowly seeping from his forehead, "Anyway," he pounced, "what d'you guys reckon they're gonna do?"

"I think they're going to attack Finchingfield," spoke up Lillian, her eyes a little dampened.

"They're definitely gonna attack the place," drew out Will, "it's just a matter of time before a detachment swings by." Ziven's blood went cold.

"Well it was such a pitiful invasion, surely they won't," he tried to sound as jovial as he could whilst imagining the decimation of his home. Will shrugged. A pit opened up in his stomach.

"Need a piss," was all Ziven unceremoniously announced as he hoisted himself up. They muttered their goodbyes, suddenly remembering to be quiet.

Exhaling deeply, he rounded a corner then stood still. Sam's mangled, charred body, two men shot dead by his hand, the explosions of the landmines, the flash of Marta's face. Jaw chattering slightly, he tried to swallow down his impulse to cry. Despair pressured his temples. There was no way he could pull off his daring escape. Infiltrating the bay and sneaking inside the outpost to grab some God-forsaken keys? He was fooling himself.

Panic punched his ribcage, throttling his lungs and pushing down his organs. Even if he did miraculously escape, what was he going to do then? The Preservative military will just steamroll them once and for all anyway. The grim thoughts harrowed him for longer than he realized as he idly walked around the outpost, not gaining any new information.

Gravely walking away, he heard people come to life around him. People were making their way towards the meeting point. Rubbing his eyes and shaking out his legs, Ziven forced himself back into character. Slipping into a main road, he found himself with all of the Perimeter murderers. He wasn't sure of the occasion, but he thought it best to follow suit. Not long after, Will and Juliette caught up to him.

"'Ello," greeted Will, "Nice piss?"

"Hey man," replied Ziven, giving a light wave to Juliette who smiled curtly.

"Can't wait to see you next season," he started before leaning in closer, "you'll help me get loads of more wins," he jabbed Ziven in the arm, laughing.

"Yeah, just you see who wins," chuckled Ziven back.

"So, you heard about that deserter rumour?" Will quickly changed the subject. He remembered the toll guard mention something about a deserter, but he didn't think it best to mention that.

"Not a clue, I tend to stay out of gossip," he shrugged.

"Sounds about right, I ain't even heard of you before," Will dismissed before talking about the deserter again, "So, yeah, there's an apparent deserter among our midst that hasn't had the courage to up and leave yet," he looked at Juliette, who was awfully silent.

"I don't know why people would want to leave, really," breathed Ziven, trying to take a neutral position.

"Exactly, mate. Although, we all have our suspicions, don't we Juliette?" he turned around to face her. She hummed in agreement.

"I think that's Tanasha waving me over, I'll see you guys in a bit," she quickly excused herself. Ziven didn't think she could act any guiltier if she tried. Will giggled under his breath. Regarding Ziven with a cocked frown, he excused himself too, following in her footsteps. Something fishy was going on.

Watching Will leave, Pecky materialized by his side, "Were they talking about that bloody deserter again?" Taking a second to process the sudden question, he nodded. "Well, personally I feel sorry for them," she added.

Not knowing what stance to take in case she had heard his earlier comment, he replied, "I think it's been blown out of proportion, otherwise surely they would have left by now."

"But with all the heat on everyone's backs, it must be difficult to leave without getting caught. Besides, even if they did then they would be hunted remorselessly," she trailed off at the end. She asked him some general questions about himself, and he fabricated that the Preservatives had taken over his village and he was drafted in. Coincidentally, something similar happened to Pecky.

"To be fair, the Preservatives did finally give us access to clean water, but it came at the cost of our service. I haven't been home in months."

"How long did they say you had to serve?" Ziven's stomach clenched at her story, adding even more reasons to hate the party. "They didn't say, and we were so grateful for their help that we didn't really ask," she sounded more forlorn as she reached the end. Ziven could tell she was trapped there. Feeling sympathy for his sworn enemy was a confusing discomfort. He didn't like to regard them as humans, but after playing cards with them, and now Pecky's story, he couldn't ignore their humanity.

It was easy to hate them all. Very easy, in fact, but it wasn't the people, really. It was their commanders, and officers, and party officials. He looked at her again, despite her saddened eyes, her jawline and cheeks remained resolute and ready. Once again his sister beamed from her. He quickly looked away.

Soon enough, they found themselves at the meeting point. It turned out that dinner was being served, and Ziven broke off from Pecky. He was quite surprised; he must have missed that the other day as he ventured very far out into the urban mess. It was structured the same as breakfast, and he had apparently caught the flow with group two. On their mismatched plates were, Ziven could only guess to be, a butchered attempt at mashed potatoes, a meal he hadn't had for a good few years now. Unseasoned, cold, and mushy, it was exactly what he expected it to be.

Accompanying the potatoes were a mixture of vegetables. Again, unseasoned, cold, and hard. At least it was more bearable than the porridge. By the side of the plate was another flask of preboiled water which he gulped down gratefully.

They left before the final group stampeded in, and he carried on with his patrol, a million thoughts on his mind. The main one, however, was the night ahead of him. Despite his anxieties and fears, he thought it best to at least try escaping. His soul would never rest knowing he had given up and failed Marta.

He knew where the vehicle bay was, and he knew where a pair of bolt cutters were. He would need to, at the very least, carve a secret way into the vehicle bay. Would he have to sneak into the outpost to get a key? He would probably get caught out immediately. Reminding himself why he was doing it, the thoughts subsided. The mental battle lasted until dusk started to creep below the horizon. Not that he could see it.

After dinner, he closely circuited around the meeting point, hardening his nerves and preparing his mind whilst making himself apparent to everyone else as they went off to sleep.

It was time. Butterflies introduced themselves to his stomach as he beelined towards the card-playing lot's building. He would have to be as quick as possible for maximum time on the other side of the metal fencing.

Making good progress, he soon was striding towards the building, when he saw a shadow slip into the front via the crumbled entrance. Slowing, Ziven squinted his eyes. Who was that? Drawing a little closer, and the same shadow, with a feminine build, stole down the stairs into the basement. Although intrigued, he had to stop himself from going any further, in case whoever it was compromised him.

Taking a few steps back, and a presence lingered to his right. Darting his eyes over, and Will's head protruded from a corner. Gesturing him over, he ducked back behind the wall. *'What the hell is going on?'*

Rounding the corner with his wits about him, Will was waiting with Lillian.

"Did Jack or Kobes tell you or something?" pounced Will, closing the space between them and whispering. Not to give a fully committed answer, Ziven just stumbled on his words in a very low whisper whilst looking about. He hoped it worked, he must have looked ridiculous.

"Right," dropped Will, "did you see her go inside?" he passed Ziven to look around the corner again.

"Yeah, I think so," he guessed the mysterious shadow to be Juliette, perhaps trying to swing the points in her favour. She was losing, after all. He was reminded of the suspicions of there being a deserter, but he seriously doubted it was more than just speculation and rumour what else was there to pass the time in that place, anyway? Apart from playing card games. It amused Ziven, to think she cared so much about winning the season. Even more so the fact that everyone else cared just as much.

Alongside the amusement of the situation, came the frustration. With all the heat on the site, how was he supposed to steal the bolt cutters? He didn't want to waste the night, so he would have to hurry whatever their plan was to clear them of the area. As soon as it was clear, he could quickly grab the bolt cutters and hopefully at least cut a way into the vehicle bay before sunrise.

"We should pursue her now, she's right in there," he jabbed Will in the elbow.

"Yeah, you're right," he gestured to the darkness, and soon Kobes and Jack sprung forth. This was a God damned conspiracy. Lillian also stepped up.

"Let's go," Jack was already in the lead, gun at hand and was bearing down the steps with everyone else following suite before Ziven had a chance to take a step.

Immediately, an incriminating gasp sounded as the thunderous footsteps launched down the stairs. It sounded like Juliette alright. It was swiftly followed by, "I'm so sorry!" a few times. She had been caught in the act.

Ziven finally decided to make his way down the stairs, and he saw all four of the others boxing Juliette into a corner.

"And what do you think you're doing?" started Jack, taking another step forward.

"Really I'm not doing anything!" Juliette started to sob. Ziven would have felt bad for her, if she weren't partly responsible for killing all of his friends. Not ones to loiter around, they quickly grabbed her by her arms and marched her up the stairs, Ziven had to take a step back.

Throwing her to the floor, Kobes continued, "How long has this been going on for? The only damned thing we have in this place and you're ruining it!" Ziven was very conscious of getting caught out by any of the other night patrollers, and he hissed at them to keep their voices down.

"Say, what are you doing here anyway? You were on night patrol yesterday, you got outran by that same Finchingfield bloke," asked Jack, still standing over Juliette.

"To catch this cheat," he defended. Then trying to quickly get himself out of the interrogation line, he then suggested he go back down to make sure she hadn't swapped any points.

"Points?" Will started to laugh, "Hold on, you thought this was about points?" now everyone was looking at him. He took an involuntary step back.

"Let me ask again, what the fuck are you doing here?" Jack started to make his way towards Ziven, a lethal look on his face.

"I could've sworn she was cheating," He started, but knew he had been caught out. Lying can only get you so far, "Look, guys, truth be told I couldn't sleep, so I was," before he could finish, Jack punched him in the face. Almost falling over, he flung his arm out for balance and instead slapped Will right around the cheek.

"Right, you're in for it now, matey," Ziven couldn't react as Will's leg swept him off his feet, causing him to fall with a mind-shattering thud on the floor. Jack's hands had grabbed him by the top of his shirt, hauling him up a little so his head lolloped backwards.

"What the fuck are you doing, Thomas?" he was sure he was in for another punch or kick or swing, but Jack just let go.

"He's not worth the effort man, he's a strange one. Never seen him before recently anyway," Kobes was talking to Jack in a low register, but Ziven could still hear them. Ziven would realize later that they couldn't beat him up or report him as that would most definitely risk exposure to their secret card-playing club.

In the meantime, though, his head was swimming. Pain was ringing out all across his skull and body and Lillian just watched him groan and slowly shift around on the floor with an unreadable expression.

To think he was playing cards with them all not so long ago.

Their attention turned back to Juliette, who had taken the opportunity to try and sneak off. "Oh no you don't," laboured Kobes as he restrained her.

"I'm sorry! I won't desert you guys, I'm sorry I won't!" she blabbered, struggling in their grip.

"We knew it, we knew you were always weak-willed," almost spat Will as he neared her, "You know what happens now, don't you?"

"No, please, I'm sorry, I've already said I won't!" Streams of tears were running down her face, Ziven could only make them out as a twinkling flow through his blurred vision.

An organ-crunching punch to her stomach. A choked cry of agony.

"Right, let's take her to Jordan, he'll sort her," they looked at each other in confirmation as they dragged her, still struggling. Be it through pain or resistance Ziven couldn't tell.

He thought they had forgotten him and was remaining as still as possible for them to leave him to grab the bolt cutters and dart. If only he was so lucky. Kobes ordered Lillian to stay put and make sure he didn't 'do anything stupid,' and there she stayed.

She wasn't a dictator and she let him sit up and stretch his legs as he caressed his head and injuries.

"May I ask," she started, "what were you doing?" That was a very good question.

"Wrong place wrong time," he grunted. He didn't know whether to lie his way out of this one too. Would he get away with constantly lying? To be fair, his entire identity there was a lie, he may as well keep it up or else the whole thing will fall, "so she was deserting after all then? I had heard rumours about it."

"You did? Well, it doesn't matter now, everyone will soon learn about it," she shrugged.

"Can I at least sit inside?" he tried.

"Sure," she distantly dismissed him.

Getting up felt like he was wrestling himself through a violent bush, except the pain was internal. He really put on a show about how much he was hurting to sell the idea that he wasn't going to 'do anything stupid'. But that's exactly what he had in mind.

Thankfully for him, the basement was out of sight from the entrance. So, after collapsing to the floor and making it audible, he slowly and quietly picked himself up, save for a couple muted grunts. A few tiptoes later and he was already creeping down the steps. He would have to do this before they all came back. Pressure mounting, he cautiously lifted the bulking bolt cutters from its place among the junk, which caused a mini land slide of smaller bits and pieces.

He held his breath; this was the last thing he needed. Making quite the noise, it surprised him that Lillian didn't come down after him. Relief joined his exhale as he slowly turned to leave. Until he remembered Juliette. Why had she gone down there? How had the others known she would be there?

Mutely placing the cutters on the floor, he crept over to Juliette's pile. The smallest of the bunch, he wondered if she had anything hiding. Observing all around the pile, he couldn't find anything significant. If she were hiding anything, it would be in the middle of the pile.

He started slowly, by taking little bits off the top and suspending them whilst trying to peer into the centre of the junk, but still to no avail. Placing them also on the floor, he picked up more and more stuff, and with each failed looking his curiosity grew bigger and bigger. At last, as he grabbed a toolbox's lid, he found a picture.

It was incredibly frayed and faded, but it was definitely Juliette on it. Her dark skin and wooden eyes stood out quite prominently. Mysteriously, the person she was with had faded beyond recognition, their pale skin fading into the background. Must have been an old friend.

Moving the picture aside, and he found a twice folded piece of paper. Opening it, and it turned out to be a map of Outpost E. He almost gasped. Delicately folding it back up and slipping it into his pocket, he carefully took the bolt cutters back, before slowly climbing back up the stairs and onto the ground floor.

She had definitely planned to desert, and she was prepared for it. Was she going to escape that night? A sense of foreboding fell upon him. Ziven could only pray he didn't suffer the same fate.

There wasn't really more than one exit unless he counted hauling yourself up to the first floor and jumping off the roof.

Unfortunately, that's all that seemed apparent. Lillian might be very distracted, probably on account of her friend trying to desert her or the fact that she got so brutally treated by her other friends, but she wouldn't let him run right out the front door. There was no way of outrunning her either, he was too exhausted. Getting beat down and functioning off of little sleep was having its toll on him.

Stopping for a minute to assess how much he hurt and how much he could take, he deemed it safe to proceed. The stairs were broken in the middle and had caved into the stairwell, and so a big leap would secure his place on the other side. Only problem was that it looked extremely weak and might topple under him charging on top of it.

He didn't have much choice.

Clutching the bolt cutters firmly, he did a short run up the stairs and jumped forwards, reaching out with his arms and legs to get ready for the impact. Thudding onto the first steps of the stairs and they gave way slightly, forcing him to chuck the cutters onto the first floor to get a better grip on the more solid stairs ahead.

Scrambling slightly, his head and limbs hurt too much to focus properly. He still managed to haul himself up and crawl along the rest of the stairs, but as more and more body weight was being put on the stairs, he could feel the ancient wood slowly cracking and slipping.

With a final effort he kicked off of the stairs that was still holding out, beaching him onto the first floor as the rest of the stairs followed through. Surely Lillian heard the crash and would already be on her way. After a final grunt, he swept up the cutters and looked around. Having wasted enough time getting up there, he scanned the available rooftops to jump onto. The drops seemed too steep or the distance too large or the roofs too unstable and crumbled. Panic rising, he saw a bent lamppost that was highlighted by the moonlight.

Wrapping his arms around it, he slid down, the bumps and juts digging into his stomach and ribcage. Almost falling off, his feet landed firmly. After all of that jumping and exertion, his legs were coursing with pain, his muscles screaming to him and his head joining in.

But he had to continue. He heard some sort of shuffling behind him where he assumed Lillian to be searching for him. Surely, she had known of his miraculous escape by now. Forcing his legs to submit, he charged down the streets in the vague direction of the outpost. Ziven just prayed he wouldn't come across any night patrollers.

He didn't stop running until his legs were threatening to give up, and even then, he committed to a light jog as he looked behind him. No one. He let himself sit down; he was spent.

Looking at the bolt cutters that were still in his grip was a sure sign of relief and gave him the will to carry on. Despite the hiccup, Ziven still managed to get what he needed. He was almost at the outpost anyway. As he neared, he realized he couldn't act like an innocent night patroller with a big pair of bolt cutters in his hand. So, he resorted to flitting past the roads and houses until he arrived at a ruin opposite the toll booth. It was there he decided to ditch the reflective straps, and he lay them under a few rocks. Mentally noting where he had hidden them, he pressed on.

The vehicle bay was large and an extension of the outpost, so it jutted out. This meant that Ziven could pick the corner where the toll booth wasn't and try to break through, without the main outpost guards able to spot him. There was definitely more of a presence, but not even they could be bothered to patrol the entire bay. Lucky for him.

Looking at the bolt cutters and a minor wave of doubt washed over him. They *were* very rusty. Could they actually break through? Only one way to find out, he guessed. Taking position, he opened them up and started to apply pressure to a barbed wire.

Clamping down, and after a couple seconds of straining the wire snapped in half. Although the barbed wire was a jumbled mess, he was careful to cut at a section where he could then carefully separate the bulk of it from each other, leaving only a few strands in the middle where he was separating. Stepping on the stragglers, he was squatting in front of the metal fence, ignoring the barbs that grazed and nicked his legs.

Inspecting the cutter blades and he found that a tiny part of the blade where the wire was cut from had indented slightly. Nothing major, but that small section was now blunt and couldn't be used to cut anything else. He would have to use different sections along the blade until it was knackered. Still, it was better than nothing.

Now with access to the metal fence, he positioned the thicker wire further up the blade. Sure enough it cut, although with a bit more force required. He would have to be economic with the wire he cut so he could get through it before the cutters became too blunt.

Attempting to create a 'flap' in the fencing, he cut another wire a little further down. Looking at the cutters, and three arcs were forced into the blade either side. The blades weren't particularly long either, about two more cuts, and Ziven reckoned it would be finished.

With the flap bending slightly already, Ziven hoped it wouldn't be too obvious. He would have to make it settle in a natural position when he left. Another jarring cut into the fence and a creak sounded as the weight of the flap started to slowly bend inwards. His blood ran cold. He was in a very exposed position. Hearing nothing else for a half a minute, he made a final effort to make another cut in the fence. His muscles shook with the effort, but he somehow managed to force the cutters between the wire.

He let out a laboured sigh. He was in.

Pushing the metal wire flap he had cut out, he was able to duck low and slowly crawl in, with some of the cut wire ends scratching along his body. Once inside, he dropped the bolt cutters with the intention of picking them back up on the way out and maybe even put them back into the point basement. He'd have to see how he did for time.

He quickly took a moment to push the flap back into place, so it looked as innocuous as possible. It was just enough to not attract attention, but if someone walked past it, it was as obvious as a sore thumb.

Allowing himself to look over the bonnet of the nearest cruiser, he spied the toll booth guard and the other two border guards. There was currently one other lingering around near the outpost entrance to the vehicle bay. Slowly and very carefully, he explored a little further up. Now he was there, he had to decide what he wanted to do, what would further help his escape.

Weighing up his options, and he could either try to sneak into the outpost for some exploration, inspect the toll booth for anything valuable, or commit some sort of sabotage there in the vehicle bay. Or perhaps all three if he played his cards right. A devilish grin highlighted his shrouded face as his nerves tingled his stomach and tightened his throat.

Post-built structures usually used the ground as it was as the foundation, no matter how unstable it was. Most of the time people had to make do with what they had. The Preservatives, however, had laid the foundation of the vehicle bay with some sort of dense, pact, material. Not quite dirt or soil, but not quite tarmac either.

Under the tires of some of the cruisers the material had been displaced, and Ziven was able to grab a few chunks and hold them in his hands. Throwing it somewhere to distract the guards was a cliché and unrealistic move, as they could trace back where the obvious chunk of earth had been thrown from. Unless he threw it outside the fencing, to mimic movement from the outside?

Shifting in between the cruisers to get even closer to the guards and the outpost wall, he threw a chunk away from everyone, so it arced over the fencing and collided with a ruin's wall. The loud, slightly echoing crumble grabbed everyone's attention. As soon as the chunk left his grip, he was rolling under the nearest cruiser, just waiting for the guards to make a move.

As expected, a couple guards broke out of formation and slowly checked out the scene, their barrels pointing the way. The rest watched them, but they never wavered from their posts. Irritated, Ziven needed something that would get them all as far away as was practical.

But the only thing that would stir them all would be an emergency of sorts.

He didn't dare move from under his cover, for they were to the left and right of him now, thanks to his botched distraction. He twisted himself round, looking for some inspiration whilst trying to stay calm.

The vehicles in the bay screamed of opportunity, but he couldn't quite press his fingers on what he could do. Facing the underside of the cruiser was a sight he often saw in the garage, and instinctively he started to fondle the under belly of the cruiser. That's when he spied an electrical wire. Preservative vehicles had what the mechanics back home called 'warning lights' and were always on. Just like the ones back in the day, they warned if something was wrong with the vehicle, but without all the complicated and expensive wiring that goes along with it. If the warning lights flashed, then people knew not to use that vehicle and to report it to the mechanic. Or at least that's how the Finchingfield mechanics thought it to be. The main take away was that those wires were always hooked up to electricity.

Post-built electrical circuits, to save time and resources, were usually all part of a single circuit to the same generator or power supply. A structure as large as the outpost was bound to have better, more efficient means of wiring, but Ziven didn't think same applied for the vehicle bay, being a simple extension of the outpost.

Straining his mind to remember what he saw on the panel in the toll booth from his first excursion: the lever, the red, yellow and blue buttons came to mind. Speculating, he guessed the red button set off some sort of alarm system and the yellow controlled the lights (considering that it was the only button that was on at the time and that the lights aren't on during the day, suggesting that they are controlled). As for the blue button, he didn't know.

Starting to form a mental picture of the bay's inner workings, he stopped playing around with the car and focused on thinking. The toll booth must control all of the electrical functions of the bay, and Ziven estimated that they all ran on the same circuit to feed off of the same power supply. Letting a smile slip, he knew that if he were right, then tampering with one element would mean all the others also going down. Thus, whatever system he messed with would bring the alarm system down with it. Now that was an excellent opportunity of sabotage. The very idea excited him, but as usual a demon of doubt preached out to him. His idea was based on assumptions and little actual knowledge of electrical systems. He would be risking himself for something with low likelihood, and he would most likely get caught out during his little act of sabotage.

But, for once, he ignored it. With Marta in his head, he steeled his nerves and got his mind into action. Victim number one would be the lights that were shining from the outpost wall. Little plastic semi-spheres covered the bulbs that were wired from the ground up. Metal casing was drilled into the wall to protect the wires against the weather.

The guards were starting to walk back to their posts, their interest faded. He had to be especially careful of the guards walking in and out of the outpost, for if he were to cut the wires of the lights he would be in their direct line of sight.

After rolling under several vehicles, he retrieved the cutters again, and crawled his way to the furthest light from the guards. At that moment, no guards were patrolling out of the outpost into the bay, but he resisted. If someone walked in on him snipping the wires, he would be done for sure.

Right on cue, another outpost guard walked out and began to loiter around. Whilst waiting for him to head back inside, Ziven planned his approach. He would launch himself towards the metal casing, use the cutters to jimmy it away from the wall, cut or disrupt the wires, shutting off the lights and hopefully the alarm system, and leg it through the darkness. Being careful was paramount, if they easily identified that it was sabotage then they would commit to fixing it quicker and probably increase security measures even more. He just hoped that after the act the alarm wouldn't be repaired in time for his grand escape, whenever that would happen. If it would happen.

As he was lying there, his exhaustion made itself apparent, and his breathing required a little more effort. He would have to be quick, efficient, and not hesitate.

The guard walked back inside. He braced himself.

Using his legs to force himself out from under the car, he scrambled to the casing, hoping the noise of his crinkling clothes wasn't too loud. He opened the cutters and used a blade to get in between the metal and the wall, and after some struggling and slipping he finally managed to make an opening, but it split the metal in half with a grating noise.

Panic rose in his chest as if a submarine emerging water. His fingers couldn't work any faster, as he jammed the cutters in and severed the wires in half. The lights flickered. *'Is that it?'*

Although hesitant and a little stunned, he was still conscious of getting found out, and he quickly spun himself round and hurried back under a car, battling for control over his breathing. In his confused thinking, he heard hurried footsteps making their way right towards him.

Before it became a bigger problem, he rolled out from under the vehicle and before he could take a breath, he was running, doubled over, cutters in hand, throwing himself out of the metal fencing all in one fluid motion.

He cursed himself over and over again. Someone had saw him for sure. Stupidly, he had lingered for a second more than was necessary. He was caught, and so was his sabotage, and his cutters, and his break-in. To top it all off, the lights were still on. He had failed. Marta wouldn't have.

Part Four

He threw the cutters as hard as he could over a building as the chasing guard struggled through the hole he made. Already calling for help, he heard multiple nearby bodies rushing over. A last-minute moment of inspiration, and he thought he could bluff his way, yet again, into safety. Unlike last time, where he ran off and bumped into the leader, he thought he would stick around. His continued survival depended on him calming his nerves and doing what he did best. Lying.

He just hoped the guard wouldn't recognize him immediately, he hadn't seen his face, after all.

"What's going on?" sounded from behind him. Turning around, and Pecky Blank was rushing over.

"I don't know yet, but I think it's that fucking Finchingfield guy again," right into character, Ziven looked clueless yet determined.

"Where are your straps?" Pecky gestured to his arms.

"Oh, I, uh, I don't like sleeping with them on," he tried to sound apologetic, "they're just over there, I'll go get them." As he made his way off, the outpost guard came bulldozing over, tackling Ziven to the floor.

Another head-jarring impact with the stony ground.

"What the fuck are you doing?" shouted Pecky, as she stood over the struggling pair. More and more outpost guards rushed out and were filtering through the streets. "He's not your guy," she persisted.

"Yeah, get the fuck off of me, man," he didn't need to act that part.

Grumbling, the guard got up and grabbed Ziven by the shoulders, "You tricky bastard," before he could do anything Ziven quickly tried to tell him what he told Pecky.

"Yeah, too right, those straps you stole off of those two men you killed the other night, huh?" Ziven struggled for words, he was terrified.

"Look, that rogue goes about in secret, I've seen Thomas before, patrolling and the like. The poor guy's had two run ins with that fucker," she placed her hand on his back.

An official walked out from the vehicle bay and saw the chaos, "Graham, tell me what the absolute fuck is going on." Graham, the outpost guard currently crushing Ziven's shoulders, let him go to address his boss, and tell him that he saw someone shifting under the vehicles with a bolt cutter before escaping through a hole cut into the metal fence.

"And I have reason to believe he is right here," he gestured to Ziven, a lethal stare in his eyes.

"Bullshit, I've just been sleeping," Ziven retorted, "and whilst you're fucking around here that rogue is getting away again!" Relishing shouting at him, he was surprised to see the official, arms crossed, staring at Graham, his swampy blue eyes sharpened by his eyebrows. They must consider all the guards to be of the same standing, outpost or perimeter.

"You go off and get your straps and your weapon," Ziven scurried off to put on his straps, of course he didn't have a weapon, but he would explain that off as the rogue stealing it if he had to, "as for you," he pointed to the outpost guard, "run along and find him. We cannot let him get away again," he remained calm and in control. Ziven wondered if he was the director.

More and more people gathered around. One of the officials waved off the idea of sounding the alarm, which would have proven if Ziven had managed to mess with the whole system or not.

"Go and fetch the electrician in case the intruder had the chance to cut a wire or something," He also mentioned the words 'back-up power' as Ziven was rushing to fasten his final leg strap, but he thought nothing of it at the time, "Get the mechanic to check every car as well," he ordered, and another person nodded and went to do as was told.

Nearing Ziven and Pecky, he ordered them to go and tell Leader Jordan what happened. As expected, he asked after Ziven's gun to which he laid out his prepared explanation which got a suspicious grunt and side eye. The official had wiry hair, which was a plague among all the balding folk that couldn't properly shave their heads after the world turned upside down.

Ziven and Pecky marched away together past the rushing guards and higher-ups, his nerves fried and his fingers shaking slightly. He didn't know for how much longer he could cope with being a hair's breadth away from being caught out. He had already had that conversation with himself, but he was now worried that his body would give up before his mind. Constantly running or scheming or walking or stressing, his body could only take so much.

Although a miraculous escape, he knew that Marta wouldn't have approved of something so stupid. He needed to get his act together. He missed his sister.

Wrapped up in his thoughts concerning the possibility of Marta having escaped in the initial attack like Ziven, he almost completely ignored Pecky talking to him.

"...real mess, huh? I wonder how long he can survive without water or food." What she didn't know was that he was in fact eating their breakfast and dinner, but he was still incredibly hungry, thirsty, and tired.

"Yeah, that guy must be nearing the end of his rope," he breezily suggested. Another few seconds of silence followed. Looking at Pecky, and he appreciated how she had saved his life, almost as if she was on his side. She really did look an awful lot like Marta, save a few features. What a coincidence. Out of everyone in that hell-hole Pecky was the only one that made sense to him. It was as if she were the only one to hold on to her humanity, just like Marta.

"Oh! That Juliette has been trying to desert after all," she said out of nowhere, "poor soul." He had to act suitably surprised, he was 'sleeping' after all. He just hoped she didn't talk about it to Jack, Kobes, or the others. That would be an interesting situation.

"Oh has she?" he nodded, "How was she found out?" He needed to know what news was being spread, and if he had been included in any of the stories.

"I'm not too sure, but Jack, Kobes and Will pounced on her as she was trying to flee, apparently," she shrugged.

"Oh damn, what's gonna happen to her now, then?"

"Well she's gonna get imprisoned, obviously," she said rather bluntly. Ziven just stayed silent. Considering how much of a trembling mess she was reduced to after getting caught, Ziven figured the prisons there were just short of torture, if not the real thing.

"I've always liked Juliette, really, she's sensible, you know? Like you," she seemed genuinely upset about the whole thing, and Ziven saw more of his sister shine through her face.

Coincidently, as they were walking out of the meeting point to where they presumed the leader to be, they came across Juliette on a chair, being closely watched by Jack and Kobes. A flash of shock slapped Pecky across the face. Juliette's head hung low.

"Where's Jordan gone?" Pecky asked, after hesitation. Jack and Kobes stared at Ziven with hostility.

"In the comms joint," stated Kobes, "trying to raise the director about this one," he kicked the chair that the empty husk sat on. It disturbed Ziven to see her like that. To see how quickly people can turn on their friends in that place.

Juliette looked up; her sunken eyes regarded Pecky. Perhaps they were friends. Pecky let her gaze linger on Juliette's eyes. Ziven felt sorrow choke his core as he looked at them. He wasn't sure why.

"Thanks," she replied and then they carried on, Ziven feeling the stares of Jack and Kobes on his back.

"Arseholes," she muttered as they went by, forcing a cracked smile. Ziven repressed a snort.

"Lots of drama going on recently, I wonder what we're in store for next," Ziven let loose. He felt strangely comfortable around Pecky, and he felt the strange want to just have a sit down and talk to her. To just relax with her, not patrolling or playing cards, just sitting by a lake, maybe. He had to close his eyes to stop the tears from rolling from them. He greatly missed his sister.

Not too long up that path and they heard the leader swearing blind, "Why won't you fucking pick up?" he shouted.

"Sir," Ziven started. He spun around; frustration was bleached on his face. "We have news from the vehicle bay."

They filled him in. Ziven didn't know if Jack and Kobes had told Jordan that Ziven was present during the capture, as if his whereabouts became questionable, then his whole charade would be broken.

Jordan closed his eyes and sighed with his full chest, "Right, Pecky carry on patrolling immediately, try to find him. Spread the word to other night patrollers," he removed his hands from his face, "Thomas," he hesitated, "you just carry on sleeping, alright? That Finchingfield fucker is on the end of his tether, let me tell you now. There's no physical way he can still be alive by tomorrow night," after a pause, Ziven and Pecky went off to do his bidding, until he perked up, "unless..." with wild eyes, he barged them both out of the way as he stormed down the road, towards Juliette.

Ziven had a feeling he knew where that was going, but he was so utterly exhausted that he bade Pecky luck before collapsing into the closest ruin. Whether the leader interrogated Juliette on the suspicion of helping the rogue or not he would have to find out tomorrow, as what little hours of rest he had left he took gratefully.

Activity and footsteps rocked him from his sleep, as the harsh sun stunned his freshly awoken eyes. Pains and sores rubbed on his muscles as he got up with a groan. Outside his ruin, people were about, heading towards the meeting point. He let his head fall back down for another minute of rest before joining everyone.

Leader Jordan, looking mighty dishevelled, greeted everyone, before addressing the rumours that were spreading. Some were interrupted from their sleep because of the commotion Ziven caused last night, and the night patrollers were being harrowed to spill what they knew.

Jordan confirmed the break in and the detainment of Juliette, who he had relocated some place safe so the entire force couldn't harass her. He ordered business to be as usual, and he also included his near certainty that the Finchingfield rogue will die soon of natural causes, and that he suspected the rogue was just trying to be as big a nuisance as possible, which was partly true.

He ended the briefing by reminding everyone that the switch with team B would happen the next day. Fear pummelled his gut. Ziven needed to exact his plan during that day and night, or else he would have to shift his plans to compensate being inside the hornet's nest. Where unknowns and uncertainties were waiting to consume him whole. Which was when he remembered the map he had access too, which alleviated some pressure.

Breakfast rolled around and he tried desperately to eat as much as his body would physically allow, which proved not too much. Downing his hip flask of water, he set the bowl and flask down before heading off, still hungry, yet strangely refreshed.

He had no idea of the structure or scheme of the switch, or if the teams got exported to patrol elsewhere, or if escape will even be possible from the inside. Not only that, but if there were some sort of identification to get inside the outpost, he would be done for. With too many unknowns, he thought it safer to escape that night.

He had to get a move on.

Leaving the meeting point with the hordes going in and out, he got a general gist of where everyone's minds were at. They were all glad that Juliette had been dealt with, but the rogue had everyone riled. They couldn't understand how he kept getting away with it. What worried Ziven was that some people were speculating that either Juliette or someone else was helping the rogue, or that the rogue was hiding in plain sight. He needed to leave before they delved deeper into those theories.

Once again, he walked between the architecture of forgotten times. Forgotten identities. Forgotten histories. So much was wiped from the UK the moment the Great Malfunction happened. So much for foreign relations or help. It was as if the entirety of the UK had been transported to some other hellish planet, where God's grace was nowhere to be seen. He wasn't particularly religious, at least not anymore, but he always had the scriptures at the back of his mind. Ziven sometimes thought that this was the event that the book of Revelations was referring to. Perhaps a little more creatively described in the book, but that's because they had no idea what a nuke was, or that such destruction was possible from mankind.

What scared him more than that, however, was the absence of his sister. It was now officially the longest he had been without her, and he needed her now more than ever. It was potentially his last day to escape, and he had ruined and failed in his past two nights to do anything.

In the first he killed two people, and in the second he failed even to cut the lights. He was a failure through and through. If only Marta was there to help him, to guide him, to even be with him. In moments like those she always encouraged him to believe in himself, but it was difficult given his past two failures.

Nearing the outpost, he tried to shrug off his wave of doubt to focus on escaping, but that persistent thought remained at the back of his head. Why was he doing it? To go home without Marta? He would probably screw up there too. Whether she was dead or alive, she wasn't with him. That's what mattered.

Rubbing his face, he thought it best to get on with it. If all else failed, he would finally rest with his comrades. Besides, he mutely knew that he couldn't bring himself to give up if he could be the slim chance between Finchingfield and the Preservative counter-attack.

Nearing the bay and he found a lot of hustle and bustle. Upon walking closer, he saw a huge oil tanker, with the distant rumblings of a truck or lorry or such that brought it there. The orange cylinder was positioned near to where he had cut the hole in the fence. Many people were filling large tubs with the oil and the others were hauling it. As the guards did, those people wore whatever they wanted to with the key distinction being they weren't holding a gun and were generally smaller. They must be the minions of the outpost, running around, hauling, cleaning, doing whatever menial task was available.

More guards were positioned all around the oil tanker and the work line and in the bay in general, all fed up with the rogue's misadventures. Peering closer at the lights, and between moving legs he saw the damage he had done to the metal casing had been fixed. He didn't know whether they had fixed the wiring also. Looking at the lights, and above them was a tiny, black, rectangular strip.

In a eureka moment, he remembered the officials talking about back-up power supplies or something, and if those rectangular strips were solar panels, then that would mean he had cut the main electrical supply and the little solar power supply had kicked in, hence the flicker. What if he had successfully disrupted the circuit? If he was right about it being a single circuit system, then that would mean the alarms had successfully been disrupted.

Well past the vehicle bay now, he smiled to himself. He understood that a lot of his claims were based on speculation, but he couldn't help feeling happy with himself.

His satisfaction was fleeting, however. With so many people there at the same time, he would have to wait until night-time, and even then, it wasn't guaranteed for his escape to be a possibility.

Eventually, the metal fencing stopped surrounding the outpost and rounded in to connect to the outpost wall. Pursuing the wall a little further up, he came across a window. It was peculiar to see a window on its own, especially it being the first he had ever seen on the outpost. Looking around, he peered through it, to reveal a corridor. No one could be seen.

Fresh cigarette butts were scattered on the windowsill, they must only have the window to smoke out of, or at least that's what they're being used for. What was more peculiar than the window was that they still had access to cigarettes. He wondered if the people themselves sought them out or if the Preservatives handed them out, as if bonuses or something.

Connected to the corridor were a few rooms, one sticking out to him. A wooden plaque labelled 'Military Operation Filings' was screwed above the door. *'Well, what do we have here?'* He squinted, both hands against the window. From what little he could see past the ajar door, he definitely made out files of sort. It might be worth pilfering through, he concluded.

Ziven would have to make moves there and then if he were to escape that night. He wanted to bide his time some more, scoping out and planning and thinking, but he didn't have the luxury. With only one last day to do anything Ziven had to make the ultimate choice. Would he try to escape that night, or play the long game, potentially being in the perimeter guard for a long while as he waited and waited...

He had enough of waiting.

Looking at the window, it wasn't particularly fitted well, it must have been a last-minute fix for the nicotine-craving employees. Considering a cigarette butt that looked fresh, or at least not as dead as the others around it, he wondered if whoever last had their break had properly locked the window again. If it could be locked in the first place.

It turned out they didn't, as when Ziven gripped the lower part of the window it pulled out towards him. There was no system to keep it propped up and he had to catch it before it swung back down and shattered. Nervous excitement bubbled within him.

Opening the window again, he stuck his head through, thankfully there was no one walking through at that moment. They must be too busy with that oil tanker. He thought to ditch the straps to try and blend in with the general workers, so he quickly dropped them outside of the window and kicked a few rocks over them.

Clambering through felt like creeping through a veil of mystery. He had no idea what waited for him. He tried to relish the excitement, instead of succumbing to the nerves. A spark of foreboding flashed as both of his feet met the floor.

Once inside, he leaned against the wall looking out of the window to act causal before peeling himself off the wall to peer into the Military Operation Filings room. It was open. What met him was cabinets and tables and big sheets of paper hanging on the walls and slips and sheets piling on top of each other. A few maps pointed to him throughout the mess of graphs and words and numbers, to which he so desperately wanted to grab there and then and run. But he resisted, not wanting to set a foot in the room until he was certain.

Closing the door, he lingered around, deciding what to do next. He could keep on wandering the halls of the outpost, but it made his stomach turn. It was all too easy. A thought snagged his mind: what if it were a trap? It all seemed too easy. Anxiety pulled on his mind, encouraging him to play it safe. As he decided to creep out the window and return with a better plan and more courage, a voice called out to him.

"You just had a ciggy?" someone, a guard presumably, walked towards him, gravitas apparent with each step. Ziven nodded, not saying anything as fear suddenly struck him. "I'll lock the window for you," came next, as he regarded Ziven with his eyes. "Ah, right, yes, of course," tumbled out of his mouth.

Smiling, he pulled out a key on a ring and locked the window. Although locked tight, Ziven imagined he could bring the whole thing off its hinges with enough force. "What's your name? You new around here or something?" he asked.

"Jamey," he answered rather quickly. He didn't want to be associated with Thomas Grant, the perimeter guard, "and yes, yes I am. I really must get going." Standing there, impersonating a lowly general staff member with his only way out locked, he berated himself for taking such a risk.

"Jamey what?" he quickly asked as Ziven started to turn around. "Jamey Thompson," he finally spat out.

"Right," he dragged on that word slightly as he carried on walking down the hall, his eyebrows narrowing slightly.

That entire confrontation left Ziven feeling extremely uncomfortable, and now his mind was spinning trying to figure out a way to leave. Perhaps his big escape would have to happen there and then, but not without the keys, or maps or direct access to a cruiser. The vehicle bay was swarming with people hauling oil from the tanker to inside the outpost.

Very flammable and explosive fuel.

He quickly waved the thought from his mind. It was too ambitious, even for him. Luck had been plucking him from any real detection, but if he pushed it too hard, he was sure his luck would run out.

Keeping his cool composure, he hunched his back slightly and slowly walked down the hall, seeing where it would take him. Bleak, solid walls with a pasty flooring blocked all around the outpost, connecting the different rooms like an awkward organ.

That very outpost was the epicentre for the military movements and plans in the area. Although not necessarily containing all the military personnel, it sure enough ordered them all over the place. He thought back to that fateful day. What were they thinking? Finchingfield had never been in a fight. He doubted there was any real fighting happening across the country, just the greedy governments stamping all over innocent lives and villages.

Simple. That's what they told all the volunteers with no training. To drive in, shoot up the place, disrupt some power supplies or kill a few people in a hit and run. Attacking the outpost itself was an ambitious target and they all knew it, but they hoped it would make a statement. A statement that Finchingfield and the other villages that joined the effort were not to be taken lightly. And now everyone back home was mourning everyone's death.

Getting closer to the vehicle bay, he saw a stream of people with big tubs full of fuel walking across the corridor. Opposite to the bay entrance must have been some sort of storage. He joined the line, lifting the surprisingly heavy tubs from where they had been plunked down in the corridor and walking right into a large storage area with everyone else. The storage room was just a large space between the corridors and rooms that had been converted to a suitable storage unit. It wasn't a higher room, just a wider one, with random blocks jutting out from the walls where other offices had been built into it.

Dumping the tub onto a growing pile that some others would properly sort out, he made his way back.

"So, the perimeter guard are switching tomorrow, huh?" he stated to no one in particular.

"You're one of the new ones, right?" replied a woman to his left. He said he was and gave her his new name, to which she pulled a face, "That don't ring a bell," she started, trying to remember if a Jamey Thompson existed. Ziven quickly spun that he was a last-minute addition, so they probably wouldn't have heard of him. His explanation satisfied her, and she snorted before continuing, "It's not so bad, they're only actually in here until the morning after, anyway."

"Oh, good," he airily shrugged and let sit before lifting another tub up. How he sounded was the complete opposite of how he felt. He now had until tomorrow night maximum to escape, buying him more time. By the next night, all the fuel should be hunkered inside the outpost, and maybe the bay would be quieter. Perhaps they would even forgive a perimeter guard from just walking in, after all they were staying the night there.

"So how does the switching work in this place? Just in case it's different to what I'm used to," he asked.

"Nah mate, they're all the same," she obliviously stated between grunts, "They just stay in the outpost for a bit and leave when the transport is ready." Thank God she decided to elaborate.

Managing to suppress his worries through the logic of yet another plan of sorts, he flaked off from hauling the fuel by quickly taking another exit after depositing his fifth tub. More pasty and mind-numbing hallways met him, it was almost impossible to tell them apart, if it weren't for the different rooms decorating the off-white walls.

What he needed to find was the place with all the car keys, he figured it couldn't be far from the vehicle bay. As soon as he located that, he would be able to flesh out a plan that could take place either that night or the night after, depending on the business of the vehicle bay.

A sudden discomfort materialized in his trouser pocket. Patting himself down, and he jolted. The map of the outpost he took from Juliette. Looking both ways down the hall, he whipped it out. Thankfully, it hadn't been damaged, just a little creased with slight tears at some folds, but the map was still legible.

The layout and annotations of the map was written in two different handwritings. A more curvy and dainty handwriting was paired with a slanted, pointy style of writing. More than one person had assembled that map.

Quickly spying the vehicle bay, it didn't take long to find his general whereabouts. Looking around some more and he found the Military Operations Filings room. A lot of the rooms were unlabelled or had question marks on them. It seemed the outpost had a lot of secrets.

From what started as a simple window of opportunity had turned right into a reconnaissance mission. He knew that was the prime time to put everything into where he wanted it to be. He knew where the maps and information were, he knew where the vehicle bay was, with hopefully disrupted alarms and lights. All that was left was to find the keys and high tail it out of there. A few rooms sprung out to him, but one seemed painfully obvious. The 'Mobilization Unit' was located the opposite end of the outpost, which Ziven was a little suspicious of. Why would they place the mobilization unit so far away from the vehicle bay?

A brief wave of comfort washed over him. Despite his many screw-ups, he had managed to make it quite far. And all without Marta. She was always there for him, and now he had to pull off the biggest stunt in his life without her by his side. Perhaps it was about time he took initiative into his own hands. After all, he hadn't died or got caught out yet. Maybe he wasn't such a failure.

Most people were helping bring in the fuel, but he still saw plenty of workers going about their day, nodding at him as he walked past. All the rooms to his sides were either offices or more filing rooms or janitorial closets, nothing of use. The map creators didn't deem it necessary to label those on the map.

Striding down the corridors, he had the map imprinted into his mind, but it was thrown off by how awfully similar the walls and paths were. With all the workers in the main halls, he didn't dare bring attention to the map.

During his journey, he almost bumped into one of the officials. Ziven quickly apologized and stood to the side to let him pass. Dull, blue eyes glared at him from an old face. The man himself wasn't old, but the years of stress and work had dropped his forehead, cheeks and eyelids. He double took Ziven, his wispy hairs floating like an aura around his head.

The man walked past, mumbling to himself as he went. He struck Ziven as familiar. But with no time to waste, Ziven quickly carried on his journey, supressing a shiver.

More guard personnel started to crop up, guarding doors and walking down the hallways. Two of such guards were stationed outside the Mobilization Unit.

"Do you guys mind me going in? Gotta get something for the vehicles. It's refuelling day, y'know," he tried. At first the guards didn't stir, until one of them asked his name.

"Jamey Thompson, now if you don't mind?"

"This hasn't happened before, has it? What's the fuss about now?" asked the same sceptic.

"The engineer wants to try something new; she said the thing should be in here," he didn't want to say that he was after keys in case they weren't actually in there.

"And what thing would that be?" his patience was running thin, as was evident by his tone. Ziven hesitated. If he messed up there, it would be the end of the road.

"Y'know," he stammered, gesturing with his hands, "the- the car keys," he held his breath.

The guards looked at each other, before shifting aside, "You got a single minute, understand?"

"Cheers," he said, trying his best to stifle his sigh of relief. Walking inside, and there were guns, ammunition, backpacks, MREs, anything anyone would need for a mission on the road. Almost in awe, he walked into the centre, admiring the ammo clips and helmets and gloves. Most importantly, however, he saw the shining, dangling keys, all lined up on a rack, some rings with multiple keys hanging off them.

Not wanting to annoy the guards, he quickly grabbed one of those rings and walked out, thanking them as he left. A thrill tingled down his neck, right in his hands were, quite literally, the keys to his escape. Now all he needed to do was grab a map in the filings room, turn on the cruiser, and he would be long gone.

But he decided not to get ahead of himself. The vehicle bay was buzzing with activity, it would be not only stupid to try something now, but it would get him killed. Looking at the keys longingly, he knew he needed to hide them and go back for them later. Marta's voice sat on his shoulder, telling him to bide his time. He was so close, he couldn't afford to screw up now, like had been doing through his rash decision-making.

But where to hide it? He couldn't go near the vehicle bay, otherwise they'll question him on the spot, and he was in no position to answer those questions. After weighing the options in his head, he accepted that the best place to hide the keys would be outside the outpost, and the only place he knew to get out was through the window he came in from.

Strafing down the hallways, he eventually found the window, a strip of light cutting the corridor in half. Could he unlock it under the guise of a cigarette break? It seemed reasonable, but he had never smoked a cigarette before, and he would look like a fool if he had to drag on it.

Instead, he rested the keys on the windowsill and fingered around the lock, the hinges, anything. It was shabbily put together, and he figured he could use it to his advantage. In the middle of his meddling, footsteps stared echoing down the hall. There was no excuse that could pull him out of being discovered there, with a set of car keys.

Panicking, he spun around, to see the Military Operations Filings room. Without a second thought he barrelled in, closing the door delicately behind him. The footsteps clattered louder and louder.

Whilst waiting for the person to clear the hallway, he looked around. Perhaps inside a perfect opportunity could arise to keep the keys safe. At least if he hid them in there, he could grab he keys, the map, and any other important documentation in the same place. The thought of minimizing risk got him looking around.

Unorganized madness made him wonder how they managed to get anything done. A wilting plant pot faded into the background. The swamp green leaves beginning to droop and crust, with the stem already darkening in colour. Ziven saw it as the perfect hiding spot.

Quickly making his way over, careful to not step on any of the sheets of paper, he planted the keys behind the pot, ready for him to pick up again.

The footsteps had reached their summit, the person was right outside. If they entered, he would be truly finished. He could feel sweat wriggle from his brow as they paced right towards the door. Ziven almost sighed with relief as they marched on, now on the decline. Still wanting to hide it out, Ziven started perusing the documents.

One was a threat report. After skimming it, his jaw dropped. A Preservative battle fleet was planning an attack on another innocent costal village, when an ambush was sprung on them. A vast number of unidentified ships 'rained fire upon the entire fleet'. Only one ship survived, after the attackers 'relented'.

Some more documents of the same nature were spread out, with red stars being drawn on them. Some were threat reports from investigatory expeditions, detailing the same aggressors. Others were transport by sea, all of which were intercepted at different points in their journey.

One line especially caught his attention: 'One of the above captains tried to raise the opposing vessel's radio, in which they got replies in sketchy French, German, and even Spanish accents, all speaking English.' He couldn't believe what he was reading. He wanted to continue, but the footsteps had vanished as he was reading, and didn't want to risk someone else travelling down.

Slowly exiting the room, Ziven looked around. Clear. Proceeding to cross the hall to the window, he hurriedly continued trying to prise the window open. The hinges and bolts were surprisingly strong, despite their deceiving appearance.

Taking a deep breath and clenching his fists through frustration, he contemplated breaking the window. The frame, the glass, whatever was necessary. Placing both hands either side of the frame, he pushed. Gently at first but mounting in pressure.

As he heard some of the frame give way, he pushed with all of his might. As his chest was starting to complain, he managed to shove the window from its hinges, ashes and butts exploding in his face. Smashing to the floor, he quickly vaulted out the window, picking up his straps. Lots of footsteps suddenly sprung from either side of the hall.

Fastening his straps whilst running, he headed for the closest road to escape into. Calls bellowed from behind him. He was still exposed. They all definitely saw him as he spun around. Through the sound of disturbed gravel he knew some of them had given chase.

He couldn't pose as someone else this time. They all had got a good look at him. This could be the end of the line, if they ratted him out. If they described him to any officials, or any of the perimeter guard. Through his carelessness he was yet again on the edge of failure.

Running through even more roads, he managed to shake them off. Sweat generated discomfort as he still felt the claws of exposure raking his back. He had gotten fitter, from all his running out. And equally more exhausted with each passing day. His lungs hurt.

The day was starting to fade, so he shook himself down and tried not to think about his image being shared all over the outpost, and maybe even the perimeter guard. All it took was for someone to recognise him. he had to be on high alert. He didn't even want to think about the complications involving the switch the next day.

Seconds into him trying to channel his Thomas grant character, he crossed paths with Jack, Kobes, Will and Lillian.

Part Five

"There the fuck you are," started Will, quickening his pace. Ziven stepped back, as Will only stopped walking when he was within five centimetres of Ziven's face. "Thought you could rat us out to Jordan, yeah?" he continued with a furious scowl.

Kobes' hands grabbed Will's shoulder and pulled him back slightly, giving Ziven some breathing distance. Ziven took that opportunity to ask, "What the fuck are you guys on about?" he tried to sound more angry than afraid, but he failed miserably.

"Jordan," answered Jack in a confident, slow tone, "Jordan knows about our little card games. Something we've kept secret for ages," he walked up close to Ziven, who was now backed against a wall, "why did you tell him?" Through his fear, one name became apparent. Juliette. She must have snitched to Jordan, after all she didn't have much to lose. He wondered why they hadn't made the same connection.

"I didn't," he started.

"Oh really now?" Will piped up again, "Any idea who did then?"

"Juliette, you fucking idiot," Ziven couldn't help himself. He was tired, fired up and afraid. At that, Will lowered his head and surged for him, before Jack struck his arm out and Kobes grabbed him.

"Not so hasty, man, remember," Kobes whispered. Turning to Ziven, he took a deep breath, "It's either you or her, and I'm willing to bet it was you." Three sets of narrowed brows stared at him, just resisting their urge to beat him to death, "You appear out of nowhere, walk in on us, and were mysteriously near Juliette when we caught her."

"And to think that Jordan thinks Juliette was helping the rogue, now that interests us," Jack's voice picked up where Kobes left off, "She says she hasn't been, but since she was thinking about deserting then we clearly can't trust a word she says."

Ziven knew, with a sinking feeling, that they thought him to be the Finchingfield rogue. It was only a matter of time before someone sussed him out, but he wasn't prepared for it. Not *now*.

"How dare you," Ziven shouted, "how dare you accuse me of being that coward. Just because I kept myself to myself and was at the wrong place at the wrong time?" he looked at Lillian. He had escaped her watch, which she probably got a lot of grief for.

"That begs the question," interjected Kobes, "what were you doing that night?"

"That's none of your business," he started, to no avail.

"It is now," grunted Will as he punched Ziven, yet again, in the stomach. It felt as if an electrical impulse shocked through his body over and over again, his insides churning and concentrating into a ball of pain. Two pairs of hands grabbed his winded body and forced him forwards as Lillian watched by the side lines. He had a hunch they were taking him to Jordan.

Their spat had attracted a gathering, some muttering between themselves. Despite knowing it was futile, Ziven gasped, "You guys are making a mistake, it can't be me who's the rogue," they ignored him, "that fucker has outrun me twice already."

"Coincidence that, eh?" muttered Will from behind him. Where was Pecky when he needed her? Ziven had no idea how Jordan would react, but he knew Jordan was done with him. Last time he threatened to report him to the director. Now it was a done deal.

He had got so far without Marta. But he knew he couldn't handle it all on his own. Recalling his close scrapes, made him realize how lucky he had been, for the most part. Pecky saved him once, too. It went to show that he wasn't fully independent, and he still relied on others to help him out, even his enemies.

Aside from the immense pain in his stomach, another emotion swelled. Anger.

They had taken his sister. He wasn't as independent as he hoped he was. He yet again needed saving. But Marta nor Pecky were there to pick him up. It ultimately simmered down. What was done was done. If he were to die, then so be it.

Stomach still twisting in pain, it wasn't long before they reached the leader, who was sorting through papers.

"What's going on here?" he shouted, approaching Ziven who was still bent forwards and clutching his belly.

"We've reason to believe that this man," announced Jack, pushing Ziven forwards, "is that Finchingfield bloke."

"They're misguided," Ziven tried.

"As if you card-playing slackers would know anything of what happens outside of your little tournaments," spat Jordan, "Now what leads you to believe such things? He beat you in a game of snap?" Ziven couldn't explain it, but he feared Jordan was having the same thoughts.

"Oh come on, sir," started Will, "can you honestly tell us you've ever seen him before? The guy came out of nowhere."

"I can't remember all of you, now, can I?" waved off Jordan, before looking at Ziven right in the eyes. There was a five second silence, as Jordan looked into Ziven's soul, "All this drama recently," he finally looked away from Ziven, "is doing my fuckin' head in. We're switching tomorrow and I've got enough on my plate than your petty squabbles."

"But sir," stepped in Jack.

"Enough," Finality was established, "I'll deal with you lot later. Right now sorting out Juliette is taking enough of my time." Jack, Kobes, Will and Lillian took their leave, but Ziven thought to stay.

"Honestly, sir, they're just worked up about Juliette, and their card-playing getting busted."

"Look, Thomas, why is it always you? All of a sudden you're waist-deep in all the shit that's been going on as of late," Jordan cast him a fed a up look, "Now if I were you, I'd scarper along before I tag you along with Juliette." Ziven kept his mouth shut and left.

Nerves fried, his mind was absent of thought as he retreated to a ruin to sleep. Picking a spot that wasn't overrun with bits and stones, he collapsed to the cold, hard floor. He let his muscles rejoice in the inactivity, as his mind simmered. Despite thinking of nothing, the back of his mind was alive and screaming. He tried not to let his thoughts surface, or he would never get to sleep. And considering that tomorrow was the big day, he desperately needed his rest.

As the night drew on, however, the less likely sleep became. Stress, worry and a slight panic cradled his brain in a rocking pram of activity. Performing breathing exercises to try and calm his nerves, all he wanted was for Marta to be by his side.

In the constantly changing climate of fighting and rushing and dying and surviving, his sister was the only one constant, the only thing he could rely on. And now it was just him. 'What would Marta do?' briefly conjured in his mind, but he waved it away. It no longer mattered what she would do. Whether she was still alive or not no longer mattered. She wasn't with him, she couldn't help him, he could no longer hide behind her as she faced the world for him.

Pecky, although only having met her a few times, seemed like the only person that made sense. He couldn't explain it, but it was like Marta was shining through her. Maybe he should tag her along with him, she must want to get out. Soon enough another voice invaded his mind. How could he disrespect his sister's and whole village's name by even thinking of saving a preservative? After all they've done? He forgot about it. He would leave tomorrow and warn everyone of the attack. Not that it would stop it.

He was fed up with fretting, bored of screwing up, as he looked upon the stars. He had put everything in place, and soon he would be long gone. It was a shame the original attack had failed so disastrously. If he could avenge all the fallen, he would. But that may be taking it a bit too far. Especially for him.

Soon enough he fell asleep, his anxieties prevailing. When he awoke it was, for the first time, before everyone else. Feeling strangely refreshed, although mentally strained, Ziven got up, stretched, let out a body-shaking yawn, and stepped out into the freezing morning. Grey clouds threatened rain and misery, but he didn't let it dampen his rejuvenation.

Taking himself to the meeting point, and some others were already there, including Jordan. Soon enough, more and more people started seeping through the cracks and roads and their leader piped up, "Right, you all know the drill. We'll have breakfast then proceed in our usual fashion," he lingered for a few seconds before walking off.

Ziven was ready to get going. He wanted to do the switch there and then, he wanted to get out as fast as possible. The card-playing lot were in the first breakfast group, so he decided to wait to have his breakfast with group three, to minimize contact with them. They were right onto him; he couldn't have his cover being blown on the day of his escape. Well, *completely* blown.

He took the time patrolling to flesh out his plan. It was relatively simple, grab the keys and maps and such in the Military Operations Filings room, go to the vehicle bay, hop in a vehicle and break out the barrier, with the alarm hopefully cut off to prevent a huge immediate response. Now that he thought about it, he hoped the guards that were already there didn't just shoot him as he started the engine. Would he need a distraction? It didn't work so well last time.

The filings room was close to the vehicle bay, he could easily distract them as a perimeter guard alerting them of the rogue or such like before quickly grabbing his bits and leaving. He would leave it up to his improvisation, and what he had at his disposal at the time.

As he passed other people, they all looked at him suspiciously and kept their distance. He had been around them for some time, it was strange to remember that they were the ones responsible for his friends' deaths. All of them.

With their staring eyes following him, his hatred for them resurfaced. They were the enemy, he had to put that fact aside slightly to blend in with them, become them. But with his escape drawing ever closer, he wanted to make that statement that they had planned from the beginning. The whole point of them all going there was to show to them that Finchingfield wasn't an easy target for them to bully into submission. Resentment seething, Ziven wanted to make that message that they had set out to. Maybe that would curb their counter-attack. Or just encourage it.

Like a lightbulb, he remembered that they were hauling in explosive, dangerous, tempting fuel. From a fuel tanker, no less. Once again, the vehicle bay was a prime target of opportunity, but he just couldn't figure it out. It must have been so painfully obvious. He let his mind ruminate on it whilst he waited for breakfast.

The bolt cutters were long gone, so he couldn't cut into the oil tanks under the vehicles or anything. The wires for the warning lights came to mind, but he couldn't think of what to do to with them. They carried electricity, but what could he use it for? It couldn't exactly start a fire or anything. Could it?

At long last, people were ringing out for the third group to scoop up their breakfast. It was just as disgusting as before, but he lapped it up fully, he would need as much energy as possible. Once all the bowls had been handed in, everyone was being called to the meeting point.

Ziven's nerves started to set in. Although he knew exactly what he needed to do, he couldn't help but start to feel anxious. Anything could go wrong. He just hoped he would keep his cool throughout the whole thing and come out alive and on his way home.

Jordan didn't say anything. With a wave of his hand, everyone marched forwards, towards the outpost. The random sensation of needing to urinate pinched his stomach, but he ignored it. He went through the plan again and again in his head; he couldn't afford to mess up. This was his final chance.

Marching down the streets with everyone, his urge to pee subsiding, he saw Pecky, her head bowed. Eyebrows narrowing, he quickened his pace, wanting to walk past her and never look back. Overtaking her, and he glimpsed a picture in her hands.

It was faded, and blotted with drops of tears or rain, he couldn't tell. It was a picture of two figures. One much darker, the other much lighter. Ziven slowed down with the realization. It was a picture of Pecky with Juliette, with 'BFFs' stylishly written in permanent marker. Juliette had the same photo in her point pile. Ziven's throat clenched.

Not only that, but Pecky's handwriting on the photo was a perfect match for the curvier writing on Juliette's map. His breathing shuddered as the full picture inflated his mind. These people were people. They clearly wanted to escape together. Now that was impossible.

Pecky turned around.

"Oh hi, Ziven," she looked at him distantly. Not due to sadness, but something else entirely.

"Good morning," he rasped, before clearing his throat. Silence ensued. He recalled back to when Pecky was telling Ziven about Juliette's detainment. How jovial, and ordinary she had acted. Just like him, she was putting on an affront. A mask, to disguise herself among the party.

He desperately wanted to say something. But he didn't. Why did he feel guilty?

Nothing else was said as they got closer to the outpost's main entrance. The barbed wire and metal fence passed him. The outpost guards stared at him. Entering the outpost from the entrance served to make him feel more isolated and unfitting of the preservative military. He couldn't wait to get out of there. Soon, he would have to pick the right time to slip out and make his way to the Military Operations Filings room. He just hoped none of the workers would remember him.

"Thomas," Jordan caught him off guard, "when you get to registration, tell the receptionist that I send my regards, I'm off to greet team B early."

Ziven stopped in his tracks, he didn't remember a registration room or anything on the map. "Yes sir, will do," he said with a smile, knowing he would be gone before it became a problem. Jordan's face dropped. Everyone else looked confused, some looking at Jordan with horrified expressions.

"I fucking knew it!" rejoiced Will, and Jordan gave a nod to some people behind Ziven. Before he could register, he was being wrestled to the floor, his hands behind his back. Forced down to his knees, Ziven craned his neck up to see Jordan, his hand on his forehead, looking at Ziven with regret, disappointment, and frustration.

"I should've known. I should've fucking known," he kicked a wall before grabbing Ziven and spinning him around, his arms still twisted behind his back, "If I were you, I'd start walking."

In a matter of seconds, Ziven's plan had been flipped upside down. With a single trick question, Jordan had finally found him out. He must have had his suspicions, especially after the card-playing lot accused him. Rage swelled within him, blossoming from his frustration.

Jordan forced him forwards, relentlessly frog marching him, "I can't believe you slipped under my radar. You jammy little shit," he spat, his grip on Ziven's arms tightening, "All this time we've been trying to find this sneaky little rogue, but all along you were right under our noses," anger mounted with each word, "You've had your fun, now it's time for me to have mine."

He was speechless. No way was that the end. Briefly, he saw Pecky, her jaw dropped and her eyes wide.

Ziven was thrown at the door of the director's office, which he remembered being on the opposite side of the outpost. As he was recovering, Jordan knocked on the door furiously.

"When he opens the door, tell him that I've found the rogue," with a final kick, Jordan left. In no time at all, the door opened and Ziven was face to face with the same old man he had met before. In the vehicle bay, as Thomas Grant. In the hallway, as Jamey Thompson. And now as Ziven Smiert. From his perspective, seeing the same person transition from perimeter guard to a lowly worker and now a perimeter guard again was enough evidence of foul play.

"These walls are thin," was all he said before standing aside to let Ziven through.

Just like the rest of the outpost, the office was bare and depressing. The atmosphere resembled that of a funeral, with the lighting to match the sombre mood. The director sighed as he sat down and motioned for Ziven to do the same.

The director relished in the silence, letting it suffocate Ziven's beating heart.

"Let's start with your real name, shall we? Jordan gave me a heads up before the transition. After some searching, it is evident that a Thomas Grant does not exist," his skeletal face regarded Ziven with expectation. He was given a choice, there and then, to come clean or prolong the game he had been playing for so long.

"They call me Patryk Kaminski, and I come from the Polish Ministry of Foreign Affairs," he put on a thick accent that resembled his grandfather's and spoke with prestige, whether or not a Polish Ministry of Foreign Affairs existed. The director looked suitably surprised. Ziven thought it best to carry on, "Ever since the UK went 'dark', we've been seeing how we could help out, and after some intel-gathering, we've decided that the Preservative Party is the best place to start," the director remained silent for a few seconds.

"Forgive me for being sceptical, Mr. Kaminski, but the likes of this have never happened before, according to my knowledge. Have you any identification?" he asked. Ziven was unsure if he was pushing it a little too far.

"No, they were lost in transit. We have a secret encampment not far from here, we'd love to have a," he rolled his eyes, as if searching for the word, "proper meeting with you. This is all rather rash, wouldn't you say?"

"I wouldn't go as far as to say that, now, Kaminski. After all, you are the rogue that has killed two of my men. The rogue that has disrupted with the electrical circuits of the vehicle bay. The rogue that has avoided detection for so long. The very same person, even, that I saw myself down the corridors the other day," he leaned in closer, Ziven could smell his rotten breath, "Now, Mr. Kaminski, you'd better have a reasonable explanation for all of that." Ziven hesitated for a second, and he could feel sweat start to prick at his skin.

"Well, director, I've been putting your outpost through quite the ordeal lately, it's true. But you've passed, haven't you? Not only did you catch me, but you dealt with every problem with efficiency," as he was talking, he subtly looked around the desk and the director's hands. Not a gun was in sight, which relieved some pressure, "I think it'll be in your best interest to join me. You can meet my comrades by evening."

There was a loud silence.

"Please, Mr. Kaminski, step outside whilst I think of what to do with you."

Ziven smiled curtly, before standing up and slowly walking out of the room. People were walking up and down the corridor, and after nodding at the guards, he started to walk off, hoping that they hadn't heard the director through the 'thin walls'. Merely a few steps away, he heard a muffled, "kill him." He immediately broke into a run, the guards already pursuing him. Some shots were fired, but either missed or hit someone else.

Ziven barged people out of the way, mainly workers but there were some perimeter guards standing around also, some who joined the chase after getting knocked over. He needed to dash to the Military Operations Filings room and grab everything he needed, but he couldn't with the heat on him. He considered losing them in the urban mess, but then he would have to sneak back to the outpost again which could prove insanely difficult with his cover finally being exposed.

Turns and corners he sped past, scraping himself on the walls as he went, using his hands to grab and throw people aside. Every now and then another shot would ring out, but there were too many workers to be fully accurate. Breaking a sweat, he willed his legs to move just a little faster. The distance between him and the guards was slowly widening, but they could always hazard a guess where he went by the noise he was creating.

He needed to disappear. Naturally, he was nearing the vehicle bay side of the outpost, where the bulk of worker activity was. By the time he was closing in on the storage area, he had gained a nice distance from the outpost guards, but at that point a few more guards had joined the rat race and were dangerously close to him. One of the people he grabbed and forced aside was a surprised Pecky Blank, who stood frozen as he made his way through.

With people right on his tail, he would have a hard time losing them, unless of course he jumped out of the window that was fast approaching. He would have to execute the jump perfectly if he were to escape, otherwise he may as well stop and hand himself in there and then, it would save the head injury. Mentally preparing himself, he took a controlled breath and his eyebrows narrowed in determination. Baring his teeth, he braced himself.

Vaulting out of the window wasn't as painful as he anticipated, until all the pain exploded as he smashed into the ground like a failed javelin. Glass and bits of frame impaled his skin, as his head pounded. Rolling over he recovered well and was on his feet again in no time. He thanked God it went as well as it did, no matter the cuts and bruises now littering his head.

His pursuers weren't so fond of his form, and they all slowed down to clamber out of the window or rushed past to take the vehicle bay exit. As they struggled, he gained more and more ground, but he couldn't escape the occasional pot shot. Now he was out of the dense halls he was a prime target for their guns. Not stopping for a second, his lungs started to pound and sore, but all Ziven could do was run.

Sprinting down the urban mess and under the gathering grey clouds, he took turns and corners whilst being chased by the enemy which brought flashbacks from the day of the attack. Separated from his allies, alone, and in danger. A small flush of anger and spirit arose within him. He would avenge all of those lost on that day.

No matter how many corners he turned, they were still on his tail. He couldn't run forever. Springing right and dodging some more bullets, he hopped into a building that he saw had functional stairs. Once on the roof, he lay low, waiting to see if they would run straight past. A few did, but the majority saw his antics and were filtering into all the houses he could have entered, a couple hitting the jackpot.

Already on his feet, he mustered his strength and leaped onto the roof of the adjacent building, loose stones threatening to throw him off. He hopped from roof to roof, attracting everyone like a beacon. Feet slamming onto the old roofs and walls, his ankles started to feel as though they were shattering.

As he impacted with his sixth roof, it caved in under him in a bellow of tiles, dust and stones. He fell right into the attic, where the impact punched the air out of his lungs and the energy out of his body. All his muscles jarred. He felt paralyzed. More roof that couldn't handle the stress then collapsed, falling on top of Ziven like an avalanche. Dust swirled around him and laced every laboured breath he took.

Everyone saw the spectacle and started to search the scene. With no access to the attic, and no one brave enough to jump on the same roof, they concluded him dead. The Finchingfield rogue isn't put down that easily, however, and they were immediately searching around in case he had managed to use the roof collapsing as a catalyst for his escape, like an illusion of some kind.

Almost completely buried in stones and debris and tiles, Ziven was ready to give up. He briefly heard people rushing and running around, and his chasers that were on the rooftops with him alerted everyone else that he wasn't there anymore or was dead under the piles of rubble. Either way, they moved on in case of the former. Some threw a few rounds into the pile, to ensure his death, all either missing or not penetrating far enough. He felt the impacts all the same.

Struggling to breathe, and with blurred vision and pain coursing through his body, the temptation to close his eyes and let all of his pains be eased consumed his head. It would be so easy.

Rain finally started to fall, like tiny fists falling from the sky. He lay there for a while, letting the rain slowly seep onto his clothing, his skin. His lungs were filmed in dust, but he couldn't cough or splutter.

Soaked and in pain, the constant hammering on his exposed body parts all built up to a crest-falling crescendo.

But then he thought of Marta, and how, if she were there, she would be willing him up. Telling him not to give up, to rise to the challenge. His fingers twitched as they started to grapple with the floor. Rain clingfilmed dirt and dust to his face and body, but he only let his sister's voice through. He could do it. He needed to.

Straining under the effort, he started to heave himself up, grimacing and shaking. Slowly but surely, the large chunks started to slide off him, influencing the other smaller bits to do the same. His back-breaking efforts clenched his core, and he had to utilize all of his willpower not to cry out in pain. It felt as though the very fibres of his being were being strained and stretched.

Finally making it so that he could rest on his elbows, his lungs bellowed forth a coughing fit, dust visibly flew from his breath. Ribcage feeling as though it had split in half, his coughing flared his throat into a wild pain. Every second that passed, the weight on his back grew heavier and heavier. His cuts and sores and scratches raging, his brain threatened to give up again and again.

With one last spurt of power, he forced the heavy chunks off his back. As they slid to his side, a sprinkle of smaller stones and tiles joined in. Exhaling with exhaustion and relief, he collapsed back to the floor, without the crushing weight.

He let himself lay there; the rain now fully free to smack down on his whole body. Motionless, he let the streams of rain filter into his mouth. The outpost and perimeter guards searched everywhere but where he was, their paranoia directing them any place he could have escaped off to. It felt like the first time he could rest without the fear of detection or imminent threat. But he couldn't let himself get carried away. He could rest once he was home and dry.

Standing up caused him great pain, but he managed it. A fine cloud of dust was disturbed as he stretched and shook himself down. Slowly, he poked his head out of the crater he had caused, to make sure that all of his aggressors had moved on.

The only way down from where he was stranded was to jump. Searching and thinking for a couple more minutes confirmed it. Sitting on the ledge with bits of stones and debris jutting at his legs, he pushed himself off, and within seconds the ground came up to meet him.

Yet again, a pulsating pain cracked in his legs as he rolled over, letting out a muted cry. Thankfully, he managed to recover well, but he suffered from it all the same. Taking his chance, he jogged in the direction of the outpost, throbbing pain tearing his muscles with each step. If they found him again, he didn't think he could muster the energy to pull off another stunt like that.

Nearing the border and he didn't encounter a soul, excluding a shocked, scared and curious Pecky Blank. As soon as they met, none of them said anything.

"So, it was you all along," she broke the silence.

"Yeah," he mumbled, wanting to leave and carry on but unable to move an inch.

"You're the one that escaped and decided to, what, cause havoc? Take revenge?" unlike everyone else, she didn't shoot him, which Ziven saw as a good sign despite her flush of anger.

"I just want to go home," he almost shouted. Hurting, sore, and scared and exhausted, he didn't have the energy for lies, "My name is Ziven Smiert of Finchingfield, and I just want to go home."

Pecky was stunned for a few seconds, and she looked to the floor, "So do I," she whispered. A few tears rolled down her cheek, "I want to go home, too."

Ziven considered his next action carefully. He had been seeing his sister in her, but now he saw himself. She was pleading, scared, and now lonely. He had come a long way since he parted with Marta. He had been mollycoddled by his peers for too long. It was about time he helped someone else, "Why don't you come with me? Finchingfield will have a place for you to stay."

She looked up, "I can't, Ziven. As soon as they see my uniform, they'll kill me."

"We're not like the Preservatives," was all he could muster. "I've lost someone close to me, too," in fact he had lost countless people that were close to him, all in a matter of minutes, but mentioning that wouldn't help him nor her, "but back at the village you can make a new start." She looked at him longingly.

He was losing time, "Look, if you could go to the vehicle bay and wait for me, I promise I'll help you." She remained silent, unsure of the situation. There was no time for him to loiter, if she wanted to take his offer, she'll be there. If she wasn't, then there wasn't anything he could do for her.

He made it to the outpost border without any others noticing him. He had grown accustomed to the surroundings and navigated his way to the first window he encountered, with a wooden board diagonally nailed over it where he had broken it.

Skulking over to it, he tried again to put pressure on it, to no avail. Even trying to shoulder through didn't budge the plank. Almost exclaiming in frustration, he grabbed a rock and started smashing the wood in the middle. After about a dozen swings, the board splintered, and with a final hit, broke in half. Dropping the stone, he slumped through the window.

Knowing people would be alerted to his position, he dashed into the filings room, swiped the keys, folded a map that encompassed Outpost E and Finchingfield, grabbed a pencil for way finding, and dashed back into the hallway.

Looking both ways, Ziven scurried down the hall, hoping that halls were cleared due to their search. Running the last stretch, he stopped just on the cuff of the vehicle bay, with a toll booth guard standing post and two other outpost guards doing rounds around it. Pecky was nowhere to be seen.

He was almost there. On the brink of his final stop of his hellish journey. He was finally there, with everything he needed. If only he could avenge the souls lost, or finish what they started. At least his survival was sentiment enough.

Ducking back into the outpost, he looked at his pencil. Post-built pencils were similar to the traditional ones, except the lead was thicker and the wood a little more uneven. Yet again, the vehicle bay screamed out to him in streams of hidden opportunity.

Another five seconds of thinking, and he had it.

It was risky, but it would be so worth it. It was just a shame that Pecky would suffer as much as everyone else.

He crouched low, singling out a key from his ring, and took his first steps into the vehicle bay. Striding through a row of cruisers, and he dumped his stuff in the cruiser behind the front row of vehicles. Excluding the isolated key.

The patrolling guards were at the far left, and the toll booth guard was looking out at the urban mess, his head leaning on his right hand. It was then when Ziven spied other guards in the distance, alert and walking around.

He then lifted a heavy chunk of the bay's flooring and, as fast as he could, heaved it onto the acceleration pedal all before jamming the key into the vehicle and turning it. The sudden jolt of life almost brought Ziven along with the thing, but he managed to leap backwards and roll behind a car.

Naturally, the outpost guards in the bay were alerted by the engine roaring to life, and the cruiser crashing out of the barrier. They immediately both, unexpectedly, ran straight inside, yelling at the toll booth guard to sound the alarm. All the outside guards were giving chase and shooting the renegade cruiser. He had precious little time left to make his escape.

With the barrier broke and the guards occupied, he leaped up. It was time to initiate his plan. The cruiser in which he dumped his map, keys and pencil into was right behind the one he set off, giving a clear passage out of the bay.

He turned the cruiser on, which jolted to life, and he slammed on the accelerator to drive clear of the barrier, the other cruiser rampaging into the urban mess ahead of him, distracting everyone in its wake. But he wasn't done yet. Having separated his vehicle from the others, he jumped out of the cruiser, grabbed his pencil, and took his sweaty, grimy, dirty shirt off. It was time to avenge all of those lost. To avenge his sister, who was willing him on in his head. And to squash any hope of a counter-attack.

Sprinting back into the bay, the toll booth guard's jaw was dropped as he was slamming on presumably the red button, to no avail. As he was fumbling, Ziven was jamming his shirt down the fuel funnel of the closest cruiser. Rolling under the car, he singled out and ripped out the live wires from the warning light and held them with a single hand.

He knew the next part was dangerous. He knew there was a very high likelihood of him not making it. But all of those thoughts were brushed to the back of his mind in only a moment's hesitation. It was worth it, whatever happened.

He wrapped the pencil in the end of his shirt that was hanging out from the funnel. Holding it in place by pressing his body up against it, he separated the live wires into both of his free hands. Carefully, he guided the wire ends to the exposed ends of the lead rod inside the pencil.

Just before the live wires made contact with the pencil, gunshots sounded ahead of him, dropping the wires in surprise, and he saw Pecky's face at the end of a pointed barrel. Spinning around, and he saw the toll guard flinching and cradling his arm that Pecky had forced a bullet through. There was no time to thank her. He was still on the clock.

Resuming his plan, he put everything back in place. This time, the wires met both ends of the pencil's lead. Almost instantly, thick swirls of smoke shot out from the sides, almost causing him to recoil back. In no time at all, fire erupted and leaped out from the pencil, engulfing the shirt in flames and scorching Ziven's body. Being thrown back with a cry, his stomach region was scored with a burning pain as his shirt was being eaten alive by the improvised incendiary bomb.

Despite his huge burn, Ziven had to grit his teeth and make his escape there and then, as the toll booth guard took a shot of his gun, aimed perfectly where he was only moments ago. Even more encouraged to get a move on, he persisted through the searing pain and fear, as more nervous shots were made by the guard. Pecky returned fire, neither of them were expecting the toll guard to try and fight back given his wound. With her covering him, he hobbled forwards.

Feet pounding as the seconds counted down, he leaped into his cruiser, another stray bullet grazing his back. Falling into the front seat, he shouted at Pecky to join him as she landed the perfect shot between the toll guard's eyes. Without another word, she threw herself next to him, squashing the map. Putting all of his weight onto the front pedal, they moved off, as the fire used the shirt as a bridge to interact with the fuel in the other cruiser's gas tank.

A staggering explosion threw the vehicle sky-high, as it let out it's fiery metallic parts all across the bay. A chain-reaction quickly took place, with other cruisers blowing up like a deadly game of dominos. Fire exploded into the sky, beating back the rain and breathing a great plume of smoke into the air. Even though Ziven was driving away from the bay, he could still feel the lethal shockwaves, and risked a look back.

He put on the breaks.

A great inferno was greedily grappling at the vehicle bay, clawing at the walls and fences and vehicles, as cruisers exploded with untold power. Some of the cruisers smashed into the outpost. With the fuel being stored so closely, and the fuel tanker with unknown quantities of fuel left right next to the bay, Ziven knew it was only a matter of time before the whole outpost went up in flames.

Figuring he was at a safe distance, he clambered out of the car, his wounds and burns still hurting and aching him. Pecky joined him, speechless. Sitting on the boot with Pecky by his side, the rain soothed his wounds. He watched the majestic flames curl and spit. At long last, the beautiful beast was joined by the deafening, awe-striking explosion of the oil tanker and fuel stores. Bits of wall, sections of metal, clusters of stuff all went up in glorious death and destruction. Seeing the sight lit a spark inside Ziven's soul.

He had accomplished that by himself. The mission was a success, and everyone who lost their lives were avenged. What's more, he saved another trapped soul lost in the system. There could have been more people in her situation in there, but he felt no remorse. It almost scared him, his lack of empathy, but what they had done had steeled him. At least he saved one. One that had also saved him.

Even if Marta was no more, he knew he had done her proud. A solitary smile spread on his exhausted, beaten face. Ziven Smiert, once a shy resident of Finchingfield. Looking at the sight of ripping flames and destruction, he was now the man that single-handedly tore a whole outpost from the inside out.

All that was left to do was go home, announcing the mission a success.

Fragmented Horizons
pt.2

Ah, Clarence, thanks for joining me.

"I wanted to see how you were doing, here, let me."

No, please don't fuss, I'm doing alright thanks. *Ah*, no please.

"It's been a couple days now and there's only half a dozen of us."

It's alright, we have lots to survive on. That Dabby is a real green thumb I'll tell 'ya.

"It's not about surviving, it's about what the hell happens next. What are we going to do here? Sit and eat for the rest of our lives as the corpses decompose and more buildings collapse all around us? Where the fuck are our allies? The relief? The aid?"

I'm not sure that really matters.

"What do you mean?"

Did I ever tell you of that boy I saw, before coming across this little grouping?

"No, you didn't. There's a little boy out there?"

Don't start up now, it's already too late for him.

"What do you mean 'too late'? Udochie, is there a young boy out there?"

As I was hobbling around, trying to find any form of respite or saviour, I saw more and more of those strangers walking about. As you know I steered clear, but there was one little boy, white with brown hair, who had blood all over him, burst out from one of the collapsed buildings.

"What?"

I know, I couldn't believe it. I was mustering the strength to call out, but before I knew it another young girl ran out right after him.

"Was she covered in blood too?"

No, interestingly. They were long gone by the time I properly appreciated everything that happened, and as I went to follow them, another of the strangers almost fell out from the way they came, clutching their chest as blood dripped and spilled from their body.

"That's barbaric."

I think they acted accordingly, myself. If that stranger was after them, then they had the right to what they had to.

"Well, yeah, self-defence, but that stranger was after the kids?"

I'm as clueless as you are. It looked me in the eyes as it collapsed to the ground. I had no intention of staying so I went away with haste.

"Did you see much more of the boy or the girl?"

Funnily enough, I did. As I was close to giving up to the elements, very close to where I found you, Clarence, I saw the boy again, weeping. I could hear the wailing before I could see the boy, but he wasn't crying for long.

"What happened?"

Give me a minute, please.

"Right, sorry."

As I stumbled into a clearing, the boy was curled up, shaking and terrified. Before long a small group of strangers cut from the shadows and seized him.

"What? My God that's horrifying."

It is. And when he struggled too much, they chloroformed him, or the equivalent of. He instantly fell limp.

"What the fuck? I refuse to believe this. Not kids, not a young boy."

I could scarcely believe it myself.

"What of the girl? Did you see her?"

No, I didn't. I haven't seen her since. Perhaps they caught her too.

"Why would you tell me this? It's just despicable."

To show you that whatever happens next isn't going to be pretty, and that there is no point getting our hopes up. Whatever happens next will be very dark indeed.

It's almost time.
"Daphnia, prepare the chambers for release."
"Yes sir."
"Has everyone been briefed on what they must do?"
"They should have been, every instructor is reporting as 'finished'."
"Perfect."
"As soon as that counter reaches zero, release them all. I'm going up top ahead of time."
"Are you sure sir? That probably isn't very-"
"Very sure, now release them on time, got it?"
  No need to wait for a response. Where did I put my cigarettes again?
"Yes, open the doors please."
"Is it time already?"
"I said open the doors, for fuck's sake."
"Yes sir."
"You two – come with me."
  There's no telling what it's going to be like outside. I hope at least that it's safe to walk.
"Wow…"
"My God."
  I can't believe my eyes. This is perfect. Soon everyone shall be released, and our presence will be established. It is imperative that these initial steps go perfectly, so much relies on it.
"Hold on."
"I don't need protecting, Elliot, I just wanted some fresh air."
"Oh fuck, that's abhorrent."
"What do you see?"
"A flaming dead body, ten O'clock."
  That's a sight to behold. Naturally they're going to be littered everywhere. A small price to pay for salvation.
"Grow a backbone, will you? There's plenty more where that came from."
"I wonder if anyone survived."
"I doubt it."

Perfect, everything appears to be in order. Our new place of operations is a little small, but it'll do the job.

"Sir, we've met 25% of our target."

Good. Now we just have to wait as the beeps and the dots come in from all over the place.

"All the organizers in position?"

"Yes sir, they're just waiting for everyone else to finish planting."

"You can call them back, if they're waiting they may as well wait where I can see them."

"Yes sir."

This is a breath of fresh air, being able to watch the fruits of our labour begin to develop.

"Speaking of the organizers, sir, one has just been killed."

"What?"

"Yes. Apparently a young boy and an older girl had stabbed her to death."

"What about everyone else that are supposed to be there?"

"It was just her and one other, who is reporting the incident and bleeding out."

"Order a team to pursue and grab them immediately."

I guess resistance is to be expected. It will be dealt with.

"Oh, and add that I would like them both alive, I have a few questions I want the privilege to ask myself."

"Any more news of the boy?"

"Not really, just that he's safe and recovering from whatever the bastard terrorists had done to him." I felt so sorry for that boy. Having been put what he's been put through.

"Still no girl?"

"Unfortunately not, I think she's long gone." Unless they got to her too. That's a sickening thought.

"So what's your assessment on the whole thing, then?"

"Well, if I've got it right, after killing that bloke, they were on the run for a while. Until the girl figured out, somehow, that the devices they were planting were giving them some sort of surveillance or beacon or something that was giving them some sort of coverage of the area."

"Props to her, even we still don't know how they work."

If only we did, it would be a hell of a lot easier to figure out their motive or background or any shred of information that we need, "That's part of the reason we wanted her. She could have been valuable. She must have seen something, or she must know something that could be of great use."

"It's alright though, I'm sure. I mean, even without her we managed to wipe out a whole bunch of them. Well, to be fair, they ended themselves pretty quickly."

I can't get the vision of half a dozen people blowing their brains out to stop repeating itself, "and how do you think we managed that?"

"In what regard?"

"You know, if they had planted those beacon disk things, then how did we manage to get close enough to the group of organizers to end their little operation?"

"You're not telling me…"

"Yes. They found out where one of the organizers was and, well, you know the rest. They also disabled the equipment, meaning that all of the beacons in the local area were disabled, granting us safe passage through."

"Well I never, so those kids were responsible for our success, then?"

"Pretty much. And we only get to thank one of them."

"Well that's a lot better than none of them. I don't know, maybe we'll chance into her the same way they did each other."

"Either way, I am extremely worried of what that… organization? Will become." Whatever the hell they were up to doesn't sit right with me.

"In other, less depressing news, we haven't had as many people die today. It seems we are stabilizing, and thanks to the police station idea that Gerald had all of our search parties are equipped with firearms."

"That's good to hear. Thanks, Yousaf."

Scrapes n' Scratches

Bated breaths stabilized his aim, as the skulking vixen sniffed between the remains of a past battle. Searching around, the black nose sorted between weaponry and body parts, trying to find a meal that wasn't too decomposed. Once it had found something of interest, it halted briefly. Its lonesome brown orbs observed an arm of interest. The winds rustled the pelt on its back as it sniffed further.

A moment later and Sean unleashed three rounds into its head and neck, careful not to ruin the salvageable meat.

Slumping to the ground, the vixen let out its last breath, unsure of how it died, only sure of the fading light as darkness approached with haste. Sean rushed over; he didn't want her mixing too long with the decaying corpses. After slinging the gun over his shoulder, he hauled the vixen into his arms, her blood running down his only sleeve, which wasn't the only thing without a counterpart.

Having already scavenged all the available ammo and even the odd granola bar, he was content with finally leaving the field of bodies, carrying his dinner with him. The battleground proved a pretty good haul; his pockets boasted two granola bars and three ammo magazines, but all for his automatic machine gun. Soon he would have to leave his full-auto pistol behind if he didn't find ammo for it. At that point it was just slowing him down, but it was a reminder of one of his proudest memories; the empty side arm was the only other thing he could share that memory with.

In one of his recent close scrapes, Sean escaped a grouping of bandits that were, he presumed, hunting, not too far off of the nearest village, Caheragh. They were a very well-stocked group of about ten people. They were making their way along the river collecting water, all with guns on their person. Sean himself was looking for a drink, after walking for so long the sight of the river caused him to drop his caution.

Running over, and suddenly five gun barrels were pointed his way. He had half a mind to go further up-stream and have a drink there, but the look on their eyes above their black, mismatched attire didn't show a shred of mercy. Sean knew a fight for the river was bound to happen.

It was down to who shot first, and Sean already had his hands clutching his rifle. Through the paranoia, he imagined all the guns blaring, and him having to dash up the stream. They hadn't fired yet, they must have thought him not a threat, something Sean was then adamant to prove otherwise. Slowly walking up the riverbed, his eyes locked on theirs, he had to suppress his chest to control his breathing.

Surprisingly, he had made it a full five paces when a sudden crash (which he soon found out was one of their water canisters being dropped onto the rest of them) caused him to break composure and run, spraying them all with his rifle. Or at least that was intention, it quickly got jammed. With multiple streams of bullets attacking his shadow, he quickly drew upon his pistol and riskily doubled back on himself, unleashing his full magazine of sixteen bullets upon the ten standing soldiers. Almost every bullet hit. Sure enough, the sudden barrage on the exposed, standing bandits forced them to quickly back off, and another long burst from his last magazine, topped with the intimidation of a maddened, running boy, caused them to retreat into the forest.

Although a very close call, he wasted no time and sprinted along the riverbank to get as far away from them as possible. He may have scored a lot of hits, but that didn't render them unable to shoot back. Sure enough, as he was running over the incline, bullets of retaliation slammed into the hill and the air, but in no time he was falling down the hill, too carried by his momentum to steady or stop himself. He tumbled for an uncomfortable while, bringing him further and further from the bandits.

Once he was at the foot on the hill, he shakily got himself up and checked for enemies. There weren't any, for now, so he cupped his hands and quickly drunk from the flowing river greedily, a grin to rival that of a Cheshire cat. He soon got going though, with bandits in the vicinity you can never get caught with your pants down. Most of the time, anyway.

That memory always amused him.

Prior to setting out, he set up a campfire and fed it with enough wood to keep it lit whilst he was away, or so he thought. The flames were already dwindling, and he had to rush over to dump the vixen and throw as many sticks and kindling as he could onto the fire.

In due time, it slowly crept back to life, and he got to work hacking at his prey. Luckily enough for him, he had managed to ransack an abandoned or massacred settlement a few months back, and he found a machete, still sharp. It was his greatest find so far.

As the smoke swelled up and the sun started to set, Sean got to work preparing his meal. Handling the machete in a strong grip, he rested the vixen against a tree, her legs pointing up in the air. Gripping one with his left hand and stretching it out, he swung down aggressively with the machete. Hacking into her leg joint, blood spurted as he withdrew it, only to hammer down again.

He kept going until he could rip the leg clean off, sinews and bloodstreams exposed to the world, with severed ligaments to avoid the hassle of cutting through bone. With the bleeding hunk of meat in his hands, he lay it down on a row of wooden sticks and branches, so it didn't touch the floor. Ineffectively wiping the blade with a leaf, he got to work savagely cutting off another leg.

Figuring two could keep him fed for that night, he thought about food reserves to keep him sustained before he acquired his next meal. There really isn't a lot of meat on a vixen leg, just at the leg joints, but it was the easiest meat to extract. He wasn't too efficient or skilled at skinning animals either, so the only real meat worth gathering were on the skinny legs.

He's hunted and eaten vixen and fox alike before, but it always bothered him that he couldn't extract even more meat for his troubles. Shrugging, he got to work, ripping off the remaining legs until the vixen was reduced to a hunk of bloody fur and strands.

As fresh blood ran down his forearms, ants started to seize the corpse. Anger flushed through him, he could never get rid of those damned pesky insects, they were always there to try and steal his hard work. As expected, the nest had clung its tendrils onto the legs he set aside, as a black swarm grew on the exposed meat. Despite the skin-itching display, he didn't fret or worry, he just grabbed the leg by its paw and suspended it over the fire.

Frenzied ants crawled with incredible speed all over the leg, a few escaping being cooked by running up his forearm, which he simply swatted away. Angling the meat lower, and flames licked the underside; some ants fell off into the bonfire. Slowly but surely, the enraged ants started to slow down. Soon, all the movement stopped altogether. Once he was satisfied that they had all died, he focused on cooking the meat.

Having claimed the vixen's body fully for themselves, Sean accepted defeat and thought it best to retain at least two legs to keep him fed for the night. Shoving the fleshy ant graveyard into his other hand, he grabbed the other leg and suspended that over the fire and saw the whole show play again. It never got old. He couldn't effectively swat away escaping ants, so he just muscled through the irritating sensations until he was able to pat himself down. It took a small while to cook his dinner, and the moon crept out into the starry playground.

At long last, he could tuck into the meat on the higher end of the leg, where it used to attach to the corpse that was now fully enveloped in gnashing ants and letting out a pungent smell. The occasional ant body would find its way into his mouth, but Sean didn't mind so much. He remembered from his shows when he was younger that insects are high in nutrition. Tearing at the meat with his barred teeth, the blood squelched as he clamped down. It could have done with a bit more time over the flames, but he was starving.

Discarding the first leg with patches of brittle bone showing through the ripped-off flesh, he moved onto the second. In no time he had both legs digesting in his belly. Usually, he would have got to work with cooking his meal for the next day, but they were so ridden with ants that he was pretty sure there wouldn't be any more meat worth fighting over. Ants weren't usually that big of a problem.

With a full belly, at least, he gathered his guns, ammo and granola bars, wrapped his empty, bloody carrier bag that would have been used to preserve food for the next day tight around his left hand, and set off to find somewhere to sleep that wasn't infested with ants.

Setting off to the crumbled barn, he walked bare footed on the ruined farmland. The rich soils had sprung up weeds and all sorts of strange plants and flowers, it made walking difficult and precarious; he didn't want to step on a thorn. Regardless of the danger, he was visited by the same comforting hands of the moon as he strolled across its illuminated path.

He ought to move on to a different area, he was running out of things to eat and live off there. As was tradition, he would sneak into the local village, Caheragh in this case, and take all he could before hiking off to the next place he would stay for a while. At first, he used to use the cover of darkness to sneak into settlements and villages and steal all he could unnoticed, but more recently he found using their hospitality against them was more profitable. And more fun. That's if they were hospitable to start with, though.

That way of life, sneaking around settlements and taking all he could, living off the land and fending for himself had forged him a new friend. He soon learned to appreciate the dark, to live for the night. It had done so much for him. A single scavenger, stalking the lands as if a moon's star on the ground. Alone, a million, million miles away from any other, and constantly shifting. A crescent smile hid on his face as he silently phased through the waves of grass. Whenever he felt the most alone, or upset, or bereaved, it was the peaceful night who soothed him. In recent nights, however, in that moment of blissful quiet, he was met by a half-thought, a sensation emitting through the tranquillity.

Tired and on his way to sleep without the pressing distraction of hunger allowed his mind to open up to the ghost of a thought, something he couldn't explain, not even to himself. Slowly fabricating in his mind, it took place behind his eyes and forced his face into creases and wrinkles and dragged his eyebrows to points. He didn't like to think about it, whatever it was, so he shook his head and tried to make constellations from the ever-loyal stars.

It was the fourth night he had spent in that barn, and as far as sleeping places went it wasn't half-bad. Looking at the derelict barn again, he decided he was ready to leave Caheragh and its pastures behind, it was running scarce on food and bountiful in dangerous bandits, not to mention the scummy Regulatory Party that occupied poor Caheragh. Pitching up on soggy, beaten down haybales and setting his possessions aside, he forced his mind to believe him to be comfortable, and soon he shunted into sleep.

Lucid dreams were steadily becoming more common. He knew he was asleep, yet he could do whatever he wanted. He relished in the control he had, but with his boundless possibilities and power, he always laid out the same story.

In his home, the one he had grown up in, he walked out of his bedroom that was littered with toys and posters and hairs from the cat. Bounding down the hallway came Conor, the best brother in the whole wide world, his nerf blaster in his little hands.

"Don't make a mess up there, you wee rascals!" chimed their mum from downstairs.

"We won't!" they replied in unison, cheeky grins on their faces. Sean accepted the blaster off of his brother, two nerf magazines already in his pocket. Conor had another blaster in his hands by the time Sean looked back up.

"You ready?" asked Sean.

"You are so dead!" Conor's little chubby face was full of determination and focus, signed off by his endearing smile.

Running off, Conor took his station and Sean walked back to his room. They both counted down from three to one, with the "*one!*" being cut off short by them rushing out into the hall to fight each other in honourable combat.

Leaping into the hallway, Sean was suddenly looking at his brother, dragging his mangled legs towards him with an unfathomable amount of fear in his eyes, face, mouth, nose and wavering chin.

Sean's lucidity drained from him in an instant, making him feel as though he was a falling bird shot out of the sky although he remained in place.

They were coming after them. Sean and Conor had made it so far together, but if they kept going at the same pace, they were both going to die. Large, silhouetted hands grabbed and forced aside the burning, crumbled, destroyed city that was their home only hours ago, clawing its way towards Conor.

They were almost there, Sean had no time. His hesitation had cost him precious seconds. He couldn't bear to look at his brother for much longer. He felt sick. His hesitation had closed the gap between them and the others that hunted them. He backed off, and started to run, as the ground gave way and a chasm split up the already cracked and ruined cityscape.

His hesitation had killed his brother.

A large crash grabbed him awake, followed quickly by a frenzied shuffling sound. Gasping, he looked around wildly, trying to find shapes in the shadows. Getting up and grabbing his rifle, he called out into the darkness. Taking his first few steps, not trusting the silence, he found himself in front of a pale arm of light, showing him some rotten beams that had collapsed, bringing some of the roof with it. As he was looking up to try and find the source of the collapse, he heard a noise to his left.

Gripping his gun tighter than ever, he stepped back, his breathing quickening. It must have been outside the barn, for all there was when he looked was the barn's wall. Slowly his eyes adjusted to the darkness, and he could see a way past the collapsed beams.

Instinctively, he grabbed his magazines before gingerly picking his way through, leaving everything else to grab later. He strained his ears harder and harder, trying to make out more sounds. What could have caused this? Was the barn giving up on itself? Almost past the pile, and he heard another noise above him, on the roof. Before he knew it, more snapping and crunching sounded above, and he found himself dashing to the other end before he could think.

Rotted beams and planks came cascading down, crashing all around him. With the exit rushing towards him, he got beaten down by the spike-point of a falling beam. It dug into the back of his calf, the splinters digging deep into his flesh before the beam broke off. Tears instantly threw themselves out of his eyes as he desperately trawled his way out of the barn.

When the cold, sweet embrace of grass met his skin, he rolled over and tried to get a good look of his injury, before the bellowing dust of the barn's collapse attacked his eyes. Grappling at his eyelids and crying in muted pain, he squinted to see through the tears. Frustratingly, the wound was right on the other side of his leg. Although the darkness masked his vision, he could still see the reflections of the moon's light on all the blood that was oozing out and smearing all over his leg and hands. Stinging to the touch, he could feel the little rotten shards of wood wriggle and stab at his muscle.

The barn was still standing, and through his blurred vision, some of the stars turned off. Focusing, and it turned out that someone was on the barn and was looking right at him.

"Hey, what the fuck?" he shouted, his course throat struggling to produce volume. He repeated himself, but the head tucked back over the barn. Angered, Sean thrust himself up and limped closer to the part of the barn that was somehow still standing. He couldn't figure out how someone managed to climb on to it without some sort of ladder, until he spied a dangling rope. No way Sean could climb that with his leg how it was.

As he tugged at the rope, the head popped over the side again. "Oi, you, what the hell are ya' doing up there?" he shouted. This time, the person put a finger to his lips, "Think you can just shush me, eh? Get the fuck down here and we can have a chat man to man," betraying his words, his voice warbled and rocked at the intense pain exploding his leg.

The mysterious person didn't entertain Sean, and instead went back to whatever he was doing. That didn't sit well with him. "Come down here, ya' bastard," he shouted, punching the wall. Being grabbed and forced to the ground, Sean got a face-full of dirt. Gasping, he barely looked before a man in serious military kit firmly put a finger to his lips, slowly and quietly shushing him. His shush had an interesting accent.

Not getting the message, Sean was quick to retaliate, before his ripped calf gave his leg in, and he stumbled to the floor again, a cry of pain bursting out from his mouth. Crouching low, the other man grasped his shoulders and held him in place as he lifted his leg up. Caught off guard, Sean kicked the man in the face.

Again, the man grabbed his shoulders, "*Silence!*" he hissed in a French accent. It wasn't often you got a Frenchman in post-apocalyptic southern Ireland. Slowly, this time, the Frenchman got his leg and lifted it up, recoiling at the sight of his butchered calf.

He shot a look at Sean, and he felt as though he could see the shock through his headgear. Calling over someone else, the Frenchman helped Sean up on his feet. "That idiot up there collapsed the barn which I was sleeping in!" he tried to shout, viscously looking between the two black-donned soldiers, the other having materialized out of the darkness.

If he squinted, he could make out another dozen of them, slowly traversing the farmland. Being prodded, the other man ordered him to move, "Bouge-toi," but allowed him to pick up his gun that he must have dropped. Now limping, and slightly scared, loads of geared up soldiers sneaked past him, their guns out and ready. It was then when it clocked that they were probably part of a governmental attack. They must be going after their rival, the Regulatory Party in Caheragh. Whoever they were.

Realizing what he was in the middle of, he started to question where he was going. "Where you taking me?" he spluttered. They didn't say anything. He couldn't outrun them with his leg being busted and causing agonizing pain. So much so that he had to stop and let himself fall to his knees.

"Merde, nous devrons le porter," the other person was also French. Next thing he knew, he was being hoisted over one of their shoulders. Some form of tool was digging into his stomach. Swaying and jerking, Sean saw the ground pass him through pained and teary vision, his gun barely hanging on in his loose grip.

The soldier had numerous items all over his person, which of the parties had access to this much equipment? Or even that many French supporters?

Knowing he needed medical attention, Sean just hoped they were bringing him to some sort of doctor or surgeon, but the likelihood was low. Caheragh probably had some form of medical equipment to help him and was his best bet if he could escape them and somehow beat the advancing army to it. He didn't put much faith that his captors would help him as much as he needed.

"Where're you taking me, for fuck's sake?" he asked again, wriggling about.

"Ferme le bouche," one of them aggressively whispered.

"I don't speak French!" he fruitlessly retorted. They didn't seem to care.

With his leg throbbing and beating, he felt tingles ravage his leg muscles and he started to sweat. It was intense. Groaning slightly, Sean felt his carrier quicken the pace.

Before long he was sat down, the sudden rush of blood hitting his head disorientated him. Focusing his vision, and the Frenchman started fretting and muttering under his breath. Out of nowhere he procured some sort of first aid kit, which was when Sean registered the slowly mounting coldness on his backside. He was sitting down on the back of a van. A military van, more precisely.

The Frenchman cleaned his leg and applied pressure to the wound for a minute, using a dense, pact tissue. With pain still splattered on his leg even if the blood wasn't, Sean had to tightly grip the end of the van, breathing heavily. The Frenchman said something else in a hesitant tone, suggesting he knew he wasn't being understood, but he proceeded to start dressing his wound with bandages anyway. Unknowing of the bits of wood deep in Sean's leg, the bandage cemented in the blood, and also the potential infection. At least it was a step in the right direction.

Movement sounded behind him, there were a few others milling around the van. They must be protecting the site, Sean concluded. Their muttering and whispering sounded awfully French. The odds of there being that many French in one of the political party's armies was low. The only explanation that Sean could think of was that the French had invaded southern Ireland, which made him laugh to himself. It must be all the pain getting to his head.

Sean thanked the Frenchman, and prodded his leg, which he received a stab of pain in reply. The Frenchman told him something that Sean could only assume was an order to stay put, and one of the others stepped up to stand by, keeping an eye on him.

Although glad they had patched his leg up, he knew it wasn't the sort of attention he needed. The splinters in his leg were bound to cause an infection. He needed to go to Caheragh, where they could understand him and his predicament.

His leg was in a world of pain, but he still thought it best to try and stand. Strangely enough, standing didn't cause him as much grief as he thought it would, it was only when he contracted or relaxed his muscle when the pain came full fold. As he stood, one of the soldiers walked over, towering above him menacingly.

With a half-baked idea and a dirty smile, Sean punched the Frenchman between his legs, and in the intense pain he dropped his gun, which Sean was quick to grab before it hit the ground, his own gun in his other hand. Devilishly, Sean pointed the guns at the others as they started up, freezing them in place.

Retorts were blabbered and shouted as Sean waved the barrels at each of them in turn, the one he assaulted trying his best to maintain what little composure he had left. Sean knew he couldn't get to Caheragh before the advancing army did. Unless he drove there.

Looking at the van and walking over, he noticed that he had no idea how to drive, and thought it a good idea to get to Caheragh alive. He would have to hold one of them hostage and order them to drive the van for him. The others could see him intently looking at the van, and when he nodded at the one who bandaged him up and jerked the gun to the driver's seat, the Frenchman knew exactly what Sean intended.

Shaking his head, the Frenchman advanced in large strides, ready to tackle Sean to the ground. To avoid this, he shot the ground where the Frenchman's foot was about to land, halting him in his tracks. Unrelenting, he re-established his control by waving the other gun to all the others. Their hesitancy to shoot intrigued him. The filthy government parties had never hesitated to try and kill him before. Why were they second-guessing now?

He felt as though he had the group around his finger, until, yet again, someone had crept up behind him and tackled him to the floor, his leg wound being punished severely.

"Que crois tu faire?" the man growled between his teeth. As the guns slipped out of his grip and he was being detained on the ground, he knew he wasn't going anywhere anytime soon. But he needed to save his leg before it turned infected; he would have to cut it off otherwise. And that's practically a death sentence in its own right.

His efforts weren't completely in vain though, now he was being forced to the floor, he was at their mercy. They seemed like a merciful group, which not only surprised Sean, but gave him an opportunity to exploit them.

Suddenly yelping with pain, he made several hissing noises as if his leg had been hit by the man. Wriggling around in the Frenchman's grip to try and show unbearable pain, he made more exotic noises as people started to run over towards him.

As expected, the one keeping him down relented his grip slightly, as he looked around, trying to steer clear from his bandages. To maintain the show, Sean swatted away all the hands that tried to help him, retreating away to sit up against the van. What were clearly questions being asked were made redundant by the language barrier, so he just sat there with a hunch, rubbing his leg and wearing a grimace.

Thankfully, they backed off. A couple of the Frenchman stuck around near him, but at least he wasn't being grappled to the floor with zero chance of escape. Looking over to his left, and he saw the glint of vans in the distance. Clearly, that man who had tackled him to the floor must have been guarding the other site.

Although he had slipped up the first time, he still wanted to hop in a van and drive to the village. He still needed whatever medicine they had. Also not knowing what the French lot wanted with Sean was another motivator to get as far away as possible. Was he a prisoner of war? Or did they think they were rescuing him? He didn't want to stick around and find out.

The first step would be to move away from the bottleneck he was in, to be in a place of better mobility. Stretching his legs and making a show of it, he stood up gingerly. His leg was in intense pain, but he really had to express that on his face. He had a high pain tolerance from his solitary scavenging lifestyle. There was no one ever with him to help him with the pain, so he never felt a need to show it.

Once he was upright and had attracted suspicious glances from his two guards, he slowly moved picking up his gun beforehand, whilst stretching his legs with every step, away from the van to its right, where there was more open space. The Frenchman were very weary but stayed put, keeping an eye on him.

He wondered how long they would put up with his games.

Giving his legs the stretching of a lifetime, he slyly eyed the van door. He had never driven anything before. His plan was probably a short-fire way of killing himself, now that he had ditched the idea of making someone drive for him. The more he stretched, the more his wound came wailing out to him. If it got infected, then he would slowly waste away. Although he knew throwing all caution to the wind wasn't the brightest idea he ever had, he concluded that an epic car crash was far better than the alternative.

With everyone's eyes on him, it would be a tricky feat to get into the van, start it up, and drive it off without them being able to shoot the van's tires or him, for that matter. He would have to be quick. Smiling in anticipation, Sean leaped sideways, grabbing onto the handle with his free hand before his feet touched the ground.

Hoisting the door open and not bothering to shut it as his hands flung towards where he suspected the keys to be, he let his gun fall to his lap. Everyone else's reaction was rather delayed, but soon enough they came hurtling after him. The van, with its keys thankfully in the ignition, revved to life, but there was no time to savour the beauty of the beast.

Thinking to close the door as a Frenchman struck his arm out towards him, whacking his outstretched fingertips on the way, he haphazardly kicked down on the acceleration, trying to remember his parents driving a car all those years ago. He vaguely remembered his parents using the gearbox when they drove, so he shoved down on the clutch before grinding into first gear.

After a worryingly bumpy start, the van zoomed down the pasture, roaring so loud it startled him. As Sean was working with the gear box, pushing and pulling the clutch, he almost crashed right into another one of the vans as people threw themselves to the side.

Spinning the wheel as far as it could, the van made a wide arc, its left headlight smashing after contact with the back end of a stationary van. The impact knocked Sean off the pedals, but after a second to shake himself, he jumped back on to the acceleration, his backside off the seat, and rampaged back towards where he van from, with the others all trying to shoot at the wheels and the bonnet.

In no time Sean smashed his way past as if he were a bowling ball; all the skittles scatted as he swept through. A triumphant laugh bellowed as he looked back at the carnage he caused. Now all he had to do was drive over to Caheragh before the army got there, receive medical treatment quickly, and vanish before the fighting happened.

To stop the ear-pummelling screaming from the van, Sean tried moving the gearstick to other compartments, successfully quieting the noise. The rancid smell of fumes crept into his nose, however, making him splutter. He hoped it wouldn't be a huge problem.

Whilst enjoying the plan he made, the bonnet started to smoke, *'Those bastards must have hit something.'* Pressing fully on the acceleration, he made it his mission to go as far as possible before the smoke concealed more and more of his vision. Thankfully, it was spiralling out of the sides, and at the speed he was going it was being whipped back behind him. It was still concerning, however, and he knew he would have to ditch the van soon.

It just depended on how long he wanted to risk it.

Screaming down the farmland, the van bumping into everything, Sean saw the barn quickly approaching. Spinning the wheel, the van reared to the side, raking through the course dirt. Spinning the wheel the other way to stabilize the van caused it to rear up the other way, and so ensued a viscous cycle of Sean battling for control of the van as it careered into the barn's side, knocking out the other headlight.

Grinding to a halt as Sean regained his composure and steadied his breathing, his adrenaline raced his heart. After a few seconds, he grabbed the wheel and slammed down on the pedal again, before he realized there must be a prole with the van. Turning it back on, and playing with the pedals again, he suddenly shot off, the thick curls of smoke that where threatening explosion got raked back behind him. Every second he wasted was another second lost to the army. All the while his wound was more than killing him; Sean felt fear gripe his organs.

Careening past the ancient farmland, more and more smoke plumed. It started to conceal his vision, as if the darkness weren't enough. He braved his fears through more and more fields, knowing full well that any second the engine could give in, or worse, explode. Breathing pacing up, he hoped he was travelling in the right direction. Through narrowed eyebrows he managed to isolate the silhouettes from the night sky, and mentally pictured what was in front of him: woodland.

Trees and bushes unearthed themselves from the darkness. All he could do was gasp before he was violently throttled side to side, his foot being launched off the pedal as the momentum forced the van through branches, leaves and roots. His skull jarred as he was thrown around the van as the van was thrown around the environment as the environment was thrown around him, his gun joining in the madness.

Eventually, the van crashed to a halt. The final impact saw Sean on his back, the danger of throwing up outweighing his poor leg, the bandage bursting at the seams. Groaning loudly, Sean concentrated on grasping his slippery focus as his limbs were rendered aloft in the air. Forcing himself up, he plucked up the effort to crawl out of the van, shards of glass scratching and scraping at him as he went.

By the time he was stumbling out, the thick plumes from the engine were attacking his lungs, and he fell to his knees as he threw up his vixen and ants. Like a beam, his vomit was highly dense and didn't last for long. Spitting and spluttering to get the disgusting taste out from his mouth, he worked out where to go by walking away from the trails from the heavily smoking van, clutching his stomach as he went.

Limping like a zombie, Sean held his head and his automatic rifle. The pain will pass, he reminded himself, the only thing he needed to worry about was his god damned leg. He had travelled very far and fast by the van; he couldn't be far off the advancing army.

Coughing up some more, he wasn't prepared for the ear-splitting and terrifying explosion that seized him up. The van's engine had finally given up with a powerful display of destruction. Turning around, and he saw a little inferno dance through the trees where the van crashed.

Joining the van's explosion were shouts of alarm all around him. Looking left and right, he saw nothing. Cursing, he knew he was right in the middle of the army. Or at least a small grouping of them, for there only seemed to be five or six as conversation, all in French, ensued as quickly as a wildfire.

"You again?" Hissed from the shadows in a surprisingly light accent. His throat jumped up into his mouth as he turned to face the voice, only to see nothing. More and more French whispering wrapped around him, he tried to peel off, but there was nowhere to go.

After shifting all of the weight onto his good leg, he let out a pained breath. He needed to go; he didn't have time to stand around. Limping forwards and hoping he didn't bump into any of them, the sound of burning slowly introduced itself. *'Oh shit,'* was all he thought before a Frenchman grabbed his shoulder and told him something. Probably an order, judging from the tone. Whatever he said he had a sure grip, it would be difficult to shake. At the sound of a single word repeated three times, everyone moved with haste and purpose away from the fire. Sean's captor muttered something under his breath.

From memory Sean knew that Caheragh wasn't too far away now, if only he wasn't being escorted there *by* the army he was trying to outrun.

Reacting to the fire, foxes dashed out from nowhere, skirting in and out of everyone's legs. They all stood deathly still, allowing the foxes to escape unimpeded. A few cries were released into the air as their paws pattered off into the night.

Sean wondered where the other groups were. Were they all in the woods, or taking up different positions to assault the village?

Another few foxes jumped in front of them, teeth barred and foaming. They were rabid. Flinching, Sean almost fell over as his weight shifted onto his bad leg. In no time at all his captor shot around the foxes, shooing them off. He then grabbed Sean and pushed him onwards.

His leg went numb, he didn't know for how much longer he could last. Sean's captor and another spoke in harsh whispers, and his mind told him that they were talking about him. Surely, they wouldn't force him into battle, but they couldn't leave him there either. They said the name of the village a few times; Sean didn't know what to think of it.

There was no way he could make it to Caheragh and still receive medical treatment before all hell broke loose. If he wanted to live, he would need to race ahead. But what if it's too late?

A few ideas crossed his mind, and he figured he could try them all if he played his cards right. Collapsing to the floor again, he clutched his numb leg and wailed at them to leave him there. "I can't go on any longer, just leave me here," he pained through gritted teeth.

The Frenchman exchanged glances before quickly wrapping his arms around their necks and heaving him up. The sudden movement knocked the acting out of him, and he was bewildered as they swiftly skirted off away from everyone. They must be bringing him somewhere safe, he presumed.

Merely seconds into being transported, yet again, by the Frenchmen, a hail of bullets and shouts of alarm lit up the forest, momentarily brighter than the fire. Being dropped to the floor, he heard the two people transporting him arm themselves and shoot back into the fray.

Madness exploded the forest, with the gun flashes lighting up the faces of friend and foe, bullets firing everywhere people suspected an enemy to be, hoping it wouldn't turn out to be an ally.

Grappling in the dirt, Sean turned himself over, the pressing numbness of his leg dominating his mind. Unable to figure out the course of action through the chaos, he retreated further forwards, trying his hardest to suppress his breathing. Bullets pinged awfully close to him; all he could do was crawl ever faster into the thicket and hope he didn't get shot.

Through the gun flashes and now the growing fire on the rightmost side, Sean got a better look at the ambushers. Their clothes were the usual level of dirty and unkempt, but they all had very clean faces, a sight not so often saw. At least not to Sean. Naturally, he couldn't get a complete look of their faces, but the flashes and glimpses were never stained by mud or dirt. They must be the Regulatory Party's soldiers based in Caheragh.

The guns they used were the common SOL-Ps, or the Sun Pipers, which were in use by seemingly all the government parties in Ireland as far as Sean could tell. Where the hell they got manufactured or salvaged from was beyond him.

He was now a comfortable distance from the action and more rational thoughts emerged, such as fighting back with his automatic rifle, but that would only be drawing unwelcomed attention to him. Managing to stand, he figured he could circle around the fighting and make his way to Caheragh.

Wobbling from tree to tree, using the trunks as support, Sean slowly made a zig-zag path around the action, that seemed to generate more and more heat. More Regulatory soldiers (or 'Reg', as San called them) fanned out as more Frenchmen appeared from the darkness to slice someone's throat. The guerrilla warfare was impossible to follow, and it seemed to encapsulate the whole forest, or at least the whole section where the French were pushing. Something must have tipped off the Reg Party that they were there. He wondered if his car-crash-turned-fire had anything to do with it.

At least with all the soldiers away from Caheragh he should have an easy time getting into the village. Well, *easier* time, it certainly won't be easy, which he was bitterly reminded of when he stalled and fell over again.

Separating himself further and further from the action, he took a second to calm his shaking. It was difficult to tell whether it was from his adrenaline or his wound. Maybe both. As he was letting out shaky breaths, someone collapsed right behind him. Spinning around, it turned out to be one of the Reg Party soldiers on his back, clutching a bleeding wound in his chest. Sean quickly got a move on; he didn't want to linger where people were getting killed.

Shoving off, he saw the movement of a Frenchman's gun pointing right at Sean. Fearing the soldier would mistake him for the enemy, Sean let loose a burst from his gun, landing three lethal hits. As soon as he hit the ground, Sean steadied his grip and finished off the squirming Frenchman.

Getting up and managing to press on despite the limb-ripping agony, and after passing another tree, Sean was suddenly face-to-face with a Reg Party soldier. About to shoot him as well, he patted Sean on the arm.

"They got your leg, huh?" he breathlessly panted, "Don't worry, I'll cover your advance. Just hurry up and get back." The man readied his gun.

"Cheers," whispered Sean as he got going.

"It's that way," the soldier looked at Sean with sympathy and chuckled, "the forest is confusing, right?"

Sean swiftly unloaded the rest of his bullets into the soldier's chest and head before limping off. It was simpler that way. He had no time for communication.

Moving on, Sean shuffled past the body. The eye of the storm was somewhere behind him, but throughout the forest there were smaller spats and stray soldiers that he had to avoid.

"Get down!" was shouted behind him, right before Sean was tackled to the floor. A murderous beam of bullets penetrated the air and trunks all over their heads. Twisting round, and it was another of the French lot that had saved him.

"Just surrender and we'll take you somewhere safe," the Frenchman tried to pacify Sean, suspecting him for a Reg Party soldier.

"I'm not one of them," Sean quickly responded, to get him off his back.

"Who are you? A Caheragh citizen?"

"Yes, I am," he lied, and taking his opportunity, he asked, "Who the fuck are you guys?" with more wobble in his voice than he wanted.

"Isn't it clear?" he humoured, exaggerating his French accent, "we're the French army, friend." Sean was speechless. What the hell were the French doing in Ireland? "Well, the France-Belgium-Luxembourg advancement, anyway. FBL for short," Sean could've sworn he saw a wink.

The Frenchman, or possibly Belgian or Luxembourger, shot up and returned fire; Sean thought it best to do the same. Propping up on his one good knee, he concentrated fire on the same bush that his neighbour was firing at. What the hell had the world come to?

So this wasn't some sort of political attack to gain power or something, this was a foreign attack? An invasion? Although they were being rather friendly with him, he didn't like the thought of hanging around people that had just invaded his homeland.

"You'd do best if you stick me with me," he shouted above the gunshots. Sean didn't agree. Ducking away, he was more encouraged to get to Caheragh then more than ever. The more he fought off the Reg Party, the quicker the foreign invaders would get to Caheragh, and the more there would be of them after the fight.

Taking a deep breath, he got himself up, ignoring the FBL soldier's advice right to his face, and grappled at the tree to spring him off to the next one. He started to see light though the trees as he weaved and trawled through more and more woodland with minimal interruptions. The main fight was behind him, and when he turned around, the fire was raging high into the night sky. That should keep them busy.

Stumbling forth into the dark-cast pasture, he grew a smile. In the distance, still quite a way away, was the village of Caheragh. Fires were dancing enticingly between the silhouettes as if beckoning hands. Right across from his bridge of shadows, the shimmering light of the moon highlighted the village. Against all odds, he was almost there.

Without any trees to rely on, he fell to his hands a few times, but he never gave up. Slowly but surely, the silhouettes gained dimension and highlights and shadows. Not yet within a good distance, but it was progress enough for him to rejoice inside.

Perhaps it was premature.

Shouts of alarm rang out behind him; the fire had spread rapidly. A great thick plume forced off the burning woods, with people of all affiliations fleeing to the field. The eye of the storm was rapidly moving, right into the pasture where Sean was watching with horror.

Now in the open, what looked like a free-for-all broke out as everyone was suddenly amongst themselves. Sean started to run as fast as he could, having to slow down consistently to stop himself falling over.

Having lost all feeling in his lower body, and with the mounting pressure of the fight drawing closer, Sean's body was shaking from head to toe. Sweat and blood loss masked his vision; he was left blindly scraping towards his last hope.

Not too far behind him were the FBL, swiftly making their way to their target now that their cover had been completely blown. Amidst the onslaught, the Reg Party soldiers were trying their best to repel them and stop them, throwing everything they had at the invaders to protect their home. Their bloody race left a trail of bodies, from sprinting FBL troops to blockading soldier. And in the lead was Sean.

As his fingernails were clogging with dirt and his brow staining with mud, he felt he could go on no longer. A guttural, savage cry involuntarily clawed into the air, bolstering his resolve for a single moment. The brutality behind him finally ordered itself, with the Reg Party exploiting the flank of the FBL, forcing them to face them.

The spontaneous front had both sides throwing bullets at each other in the open plain. Sean didn't want to look back, hearing it was hard enough. But at least they were confronting each other and not making quick progress to Caheragh, and now both sides would be considerably weakened. Or at least that's how Sean took the development. *'At last, a slight break'*, he thought.

Out of the flickering shadows ahead, from the now defined Caheragh buildings and posts, a wave of soldiers marched towards the conflict. Be them reserve or reinforcements, Sean couldn't figure out, but either way they were heading for the fight.

Unexpectedly, the few dozen guns pointed outwards, crouched, and opened fire across the field. Forced down by the shock, Sean's head and body pressed against the floor as the beams of death reached across the field, from the outskirts of Caheragh to where the main battle was raging.

Braving his fears of getting his head blown off, he inclined his head slightly, fighting his whole body to do so. Whizzing over him were the speeding bullets, but they were high enough for him to feel comfortable having a better look. He should be able to crawl over, but would they take pity on him? Kill him? Could he shoot over at the FBL and pose as a wounded Reg Party soldier? He would do whatever was needed to get the medical treatment that was straying further and further out of his grasp.

He didn't have a choice. Crawling past them wasn't an option, it was too wide an arc to secure not being noticed.

Before too long, the FBL were returning fire to the newcomers, and now Sean was even more frightened for his life. Getting louder and louder, the gun shots pinged into his ears as the bullets leap-frogged over him.

"There! Right there!" called out from the Reg Party line in front of him. They must have saw him. Thankfully, they didn't rain fire upon him at sight, they must have been too suppressed to spare any firepower.

"Wait," Sean slit through gritted teeth, "I'm with you," he found his voice. Ahead, a few of their heads tilted, but they thankfully didn't relent their fight against the FBL. Besides, what threat was a beaten, half-dead teenager, anyway?

"I'll go ahead," he managed to hear one of them whisper, and truth to action one of them doubled over and drew closer.

"Thank you," Sean uttered, "thank you so much," he repeated as the man became distinguishable, "I'm with you." The man grabbed Sean and dragged him, much quicker than he had been moving to the safety of behind the others. As Sean collapsed onto his back, he spluttered and gasped, thanking the man.

"Don't worry, I got you," the soldier quickly patted him down, searching everywhere for wounds but missing the only one, "Who are they? The Green Liberal Coalition?"

"A bunch of Frenchmen," Sean spluttered, breathing heavily in an attempt to combat the extreme breathless and adrenaline that was bursting his head and chest.

"What?" he recoiled, and the others that overheard faltered, not believing what he said.

"They call themselves the FBL," Sean tried getting up, and the soldier backed off a bit.

"How's your unit?" the soldier asked, trying to grab at his chest.

"Fuck're you doing?" Sean reacted, falling back down.

"Just checking your unit," he said slowly, and made a second grab. Finding nothing on his chest or dangling off it, he pulled out his sidearm (that very few had, Sean noticed) and held it outstretched to Sean's forehead.

"What unit are you in?" he asked again, remaining his calm tone.

"Your one, mate," Sean managed after a long hesitation. He was definitely going to kill him.

Not waiting to get his head blown in, Sean swivelled around, throwing his arm out to bash the outstretched pistol. Two rounds were shot into the ground as the soldier was thrown off and punched in the face. He quickly pistol-whipped Sean around the head and slammed him into the ground, a look of outrage and disgust bearing down on the boy. Before he could line up another shot, a flurry of bullets slammed all around them, hitting some of the others that couldn't spare a moment to help their ally's tussle with Sean.

Hunching over, they both squinted their eyes shut as the bullets flew past them, teasing death in their whistles. The soldier returned fire, equipping his SOL-P, but he kept a knee on Sean's chest, digging into his already exhausted ribcage. Struggling, Sean clawed and wriggled, but that only got a smack on his head with the butt of the sun piper.

Holding the sun piper in one hand and raising the pistol with his other to end Sean, he yet again went to hit the gun out of the soldier's hand. Reacting in time, he withdrew the pistol higher, but in the sudden movement he threw his other hand backwards to catch himself, only for the sun piper to get in the way.

Staggering and tumbling, Sean reached forwards and clawed the pistol into his hand, and without wasting a second, he emptied the clip on the horrified face that had just turned around to face him.

A few others that were raining bullets on the FBL spared a second to turn around to see Sean still alive, and their friend's face turned inside out. Before they could react, Sean was already half-crawling and half-running behind the closest building, the pistol still in hand, even if it was empty.

On his feet again, and his legs, let alone his wound, were threatening to fall apart. It was pure agony. Tears rolled en mass down his determined face, he could no longer twiddle his foot without a burst of pain in response. He could feel his leg stiffening, and the splinters making their home in his muscle. At least he was finally in Caheragh.

Looking around wildly, all Sean saw was patchwork buildings and scrambled together stalls and stands. It was quite impressive, all the other villages are barely distinguishable from the destroyed ones. Going past signs and makeshift sleeping areas, an unsettling breeze came over him. Where was everyone? He expected to see them huddling in their homes or being closely guarded by a few soldiers. But there was no one.

They must be hiding, he assumed. Exploring more and more of the village, poking into the different buildings and stands, no life could be found. And his was slowly fading. Approximately now at the heart of Caheragh, in the middle of a cleared, solid flooring which he thought to be the village plaza, he heard a muffled thud.

"Hello?" he barely managed. With no response, he tried again, "Any one there? I really need some help here! Anyone? I heard ya', no point lying now." Still no response. It was only after he opened his mouth was he conscious of attracting the wrong kind of attention.

Briskly pacing over to where he thought the noise to come from, he entered a building that had solid doors and lighting. A narrow hallway with broken stairs to the right met him. Bumbling down the hallway, and he noticed the flooring had many cracks in it, all originating from under the door to his right, under the stairs. The door was not an original part of the house for sure, it was crudely cut, and the hinges looked like they were robbed from another house entirely.

Grabbing the handle and opening the door, the smell of dust, dinge and stuffy air met him. Coughing, he looked down the hole that had been hastily dug out, snaking off at a steep decline. "Hello?" he called out. He wanted to explore, but with his leg shouting out to him, curiosity could kill the cat. Lying down and craning his neck so he got a good view of the hole, and he saw a faint light from a chasm at the end it. "Hello down there," he shouted, but still, there was no answer. He was sure the thud must have come from that house, there must be people down there. Maybe they were his only way to get help.

Bracing himself, he went bottom first into the hole and allowed himself to gradually slide down the tunnel of pact mud and stones, keeping his injured leg in the air. Half-way down and brief shuffling sounded, but there was no telling if it was just his clothes. He couldn't stop to think about it.

Slapping the bottom of the tunnel, a whole room met him, with only a few measly beams keeping it up. Not that it really needed supporting, it wasn't tall enough to properly stand in, which Sean understood from seeing a couple dozen people with gags and tied up arms, all being threatened from multiple crouched Reg Party soldiers. Dirty, aching faces of all ages and gender were cramped together in the chamber, looking at Sean with a silent desperation. Speechless, he sat still, momentarily forgetting the reason for being down there in the first place.

The pain quickly reminded him. In a small voice, he asked, "My leg is injured," dozens of eyes were staring at him, some angry, others terrified, "I need immediate medical help before I can go back to the fight," his breathing wobbled, but this time not because of the incarcerating pain.

The soldiers keeping the citizens hostage looked at each other, "Come with me," one ordered, and together they awkwardly escaped the tunnel. Sean's eyes were pried wide, and he couldn't shake off the image of dozens of people hunched and crouched over, tied up with tear-stained cheeks.

Thankfully, the soldier wrapped Sean's arm around his shoulders and assisted him as he led them to yet another building, not far off. Getting louder, the sounds of guns was overbearing any cry of pain or death. The FBL must be advancing despite the harrowing overwatch of the Reg Party line.

The building the soldier led Sean to was hardly being kept together, and its inner walls had collapsed long ago to create an impromptu open-floor plan. A lone table was sitting in the middle, the high moon's light resting on it.

The soldier quickly departed to stomp on a hatch in the floor that Sean hadn't noticed. When the hatch opened, a soldier popped his head out, "What?"

"Got a wounded here, must have forgot the correct hatch. Bad leg injury. Not one of ours though," The hatch soldier stopped climbing and looked around until his eyes caught Sean.

"Oh," the hatch soldier quizzically said before ducking under the hatch. Half a minute later and someone else stiffly crawled out from the hatch, coughing dryly. A narrow, spectacled face with short, black hair snapped his head over to Sean, and his anxious expression broke into surprise.

"Don't worry, I've got you," the medic quickly caught Sean's failing body and hauled him onto the cold table. The soldier slowly walked away, leaving Sean to his fate.

Getting right to work, the medic inspected his whole body before focusing solely on his leg, turning him around. His sodden bandages should've slipped right off, but they were almost stuck and integrated with his wound, his sticky blood gluing it tight. What ensued was pain, pauses as the medic rushed off to get something else, occasional blackouts, lots of weird sensations, and an unmatched agony.

In his pain-induced stupor, the fading face of the fretting medic was replaced by his brother. That day, those dreams. Conor looked at him. Sean looked away. What was I supposed to do? Die?
I should have died with him.
What was I supposed to do? It was an impossible situation for a kid.
I should have saved him.
What was I supposed to do? Conor was slowly dying, anyway!
I shouldn't have walked away.

Now Conor was looking at him, and Sean was the one on the floor, with a mangled leg, tear-stained face and on the end of his rope. He just wanted one more day, one more nerf war, one more laugh, anything. Conor walked away, and was replaced by the medic, sweat on his forehead.

After what felt like a long time, instead of the intense soreness and the constant scratching and ebbing and digging, he felt the insane pressure of the muscle and skin being forced back together and aftermath of the splinters and blood loss and chunked off flesh. During the operation, the medic must have noticed the splinters, for the scratching needles had been replaced with an extreme soreness, although the worry of infection being relieved was a comfortable trade. Instead of being better, the pain had shifted itself. From stabbing to sore, from explosive to tight, from flaming to electrifying.

Nowhere to be seen, the medic must have finished. Flipping himself around, Sean looked at the moon-laced buildings. A beckon flushed within, he could easily slip away there and then, if he wanted to, he was completely alone, if the presence of his brother in his mind and the ever-closer gunshots and battling were excluded.

It wasn't in the forefront of his mind, but he knew it was somewhere. An impression of the emotions, a stain of the regrets stuck in his brain. Maybe it was always there, but this time he was truly alone to appreciate the company of his thoughts. At least he had never felt more alone.

He had gotten used to it. To think that he spent every day with his brother, to spending every day with no one. Alongside his leg, a new heavy beat chimed in. A thud in his chest. Looking out into the tempting darkness, it called to him. A strangely familiar feeling.

Dangling his legs off the table, he took a deep breath and braced himself before his newly bandaged leg firmly planted onto the floor. A sigh of relief, the pain was of similar calibre. Standing up proved manageable too, but as soon as he worked his muscles through walking, he froze in place, his face screwed in silent pain. He should've expected that.

Back to limping, Sean left the sanctuary of the building, and took his first steps into the drapes of dark concealing the alleys. By the sounds of it, the FBL were at Caheragh's front door. Strangely, he didn't want to quickly run off before the action took to the streets. He found comfort in the invisibility, comfort in wearing the moon's cloak. Flitting between roads and stalking in the alleys, Sean's mind was silent.

The thudding intensified, and his breathing involuntarily shuddered, wavering the comfortable control he briefly held. What was it? In the absence of thought, an image nearly formed, if it weren't for the shouts that echoed all throughout the village, "Defensive positions!"

At once, all of the remaining soldiers holding out fell back into the village, quickly plastering behind walls and ducking under cover. Following suit, the FBL chased them, only to be disadvantaged by the lack of cover. Pulled away from being consumed by his thoughts, Sean tried to pick up the pace. He had to make it out of Caheragh before getting killed.

Peeking out from the alley, and the whole street had come alive with risking guns trading bullets. Preparing himself to dash across the street, and a bulk of Reg Party soldiers, that Sean had just saw clambering out of another hatch, ran into the street and took defensive positions behind upturned cars and over-spilling furniture.

Hoping for them to act as body shields as he ran, he pushed off the floor and practically hopped with full force across the street. At that moment, a flurry of bullets smacked all around them, one penetrating deep into one of the soldier's shoulders. Leg buckling and the intensity of being shot at swept Sean off his feet, falling at the bleeding body of the soldier.

Locking eyes, and the grunting soldier motioned at his gun. Frustrated, Sean knew that right there he was pinned, with the storm of bullets closing off a safe escape. Picking up the gun and resting in on the car's smashed out windows, Sean let rip.

Unable to properly kneel or position himself, he couldn't clearly see his targets, he just knew to keep firing at the muzzle flashes down the street. Sean never thought he would be fighting alongside the Regulatory Party, or any government party for that matter, but now it was a matter of life or death.

"If we stop firing, they'll think we're dead," heavily breathed one. The others didn't say anything, but complied anyway. Withdrawing their guns and remaining deadly still, they watched as the wounded soldier's eyes started to stare up at the night sky. Some people's bodies just couldn't handle the shock of being directly shot. Sean didn't stare for long.

Surprisingly, the effect they wanted was what they got, the only bullets hitting near them were missed shots from other targets. Even so, they all seemed content with staying still. Except Sean. Deciding to keep the dead soldier's SOL-P, Sean manoeuvred himself to be able to pounce off and make it across the street.

Sticking an arm out and grabbing the car to move off, one of the soldiers angrily whispered at him to stay put. Sean knew that as soon as he left, fire would be concentrated on them once again. Taking a second to think about it, Sean legged it. Within seconds he had managed to limp it across to the alley, and within milliseconds bullets returned full force, condemning the soldiers. He didn't look back; he didn't need to.

Scrambling away in the alley, the thudding returned, right on cue as the haunting image smacked him in the face once again.

He felt exposed, but not by the enemy, by the darkness that flowed and threatened to consume him from the alley walls. Resonating from between his ribs, the thudding shook his organs and head. Half-running, Sean was suddenly on another street. Two hands wrapped around him and yanked him behind cover. An FBL soldier quickly examined him, saw his leg injury, and sat him down, "Qu'est-ce que tu fais ici?" he shouted, probably out of impulse more than anything. Sean's mind was still occupied by the intense emotion that was the image. It twisted and formed like putty and had his emotions on marionette strings.

The FBL soldier muttered something else and reloaded, right before an explosion wracked the other end of the street. Staggering, it managed to pry away the draining thought from Sean's mind. Poking his head out the side to see what happened, and the FBL soldier quickly shoved Sean back behind him. In his second of sight, all Sean saw was fire, death and destruction.

By the confusion on the FBL soldier's faces, it couldn't have been from them. But it was a critical hit on multiple Reg Party soldiers, too. So who threw the grenade? If it even was one, the aftermath was devastating. Another explosion blew up on the other side of the village. Confusion broke out quicker than the shockwaves, and Sean quickly renewed his mission of getting the hell out of there.

Running away, he took advantage of the lack of shooting. He must be so close to the end now. Desperation allowed him to push against the shooting pain of his healing leg. Passing more and more battered and broken buildings, yet another hatch innocently zoomed past him.

Bricks sparkled. Stopping to double-take, Sean's vision focused as he bore witness to their food store. Tins and cans of food and water, and other DIY meat storages packed the building. Not only could he escape Caheragh with a healed leg, but he could run off with supplies and food to boot.

Changing course, he stepped inside the building and shook the tins and cans, trying to differentiate the water from the food. He figured he would leave the meat, it would be a hassle to carry without his plastic bag, anyway. He also decided to drop the empty pistol he took from the Reg Party soldier he killed earlier. With an armful of water and unidentifiable food, Sean popped out of the storage room and hurried off before he found himself standing still, his ribcage thudding.

He had made it. Beyond him was the open plains, delicately stroked by the moon's grace. Hands of dark gestured to him from the black slits between the grass blades and the space between the stars. 'Run,' it called to him. Welling up, he took a step into the grass. The comforting cold embraced his feet like his mother's voice once did his whole body.

No matter how much he tried to tune into the solace, he couldn't ignore the relentless thudding and the persevering ghost of a thought. Closing his eyes, a lone tear trekked down his cheek, slowed down by the grime and dirt. The image was clearer now. A blot in the middle of a mixture of greys.

Opening his eyes, and he was there again.

Conor looked at him. As all the rehearsals performed, Sean went to turn away.

"I know you can't save me," Conor spluttered. Sean looked at his brother. How could he have forgotten this moment?

"But please try to save all the others, please?"

Time stood still. His mind blank yet hosting a cacophony of thoughts. All he could do was look into Conor's eyes and regret how he had failed his brother's last wish.

The darkness was there again, the moon, the stars and the grass, but that's all Sean saw as he stood on the brink of Caheragh, his dropped tins at his feet and his chest rapidly rising and falling. The hands had subsided; the voices snuffed out. Breathing heavily and wiping the tears away, Sean turned around. He knew what he had to do.

Walking over to the hatch that he passed, he flung it open with relative ease. "Hello?" he shouted, "Anyone in there? I'm here to help." He didn't want the ordeal of falling down there and having to struggle his way up again. They would have to climb up themselves. He knew there were people down there, they were just scared.

"I'm not going to hurt you, I'm part of the FBL," he called out begrudgingly. An official-sounding name would encourage them to come out, "We're here to rescue you, now move!"

At that, he heard shuffling and murmurs. Soon enough, people started pouring out, gags and hand ties still bounding them. Sean got to work freeing them, the knots were tight but manageable.

Rapid footsteps echoed through an alleyway; Sean dropped what he was doing and raised a SOL-P that was laying by his feet. A soldier in fully black uniform sprinted forth, his gun pointed at the squabble. Acting first, Sean brutally sprayed the approaching soldier. Although dressed like the FBL, with the black uniform, he didn't have any of the equipment that all the others had. Deciding to ruminate on it later, Sean calmed everyone down and told them the plan.

"As soon as the last of you are free, I'm going to escort you out of Caheragh, and then I'll go back and free the others." The final hand ties dropped to the floor and all the gags were released. It was time to go.

Leading the charge, Sean quickly limped to the border. Bolstering his face, he didn't want any of them to see he was in pain. He wasn't sure how far he wanted to lead them out. Excitement and relief emanated off everyone the moment they hit the outside world.

"Keep going, I'll direct the others out towards you," Sean went to go back in.

"I'll come with you," offered someone from the crowd, a young adult by the sounds of it.

"Yeah, I'm coming too," chimed in another. More and more support stepped forwards. Sean tried to wave them off, he didn't like the idea of having to rely on them or being responsible for anyone.

"We know where the other hatches are, you'll get killed on your own," Sean knew he was beat. Without saying anything else, he slowly limped on, allowing whoever wanted to come along follow him.

"If you see anyone's guns lying on the floor, just take 'em. Bastards won't need them anymore," he announced as they passed the strange FBL soldier, his gun still lying there.

Moving on, they drew closer to the action. The thought of leading everyone through daunted him, "Alright, let's split up, we'll be harder to kill that way and can cover more ground."

"Are you crazy?" someone retorted in an aggressive whisper, "Only like three of us actually know how to wield the guns we're holding!"

"Just pull the trigger, it's not that hard," Sean picked up his pace. He heard pitter patters of footsteps still close to him, but the majority were making their own way, thankfully. *They can follow me at their own risk, I ain't babysitting anyone,*' he thought. He just wanted to free everyone and then he could finally leave.

Readying his gun, he withdrew the magazine to find it had a grand total of four bullets left in it. Cursing, he would have to be careful. As their munitions began to run dry, the FBL and the Reg Party were being more conservative than ever, with the sounds of bone-breaking and knife-sheathing becoming more frequent.

Trying to slip into different store fronts to creep along the former high street, Sean was adjacent to the hand-to-hand combat that suddenly ensued. FBL combatants shoving small blades into the ill-equipped soldiers with not nearly enough ammo to fight them off. Bullets still scattered the air, a few even dangerously pinging near Sean, but it was not as heavy as it used to be.

That was until an unexpected flood of bullets poured down, suppressing Sean into a shop and penetrating FBL and Reg soldier alike. Managing a peak down the road, and more of those strange FBL-looking soldiers were shredding everyone in sight.

It was barbaric. *'Those idiots are going to get themselves killed,'* Sean thought, regarding the civilians who followed him and got stuck in their own shops. He reminded himself it was their fault they tagged along.

"FBL man," one called out, barely audible above the gunfire. It took Sean a moment to realize they were referring to him, "FBL man, what do we do?"

"Get out of there, obviously," Sean shouted back. He didn't have the time nor energy to help them all, he needed to open more hatches to get out of there as quick as he could. What they wanted to do after was up to them.

He was pretty sure there would be more hatches if they kept going, but with the lunatics down the road, he needed to get away as quick as possible. It only took a few moments to find a fire exit, calling for the others to do the same.

"There's one over there," a woman called, jogging over to what looked like a big hall once they all spilled onto the quiet street. Following, they entered through the busted doors and ran across the laminated flooring. Behind the curtains on the stage was a hatch, cleverly disguised as a stage feature. Yanking the hatch open, Sean called out inside.

"We'll go in," the woman nodded at Sean, and the two others jumped down after her. *'Maybe they're not such a hindrance,'* thought Sean as he heard them freeing all the trapped civilians. He wondered how the other groups were getting along.

As the large huddle was climbing out of the tunnel, with aches and pains, a beaten FBL squad burst into the hall, quickly taking defensive positions. Two were bleeding, the other two exhausted. Sean only had four bullets, there was no way he could land four perfect head shots without at least one of them shooting him back.

Frozen, Sean stuck his arm out in a protective manner. As soon as the FBL noticed them, they rushed over, keeping one person at the door.

"Are you guys okay?" one struggled in English, letting his gun down and reaching his arm out.

"Yeah, we're fine, just leaving," Sean began to exit stage left, but his difficult take-off allowed the soldier to grab his arm.

"Are you guys civilians?" he continued. The huddle confirmed him in unison, and then the soldiers talked in between themselves.

"Are these your guys?" one person asked Sean, gesturing to the soldiers. Sean didn't say anything.

"Come with us, we'll take you to an FBL recovery camp where we'll patch you up," the other FBL soldier said, "We'll bring you safe, come now." The huddle started moving along with them.

"Hey, we can't trust them! We don't know where their gonna take us, it's better to-"

"Any Party is better than the Regulatory Party right now, they're our best bet," pleaded someone.

"But, no, how do we know? We can't trust them!" Sean shouted.

"And what makes you trustworthy?" It was pretty clear to them that Sean had lied about him being part of the FBL. Sean remained silent and watched them go, the FBL herding them away. Sean couldn't trust the FBL. He hardly trusted the civilians to do what he wanted to do.

"But please try to save all the others, please?"

It wasn't about what he wanted to do.

  A colossal explosion threw the right wall of the hall on its side, blowing the bricks and mortar in. Collapsing onto his leg, the whole pain entourage overloaded his brain. After raising his gun, he shunted off the rest of his bullets into the sudden aggressors that ran through the hole they made, all of which missed. By the time Sean was up and could register what he was seeing, the FBL had neutralized the few other strange soldiers that attacked them. Seeing them dead on the floor like that made a light bulb go off in his head.

  They were the bandits. The black-wearing, heavily armed bandits. What the hell were they doing attacking Caheragh? As an FBL soldier helped Sean recover onto his feet, the thought was quickly dropped.

"I'll," he took a deep, shaky breath, "I'll go and free more hatches."

"Cameron will go, too," the soldier motioned for Cameron to join Sean.

"Yes sir," Cameron rushed over to Sean, with surprisingly good English, "Caheragh's guards are all trying to flee, what's left of them, anyway. We must deal with this new threat. Any idea who they are?"

"Bandits," Sean replied, already hobbling as fast as he could.

"Allow me," the soldier offered to help Sean, but he refused.

"I'm a'right," he dismissed, annoyed.

Further up the street, they only knew they were at a hatch by the sight of the civilians Sean freed helping the formerly imprisoned. He was pleasantly surprised by the sight.

"There are still a few hatches left," a young woman announced, looking at Sean, her determination outweighing her fear.

"We'll get 'em, don't worry, all of you take these lot to the others outside Caheragh," Sean replied in one breath, needing a second to recover it afterwards.

"No way we're leaving you," she raised her voice. Sean didn't have the energy to argue anymore, and he was starting to like them helping out, so long as he knew what they were doing.

The newly freed civilians mostly were led out of the village, a few remained to help out. Sean motioned for the young woman to lead them to the next one, when the FBL soldier pushed Sean to the ground, saving his life from a hail of bullets. Heroically, he then stood tall, and retuned fire. All civilians with guns did the same. By the time Sean was up, the threat was dispersed. Slightly shocked, Sean regained his composure and ordered everyone to move, leading the charge to the next hatch, being fed directions by everyone else, the FBL soldier by his side. It was strange working with everyone as a unit.

Before long, they found another one, on the brink of the Reg Party's final stand. A stand-off in an arc that spanned across multiple streets and open spaces, with the FBL trying to advance where they could. Without plentiful ammunition, the sounds of dominating gunfire had dropped, but that only rose the tension ever higher, especially when spats of shots could be heard across the village.

The stand-off wasn't exclusively the FBL vs the Reg Party though, the bandits were converging on their position, having gotten bored with the smaller groups of hunting FBL and fleeing soldiers. As if waves, they would charge themselves across the streets and roads, establishing pockets of control, seriously disrupting both sides. Observing the suicide runs, Sean speculated their crazed behaviours must be the result of some serious brainwashing. Looking at them made Sean sick, he couldn't believe any one in their right mind would do what they were doing. Not even regular bandits were that crazy.

Trying to ignore the disturbing fight, Sean got to work with opening the hatch, which proved harder than the others, as if it was stuck or locked. Struggling with the hatch was no use, and Sean laboured back, defeated. The soldier then gave it ago, but soon resorted to booting the hatch with his foot and shooting the edges, to bust any hinges. They finally got through, and the hatch door fell through the tunnel.

But their efforts had attracted unwelcome attention. The neighbouring fight was leaning in the FBL's favour, as they had finally overrun the persistent, trapped Reg Party soldiers. During their surge, a grouping of hiding bandits burst out from a building behind them, raining fire from right behind the FBL's advance.

As the hatch gave in, some bandits clocked their group.

Unsurprisingly, they pointed their barrels towards them, but before they could steady their shots, Cameron pounced forwards, with Sean not far behind. By the time Sean was shooting, Cameron fell, being caught by the civilians behind him. All those with guns shot back, the noise was head-hammering, but the reaction of the bandits made it worth it; watching them break off and run was very satisfying.

The scumbags had shot the FBL soldier mortally in the chest, and some other civilians in less lethal places, but in return the three of them got gunned down. In the hysteria of getting shot at, the civilians started acting on their own accord, out of panic, fear, or a sudden urge to get on with it before they all got killed. One way or another Sean felt his grip on them all quickly deteriorate.

Some fled, whilst others started shouting at the people from inside the hatch to come out quickly, which they were quite resistant.

"We don't have all day! It's me, Jenny!" a woman shouted down, and yet they didn't move.

As that fiasco was playing out, Sean and a few others were tending to Sam. But Sean's efforts were in vain, as the man bled his life through the many bullet holes. Frustration again fizzed in him, without the FBL soldier and with everyone taking autonomy over the operation, everything was bound to fall apart.

Laying the FBL soldier down and resting his gun on his chest, Sean quickly tried to raise his voice to round everyone up, but no one paid him any mind. Hurriedly, a group of people dashed down the tunnel to extract the civilians by force. Very few stood still.

Sean could do nothing but wait and watch as people ran off, trying to escape Caheragh while they still could. With the remaining few left, he tried to reassert his position, "How many hatches are left?"

"Not that many, I don't think, we'll be done in no time. I'm sure the other teams have freed plenty of hatches by now," a middle-aged man shrugged. Sean wasn't keen on taking their word for it, he would have to check for himself, or his brother's words would haunt him forever.

A cry of alarm echoed out of the tunnel.

"You alright down there?" jumped Sean, trying to get a good look down.

"Oh my God!" shrilled someone.

"What?" Sean shouted down.

"They're all dead!" Sean's blood ran cold.

"Wha'd'ya mean they're all dead?" he started climbing down, to see with his own eyes. Upon reaching the pit, a stomach-turning smell squeezed his lungs as he crouched in front of blood-soaked walls and beams, all surrounding a bloodied heap. He was almost sick. Managing to hang on he briefly observed all of the bodies for any sign of life. They were too late. Was it the bandits, or the Reg Party? He was more inclined to believe it to be the bandit's gruesome handiwork.

The others that were down there helped him up to the top, where he remained silent. They had failed to get to them, how many hatches had been victims of massacre? Hardening himself, he reminded himself that he was hardly to blame. He was lumbered with the prolonged protection of everyone and had to constantly evade and fight groups of bandits or soldiers. It was far from pleasant, though, and he dearly hoped they wouldn't stumble onto any others.

"Alright, let's move," he swallowed, leaving the hatch and not looking down when he walked over Sam's corpse.

The Reg Party's final stand was drawing to a close, with little opportunity of retreat. If the bandits hadn't been there, the FBL would've won the village over already, to put it under their subjugation instead.

"Hey!" someone shouted from behind them. Turning around, a spry man, probably in his twenties, stumbled towards them, flailing his arms for balance, "I think we've got all of them."

With everyone's attention, he stopped, throwing his hands to his bloody knees. Paranoid of the appearance of bandits, Sean waved his right hand forwards, as if to grab the information from him himself.

"I think we've got all the hatches; we've got citizens all grouping outside Caheragh," he stopped to gain his breath.

"Any trouble with bandits?" Sean jumped in.

"Not that I've heard of," he looked up, working his face into thinking.

"Right, we better move before we do," he turned around to address everyone, before shoving his head back around again, "are you sure we've got the lot?"

"Positive, I've been around this place twice." He was hesitant to take his word for it. He had plenty of motive to lie about it, and Sean hadn't himself seen that all of the hatches had been liberated. He would have to check himself, but firstly he needed to get all the currently freed civilians to safety.

"Right people, listen up," he raised his voice, "we gotta shove off and leave this place to the FBL." No one argued with him, but not many listened to him either.

Brushing him off, a few picked up their weapons and ran off to assist the FBL, joining their ranks of guns. Others took the opportunity to flee, ditching their guns, letting their fear take the driver's seat. Spluttering in frustration, he tried to salvage the situation by raising his voice a little louder, "We need to go! Everyone follow me, Caheragh is lost, let's not go down with it," he was already running by the middle of his sentence.

People followed him, the messenger included, but he was still bothered about those who wouldn't follow him, for those he couldn't save. The thudding returned. The damned thumping. Conor flashed through his mind. Almost running into a wall, he hastily halted himself, breathing heavily. They were almost out of the village, just a little further, they would all be out, and after checking they had all been liberated Sean could finally leave without the guilt plaguing him. Or so he hoped.

"Help the others. Not yourself."

'For God's sake,' he thought as he turned around, at the brink of Caheragh, the hopeful survivors behind him. It wasn't enough just to send them on their way. If he really wanted to help them, he'd help save their home, too. He didn't trust the FBL, but they seemed to have purer intentions than the overtly awful Regulatory Party. One even died for him. The enemy of his enemy was surely his friend, right? He would have to find out.

Looking around, and he could see the mass groupings of all the civilians that made it out relatively safely. Squinting, and he could make out people being treated and patched up. The familiar feeling of being beckoned out of Caheragh returned, but not by the tempting tendrils of self-intent, but the shining warmth of desperate people helping desperate people. He had to help them, he owed Conor that much.

"Change of plan," he announced as he jogged towards the civilians. Groaning and muttering was the response to their indecisive saviour, "we're going to regroup with everyone and form an offensive to drive the bastards out of Caheragh for good."

Upon entry of the evacuation point, ragged cheering rasped from the people he had saved, but this was no time for celebrations. Speaking up, he outlined his plan, for every able-bodied person to take up arms to assist the FBL offensive. Those that listened to him did so with doubt.

Coming off from the second bout of numbness that he didn't even notice, his poor leg throbbed. He could have walked away there and then, but in front of him suddenly were dozens of Conors, all hurt and broken in different places. The only difference being, not everyone trusted him, which was especially apparent when one of his loyal followers spoke up, "I'm done with your shit, man, lying to us, telling us this and that. I'm done. Like you said yourself, our home is gone, there's no point going back now."

"I was wrong," he tried, but got shut down.

"Thank you for everything you've done so far, but as a village I'm sure we all want to leave this place to the dogs," he was tired, putting pressure on an arm wound. Sean slowly turned around, it seemed most agreed with him.

A disgusting harrowing of bullets sounded in Caheragh. Shouting and cries of terror was cut short.

"Do you hear that?" Sean called out, "That's the sound of your oppressors being destroyed," he narrated his inner thoughts to them in real time, "The FBL have come all this way to help you all, we can't turn our back on their efforts."

"What makes you think they're here to free us?"

"We'll just have to trust 'em," Sean said with a hollow chest, "So come now, let's take Caheragh back, make a statement, and if it comes to we'll fuck the FBL off as well." His voice took on a booming quality, as if he was trying to rouse the dead. By the look of them, he may as well might have been.

Slowly but surely, people started standing up, most with guns, some without, all looking at Sean with firm determination on their scarred faces.

"In these broken times," Sean said mostly to himself, "we must fight for unity. May the road rise up to meet us." He could scarcely believe what he was saying.

Already departing, Sean lead the scuffed, hurt, and winded Caheragh civilians as they walked across the blood-soaked soils to send the blood-stained hands of the Regulatory Party away from their home.

Picking up magazines in passing, a desperate struggle of Reg Party soldiers came tumbling from a side road into their path, which Sean let the civilians take their revenge on. They were nearing the epicentre of the fight for Caheragh; The FBL were clearly winning, but it was not over.

A flurry of bullets slammed their advance, forcing them to take cover. Peeking over a car, Sean saw four civilians, those who had branched off from him to fight a small while ago, sprinting towards them. Sean peered closer, if they were running, who was chasing?

Gun flares lit up the defining edges of multiple bandits, shooting a disjointed harmony at the civilians.

"Fight back!" Sean rallied, leading by example as he held down the trigger. The sweet sound of the others opening fire fuelled his heart. Before long the bandits scurried off, having got away scratch-free, by the looks of it.

Vaulting over their cover and pressing on, the civilians fired into their group, not letting that close call shoo them off. In that moment, Sean felt like part of a unit, and he felt proud. But he knew it was stupid keeping everyone bunched together like a walking target, they needed to split up. But what if they got lost, or got killed or pursued their own motives?

Battling off another small hunting group of bandits, Sean also fought with his mind. They had to split up, but he didn't know if they could get the mission done properly. *'I'm just gonna have to trust them,'* he thought disdainfully.

"Alright, split up into four groups, quickly," he ordered, not bothering to micro manage the task, hoping instead to test their ability. Having quickly and efficiently sorted themselves into four distinct groups by the time he turned around, Sean smiled, "All converge where the FBL are, and don't fuckin' get killed."

With their orders, they all filtered through the streets, still scavenging magazines where necessary. Recovering from bending down to pick another up, Sean's group were nearing a huddle of injured bandits taking refuge in a building. Halting, Sean raised his hand. Darting quietly ahead, he backed himself against the wall.

"The Party's gone, what's left for us to stay? What's the point?" asked someone in a raspy voice.

"Exactly, the French have cleared 'em, let's just leave, I mean it wasn't a full failure, was it?" chimed in another. His voice was strained, as if we were performing hefty work.

"I know, I know," an older man cut in, "I haven't received official orders yet, but I think it's high time we fucked off. Help him up, we're leaving."

Sean didn't like the idea of the scummy bandits getting away scot-free. Pouncing, he unleashed four rounds before the gun clicked, in his rush missing every shot. Backing off, he shouted, "Engage!"

The civilians ran forwards, some firing pre-emptive shots at the building. Frantically reloading, Sean did not want them getting away and starting an evacuation. He wanted all of them dead. Joining the back of the pack, all the civilians rained fire into the building. Twitching on the floor were two bloodied corpses.

Shoving past, Sean ran across what used to be a rather wide hallway and into the kitchen. As suspected, the back door was open, swinging slightly.

"After him!" Sean rallied, already out of the door and scanning everywhere he could see. It didn't help that the bandits sported fully black uniform, "he must be out here somewhere."

Combat could be heard not too far away; another group must have bumped into more bandits. They had infested the streets, but why? To flee, or to hunt?

"Spread out, and filter through the streets," Sean ordered. He hoped he would be the one to come across the bandit, but at least the others would help pinpoint him, even if they failed to kill him.

Running into the road ahead of him, Sean peeled his eyes for any movement. He realized he was getting further away from the action the more he pursued the one bandit, but at least the other groups were on their way. He hoped he could trust them to get the job done.

"He's here!" sounded a few blocks behind him. Eyebrows reeling up, he pulled together his strength and ran over. The shooting ended as quickly as it started; as soon as Sean's barrel entered the road, all he saw was two wounded civilians.

'Dammit,' he shouted in his head. They weren't dead, so someone else would have to tend to them. There was no way Sean would let him get away.

"You, help those two," he ordered a passing civilian, pointing to the road that was already behind him.

He looked down streets and alleys until at last, he spotted a bandit, his balaclava off, leaning against a wall, breathlessly panting. Instinctively, Sean readied his aim and unleashed a burst of five bullets. He fell and splattered against the floor. A sigh of relief relaxed his shoulders, allowing his exhaustion to return.

Taking inspiration from his victim, he leant against the wall and allowed himself to slip down it until he was in a crouching position. His gun felt heavier, even if there were less bullets in it.

The final battle was reaching its last stretch, as the other groups audibly joined in. At least the bandits wouldn't be going anywhere.

As he sat there, in that dark, cold alley, he once again looked into the darkness that surrounded him. No longer did it bring him solitude, no longer did he want to be an agent of the night. For although the same corruptive darkness had spread itself thick around Ireland, and probably the UK, too, all wasn't lost. To surrender in the dark was to hide from the pain and hurt and loss. Without those things, Sean thought peace, and happiness would develop. But it is with those things where goodness can truly flourish. You cannot have the good without the bad, and by using the enveloping dark as a blanket, then no goodness will ever be found.

He realized then and there, that what he was doing felt right. Freeing Caheragh of the oppressing dark felt good. He looked at his cold, silent suit of armour. What he once regarded as the shield of all grief, was the barrier between him and happiness. He couldn't ignore his grief.

After all, darkness is nothing, just the absence of light, and Sean had had enough of being empty.

Getting up, he wiped his tears and gripped his gun, just as he heard in passing, "All units evacuate immediately; leave this place to the kamikazes." Shit, he had killed the wrong guy. Setting off, he exited the alley, to find that his group had gone off to the battle. Five bandits were ahead of him, talking into small walkie talkies.

Steeling his nerves and shaky breath, he unloaded the rest of his magazine into the lot of them, two managing to run away, the other mortally wounded or dead. Feeling rather proud, he pursued, reloading his Sun Piper. Rounding the corner, his pride was dashed as he ran into what he suspected was an aforementioned kamikaze soldier.

Two automatic rifles, a heavy-looking vest, many extended magazines in straps and what looked like explosives decorating him like baubles. Sean immediately allowed his momentum to throw him clear of the road as the beast fired both guns at him. There was no way he could take that thing down by himself. He would need the FBL and the civilians to back him.

Scraping himself up, he ran as fast as his legs allowed to the eye of the storm. He couldn't believe the fight was still raging on. The Reg Party had all gone; those bandits really knew how to take up the mantle.

Bumping into a few civilians trying to take refuge in a collapsed former coffee shop, Sean yelled at them to run.

"We're injured," one spluttered, rocking back and forth slightly, applying pressure to a shin wound. *'Tell me about it,'* he thought dismissively.

"You'll be worse than injured in a minute," he shouted, not stopping to help them up.

By the time they were on their feet and running, the kamikaze soldier had thundered onto their road, and without hesitation he let loose. Lowering his back he skirted along the ground, his feet barely touched the floor as he tried to throw himself clear of the road, but there was no alley or escape in sight.

Thinking he was bound to die, as the two separate bullet streams came closer and closer to severing him in half, a group of FBL soldiers appeared from the end of the road. Falling flat on the ground, he let the FBL shoot down the kamikaze soldier. For a single person they sure had to fire for a long time.

Recovering, Sean walked over to the soldiers that had saved their lives.

"What's keeping ya' fightin'?" Sean asked, the adrenaline now boring into his tired skull.

"Kamikaze," one strongly accented man replied, pointing his gun to the fallen soldier.

"They're retreating," one struggled over his breathlessness and weak English. So the message of retreat had reached everyone.

"Well, let's not let 'em, them," he said firmly, narrowing his eyes and hefting his gun up, "let's go."

The soldiers had been attempting to flank the heavy resistance, to free up more soldiers to push against the bandit's main resistance. The injured civilians from the coffee shop decided to try and escape the village, to lay it out with the other civilians that couldn't join the attack. Sean didn't argue with them, and let them slip off as if he hadn't noticed.

Although exhausted, Sean was looking forward to finally regaining eyes and control of the civilian attackers again, to make sure they were properly motivated and fighting to the best of their ability.

Going round the houses, they were getting close to their target, when another grenade was set off. A disturbing amount of strangled cries and pained shouts exploded after the ear-punching bang. They picked up the pace.

Cutting into a side alley, they spilled out the other side to meet and slay a group of lying wounded bandits, their guard distracted. Trampling over their corpses in the same second they killed them, finally they were standing where they were meant to. The only problem being that the bandit's front had disappeared, and the FBL that were on the sight were squirming in pain.

The bastard's had blown them up and left.

"Let's go after them, they must be on the ropes, now," Sean tried to muster their support, but they looked at him, slightly horrified, and dashed off to help their recently exploded comrades.

"Where are the civilians?" Sean quickly shouted, he needed to regroup with them before running off now that the FBL soldiers had ditched him.

"Across a few streets, they're fending off the bandits well but it'll be impossible to get to them without getting killed," one of the soldiers answered him.

"What if they're in trouble?" he thought out loud.

"We're all in fuckin' trouble, just trust them," the soldier shouted, turning his back on Sean to assist someone missing an arm. Maybe he was right.

Nevertheless, Sean chased after where he suspected the bandits had run off to. Although they were trying to retreat, they surely had to free the main bulk of their forces before doing so, so Sean proceeded onwards. It wasn't far at all; he was practically bordering it. He just had to find his way in, through the collapsed or bordering building and alleys.

Multiple bandit bodies flooded out of somewhere further up, and he started shooting. Frustratingly none of the shots hit, and he was soon out of ammo. They stopped to shoot back, and Sean had to dive into the fallen face of a corner shop, shots pinging off of and breaking the exposed bricks.

Rapidly reloading his last magazine, he dived behind a counter and propped his gun on a till, anticipating a wave of guns to come careening into view. To his surprise, he only heard the pattering of their footsteps in the distance as they ran. Grunting and scrambling up Sean ran back into the open, shooting into the fleeting shadows.

He kicked the ground in frustration, they had got away. But, at least they highlighted a way in. Chasing that lead, Sean ran face-first into some FBL soldiers. Falling on his backside, Sean quickly asked where they were going, and it turned out to be chasing the escapee bandits. He was pleasantly surprised, he thought he was the only one taking up the mission of hunting every last one of them. He almost instinctively went to follow them, to make sure the bandits died, but he thought it better to trust them to get the job done and finally find his civilians.

Slipping in after them, Sean made it to the other end of the alley without any more traffic. He entered what used to be a relatively closed, private road that bent around to the left. Gripping his gun, he jogged over, and a blinding array of muzzle flashes that connected to bright beams laced the air between the houses, as if a cobweb of golden gore.

Both sides were pinned down. The civilians, who had a lot more ammo than the FBL, were lacing the faces of the opposing buildings with wild shots, with the fire power from the bandits dwindling. They must be trying to peel off from the fight whilst trying to keep the main source of power busy.

Being in the middle of the road was not the sort of position Sean wanted to be in, and soon enough bandit barrels started targeting him. Instinctively he jerked out of the way, and in milliseconds had his back against a house on the bandits' side. Taking his opportunity, Sean slipped into a house.

In his absence, the civilians were doing a good job, but not a great one. They had locked themselves in a fire fight with the bandits, and it wasn't sustainable; as soon as they ran out of ammo, it was game over, and the way they were throwing their bullets up the wall, it wouldn't be long.

Presuming the FBL were out flanking and bumping into pockets of runners it, was up to Sean and his civilian fighters to stamp out the main force, or at least keep them there until the FBL could properly support them. They must have assumed that they would be behind the bandits by now. Those kamikazes must be giving them a run for their money.

Sean opened the back door, after tiptoeing through the joint, and peered out. The house along that row shared a communal garden. It was large, with a few trees and a lot of shrubbery. Looking down the gardens, he could see a few bandits run off out of the garden and onto the street.

Making his move, he darted to a couple of trees, before nosing his gun out and taking aim. Another bandit left a house. Just as Sean was about to let loose, he spied a rusty ladder set up against the house. He had a great idea. Swallowing his frustration and letting another bandit go, he took a chance and ran over to the ladder, throwing himself up it.

It must have been propped up to work on the gutter, for that's only how far it reached. Tossing his gun onto the roof and letting the gutter catch it, he jumped, planting his upper body onto the hard, uncomfortable roof. Swinging sideways, he managed to land it, but not without anyone noticing. Grabbing his gun before the guttering was shot off, he rolled over and propped up on his elbows.

More gunfire nicked the edges of the roof, but he persisted regardless. From the angle of the incoming shots, it looked like the bandit was right under him. Leading with his gun, he let it hang off the roof, his one hand barely on the grip. Hoping the angle was sufficient, he pulled the trigger, the gun recoiled viscously, threatening to slip from his grip.

The sudden retaliation from Sean shut the bandit up, and allowed Sean time to readjust his grip, poke his head out, and shoot him down. More bandits were quickly running off from further down the street, but there was no way he would land those shots.

Again, a bandit ran over the corpse of his recently fallen counterpart. Already steadying his aim, the bandit stopped, just before Sean was about to kill him. A kamikaze soldier stomped down the garden, both guns hanging from his hands, intimidatingly casual. The other bandit procured a grenade from his pocket, and handed it over to the kamikaze soldier who must have used all of his already.

More and more bandits ran from the house, it wouldn't be long before they would have all gotten away. In slight desperation, Sean lined up his shot. The grenade had graced the kamikaze soldier's evil hands. Sean pulled the trigger. A direct impact with the grenade set off a fiery explosion that swept everyone off their feet. Fire latched onto the trees, and death embraced all of those within the immediate vicinity of the blast. Must have been an incendiary bomb. Disgusting.

Even from the roof, Sean felt the impact of the grenade as it vibrated through his sweaty, matted hair. A smile of triumph rose as he looked at his handiwork. The kamikaze soldier was dead, both of his forearms ripped to shreds, as were the few others that got blown to bits. Everyone else that got flattened shouted cries of alarm to all the bandits that were about to attempt an escape.

Taking advantage of the flash fear, Sean sent one bullet to each of the incapacitated, ending their suffering and the hopes of those on the side lines. He soon ran out of ammo, though, and that was his final magazine. Thankfully, everyone who was in the garden was dead, which maintained the illusion that anyone who stepped out would die. He hoped they wouldn't try and test it.

Sean shifted around and crawled to the other side of the roof. Waving, he tried to signal the civilians that were still raining fire at the mostly empty windowless windows and doorless doorways. He had no idea if they could see him, but he waved like a madman regardless and beckoned them towards his side of the street. Slowly, the gunfire dribbled away, with beams being cut off or spluttering. He soon thought to give up, but in that instance a sudden horde of civilians roared and charged out from the buildings, all taunting and waving their guns.

Such a sight warmed his heart and strengthened his spirit. Returning to his post, he watched as the bandits rushed out in full force, trying to return fire at the wave of inexperienced and enraged people. It was a glorious sight, especially so when the civilians burst out from the building and chased them all down.

Sean climbed back down to the ground, and immediately picked up two magazines that were on the floor, reloading his gun as he went.

"Hey!" someone called, that someone being one of the civilians that Sean recalled from earlier, but from all the madness he forgot their interaction, "We got 'em runnin'!"

"We sure do," Sean smiled, watching the civilians gun down the escapees. He exhaled as he let the civilians have at the bandits.

An FBL soldier jogged over, there must have been a few with the civilians all along, "What's your name?"

"Sean, who's askin'?"

"You've got quite the reputation on your head, kid," his accent was invisible, Sean could have mistaken him for an Englishman, "Find me after we're done here, just gotta clean up the mess." Sean had half a mind to reiterate his question, but let it slide.

And with that he left, running to the front of the offensive. Sean let him go, he had a sudden thought on his mind, anyway. They had cleared out the main bulk of the bandits, which was good, but where were all the kamikazes that were supposed to support their escape?

Another explosion staggered his soul. There they were.

His instinct to run over was shot down when he saw two rows of civilians get savagely shredded by two blazing barrels; a kamikaze soldier stepped forwards, ready to widen his angle of attack.

Trying to cut the threat down before it did any more damage, Sean emptied his magazine on the soldier, with most of the shots hitting his chest. Still standing, he reloaded his guns, his ballistic vest shrugging off the bullets effortlessly. 'Shit.'

Sean dived for cover as the kamikaze aimed one gun at him, and the other at a valiant group of FBL soldiers. Civilians scattered; the Kamikaze ready to pour another wave of death over the garden. Sean braced himself as gunfire yet again rang out. But this time, it wasn't the bone-chilling spattering from the kamikaze, but the valiant booming of the FBL.

Spraying him from head to toe, his head got knocked back, spurting blood. Collapsing, his guns continued to blaze until he hit the floor, a final cry of vengeance. With that death, a safe zone was stablished, confirmed by the sudden silence and absence of bandits.

Sean suppressed a sudden laugh. His body was shaken and damaged, and with that threat relieved, Sean's mind could focus on the intense pain in his leg, and the utter exhaustion of his lungs, *'I'm bloody knackered,'* he thought to himself. He couldn't handle much more.

The aftermath from that one soldier was hectic, with murdered, wounded and bleeding civilians hurrying to do what they thought they had to. Sean panted over to the FBL soldiers, hoping to pursue and cut down the rest of the stragglers, hoping no more kamikaze soldiers were waiting to wreak havoc.

"We need to regroup here, with the civilians, and secure Caheragh," Englishman tried, but got rebutted by his counterpart.

"No, we must escort everyone out to regroup with the civilians on the outside, they're sitting ducks out there!"

"We have to go, I mean come on, what if they come back? All our work will be for nothing" a third butted in, trying his best to string a sentence together.

"What if we chase the fuckers out, then they'll have no chance of hurting anyone," Sean suggested, and they all turned to look at him, all with different attitudes.

"Surely they're long gone by now, there's no point, if we stay here we can defend Caheragh," the Englishman stated.

"No, he's got a point," the third FBL soldier agreed.

"They're bandits, they'll come back and finish us off if we don't act quickly," Sean's leg had finally reached up to his brain and was grappling with the off-switch. His bodily shut down was visible, and they looked at each other, regarding the infamous Sean that had literally given his all to help the civilians, not just the village.

"How about this," the second Frenchman suggested, "we escort the civilians out, and we radio to everyone to flush out the rest of the bandits, sound good?"

"Very," Sean started to lose breath.

Not waiting for anyone's response, the Englishman hauled Sean onto his shoulders, grunting under the effort.

"Everyone, we're leaving!" he shouted, letting the other FBL soldiers in the area rally and escort the civilians out.

Although he remained physically conscious, his mind was absorbed in an inky black, faint memories of the insane battle that had just ensued floated around. Cries of pain, smiles of triumph, and smells of blood. Conor floated around his subconscious, the memories and dreams concocting together. He did what he had to, he helped the people. Shining through the myriad of murder and death in his memories, was the hope and happiness.

Before he knew it, he was lying on the grass, the night sky being slowly taken over by the warmth of the rising sun. Conversation was hushed as Sean sat up, his mind swimming.

"Holy shit," was his first words as he saw what remained of the civilians and the FBL. What once was a bustling village and many ranks of sneaking Frenchman, was now a battered group of civilians and a few squads of FBL soldiers.

"What happened?" asked Sean, as a few familiar FBL faces walked over to him.

"Blacked out," one of them said, their accent escaping his thin smile.

"At which point we brought everyone here and the rest of us killed off the rest of the bandits that were in the village, mainly kamikaze soldiers," finished off the Englishman.

"Did you get them all?" Sean asked, rubbing his eyes and checking his leg.

"Of course not, so many were already long gone. Those vile kamikazes stunted our progress. But it wasn't all bad, those survivors will act as a message, a deterrent," another piped in, who Sean didn't recognize at all, "The massacre of Caheragh will not be in vain. It appears we have more than one enemy out here."

Someone had rewrapped his bandages, and cleaned up his leg. It was then when he properly realized that they were with the vans, where he stole one and crashed it into the forest. He couldn't see the forest from where he was, and he didn't really want to.

"Yeah, I guess so," he grumbled as he stood up, clutching an FBL soldier's arm for support.

Finally up, and another, more hearty cheer greeted him, some whistles joining in too.

"Get in the van, we're leaving this place," the Englishman said aloud, but looked at Sean.

"Where are we going?" he asked, flinching at the thought.

"We're going to an FBL recovery camp, where all of these lot will find shelter, food, water, everything they need," someone else cut in.

"And where you will find an office with your name on it," the Englishman smiled, "Sean, I'd like to have the privilege of asking you to join us. Your humanitarianism cannot go wasted," he emphasized each word as they left his moustachioed mouth, "We need people like you to help these people. Who better to do that than yourself? Someone who's lived through whatever the hell is going on."

"Hold on a minute," Sean interrupted to stop the gushing of compliments, "you want me to go back to your little camp and work for the FBL, have you forgotten that you've invaded my lands?" He laughed, he was ready to wash his hands of them, no matter their brief alliance in the face of greater evils. Bodies of power never bode well anymore, no matter how many promises they made.

"Invaders?" another laughed, "Buddy, from what we've seen, we are the ones doing the least invading." He had a point. The Regulatory Party could not get away with what they've been doing. Caheragh was just one of the many communities they had under their control. How little he wanted to admit it, the FBL were the best equipped to topple their tyranny. With governmental parties conquering through any means possible, it seemed the FBL were the only genuine body out there, even if they were foreign. He would have to think about it.

"At least get in the van, come back to camp, get some food, water, stay the night, sleep on it, and make your decision then," offered the Englishman.

After another few seconds of hesitance, he asked, "On who's authority is it that I come back to your camp and join your team?"

"Well," he started, seeming pleasantly surprised, "on coming back to camp? It's on all of us. But joining our team? That is a request directly from the," he paused, searching around for English term, "Commanding Officer, Fotso," he gestured to another that Sean half-recognized from earlier in the battle.

Sean didn't say anything. Most of the people were in the vans; there was a lot more space than turned out necessary. Sean cared for those people, he realized suddenly. He smiled; he knew his brother would be proud. Conor was making him a better man even beyond the grave, now that's what you call the best brother in the whole wide world.

***

'How am I supposed to do this?' thought Sean as he flicked a stray ant off of his desk. Numbers and lines and words marked out that month's food supply that was arriving the next day.

"Hey, Sean," Robin walked up behind him, holding some files, "have I got some news for you." Sean looked up from his desk, his eyebrows in a forced frown from trying to work out how best to distribute the resources.

"What's happened?" he asked, trying to relax his facial muscles. Plonking the files down on the desk, Robin positioned himself in front of it, his hands in his pockets.

One was a scout drone's report of a trip to Caheragh, "I'm sure you remember that place," he chuckled.

"I sure fuckin' do," he lifted up the thin piece of paper, he was surprised it could hold the ink's weight. Bandit activity was sighted. It appeared as if they were looking around, but not just rummaging. They appeared to be searching in teams. About half a mile from the village, and a larger group of bandits were hauling big crates and sacks and other such portable storage options.

"Our guess is that they're setting up camp for an offensive somewhere."

"You're probably right," Sean breathed, picking up the other pieces of paper, "These the potential targets?" Robin confirmed, and skimming down the list they were all FBL camps or hotspots, "Why does this concern me?" he asked, he really needed to get back to the distribution of food. With all the fighting going on, supplies were starting to stretch a little thinner.

"Because," he dragged out, "if you read this week's briefing, then you'd know that one of our refugee camps had been overturned by the people, who then declared themselves the Lakeland Warriors. We thought to just let them have it, they were pretty much all healthy and all, anyway."

"I still don't see how I get wrapped up in this," his leg had just made as full of a recovery as it could, he didn't exactly want to start collecting such devastating wounds, "just bomb the shit out of Caheragh or something."

"You know what the United Nations think of that."

"The fuckin' UN..." he tutted.

"Look, Sean," Robin tried, "anything can happen out there. We've a fear that the Lakeland Warriors will migrate to Caheragh, the closest village that they don't know is swarming with bandits." That was a very real possibility. They would get massacred. With Sean silent for a few seconds, Robin gently pushed, "We also need you, the civilian Supporting Officer of the Caheragh people, because you're excellent."

Another few moments of consideration (whilst trying to ignore the sickening flattery) and he shook his head whilst rolling his eyes, "Fine, when're we leaving?"

"Soon as," he smiled, scooping up his files and swiftly walking off. Sean slumped in his chair then lightly chucked to himself. Glancing back to his sheet of paper that he was working out how to distribute the food on, he had a sudden genious idea.

Scribbling it down, he stood up, proud.

"Right then," he said to himself, taking the paper and walking over to the camp head, Max. He read it through, nodded approvingly, and walked off with it. That was the usual procedure, so Sean was sure he did a good job.

As he walked through the camp, he slipped past all the civilians, from Caheragh and other places. Pretty much everyone knew him, he was practically a hero, not that's what he wanted. His true satisfaction arrived when seeing the bruises and wounds fall from the innocent who had suffered at the hands of the government or bandits or whatever evil force thought to try their luck.

Sean was happy there, something he thought he could say when the moon was overhead and the stars around him.

Sighing, he went to his bed space, picked up his gun, and waved to Billy. He never thought he'd go back to Caheragh, but at least this time it'll be different. Those bandits will pay.

Fragmented Horizons
pt.3

Dear diary,

I would like to thank you for listening to my rambles over the years. My struggle with anxiety and my bout of post-heartbreak depression. I am going to have to make this quick because I am bleeding out, and slowly dying.
   I do not regret my decision to join them, they have done me better than I could have done. They supported me through my mental health issues, they gave me a place to stay and looked after me with great care. I owed it to them.
   But I have detailed that many times before.
   As we were preparing to pack up and head back to base, the organizer, Theresa, got stabbed in the back by a literal child. A young, crazed boy as a girl grabbed me and forced a knife through my back, before stabbing me several more times. They then threw us to the ground and stood over our bleeding bodies.
   After that they beat the operating systems pretty well, I suspect them too busted to be of use to us anymore. So much for the plan. After that they dashed, with Theresa managing to hold off just enough to watch them go before collapsing herself.
   I only managed to report the incident through my radio before collapsing and falling into a mental monologue.

I am grateful for all they did for me. It isn't the length of your life but the depth of it. If only dying didn't have to be this painful.

I just want to die now, I don't know why my body is clinging on to life, when I am lying in a pool of my own blood.

Still, thank you diary, for being the only thing that didn't try to jump down my throat whenever I talked about my mental issues. Well, before them lot came and helped a year ago.

This is it. Thank you.

My dearest boy, I can't put to words how much you mean to me. How desperately I wish to see you prosper and develop. Only weeks ago I envisioned your first communion, your confirmation. Your wedding, your first time wearing a suit, your first job. Now all they do is block my throat as you eat your cereal.

Such innocence, such naivety. So ignorant to the climate that storms the geopolitical mess that swarms outside. I fear I will get lost in it as soon as I depart from you. Within the next hour or so your grandparents will pick up where I have brokenheartedly left off.

You mean the world to me, my sweet, sweet child. Fate has decided that we are to never see each other again. My hand is forced. How much I want to hold you just one last time. But I cannot, for that would doom us both. At least my parents will get to see your first communion, your confirmation. They'll walk you down the aisle and pick out your first suit as you get ready for your first job.

As my shaky hands pick up my black headscarf and scrape on my black gloves, I cannot believe myself to be doing this. I have always known that I would lay my life for you, but I hoped it would never come to that. My black attire, as dark as the blackmail, clings on to me like sin. And yet it has all to begin. I know not what they intend to do, but I know that it is for a promised future of prosperity. One that will affect you, my beloved boy. I hope that history is kind to this moment. And that the future is kind to you.

Words cannot begin to develop a proper sentence to describe how dear you are to me. Actions speak louder than words, after all.

I love you, and please, go forth and achieve all that I know you are capable of.

I'm so sorry, I'm so, so, sorry. It was either us both or just you and I couldn't handle it. I mean I had just killed someone! I can't handle it. I need to stop running before I throw up. What has the world come to?

This organization of people stalking around, planting tracking beacons all for what… domination? Power? Who the fuck are they? I don't even want to think of what I saw in that room. All the information, all the dates and plans. The room where we took revenge for everyone that had died. For the society that had been reduced to rubble.

And that poor boy. All he wanted was to find his mum. I can't forget how he recalled the last time he saw her. Such an innocent setting. Now she is probably dead under the rubble and urban mess.

Fuck, it's just horrible.

Oh no, there are more of them. Where to go?

There looks promising. I need to get clear of this whole area, the county, even. Maybe everywhere isn't as bad as this. I need answers, and I'm going to get them. If I don't die in the process.

All this time I haven't seen a single survivor. Is it just me? Me against the world? I can't do this, I'm gonna be sick.

Oh my God, there are more of them. They're everywhere. I can't do this.

I'm sorry, kid, I couldn't save us. I couldn't find your mum, Theresa. I couldn't do anything.

And now we're all going to die.

Author's note:

Thank you so much for reading *Haunted Footfalls*, and thanks again to everyone who proofread it and talked to me about it and listened patiently to my rantings. This has been a project that I had been working on for a couple years now, give or take.

I feel it is important to bring up once again that any parallels to real life are fictitious and bear no resemblance to my own world views. The US army may be the UKLA's enemy in White Noise, and Sean may have a disregard to the United Nations, but it is all in the sake of telling the story.

There will be much more. In fact, alongside this I've been working on another project, an actual book-length book, if you know what I mean. So if you liked this, then you're going to love what's next in store for the *Dark War*.

Also, I have enacted my own liberties on geographical locations, for I have never been to Finchingfield yet have the audacity to write about it, but I'm sure it's a wonderful place. Just don't expect exact precision from any real-life places I drop into my tales.

The *Dark War* series is not a reflection or statement about modern times, it is merely my own morbid fantasies for the sake of entertainment. You don't need to worry about any of the contents of this book. Not yet, anyway…

Acknowledgements:

Operation Backseat in White Noise is inspired by the incredible real life Operation Tombola that I read about in *The Italian Job* by Damien Lewis. Such an incredible story, it really got me into the whole military writing scene. I've always loved action writing, but his books really gave me an insight into what real military action looks like, sounds like, feels like, so if you want more military goodness that actually happened then I shall direct you to him (and Cameron Spence, if you want a first-hand, entertaining account).

I shall like to acknowledge my cousin, Chloe Coley, who has been with me for my entire writing ambition, even before I started penning this book! I've been harrowing her with proofreading and questions and requests, and she's never let me down. I would like to extend a formal, sincere thank you.

Thoughts on War:

The theme of war is one that plagues our games, books, TV shows, music, and, depressingly, our headlines, too. You don't need me to explain why war is bad, but I'd like to say that war, in this day and age, should never be more than a genre, such as fantasy, or sci-fi. Not a persisting reality.

I may have just constructed multiple narratives that display it to be exhilarating and perhaps even enticing, but just know that none of these characters made a single footstep that wasn't laced in defeat. As in war, there are never really any victors. Just those that are left.